Bodybuilding
The Weider Approach

Bodybuilding
The Weider Approach

Joe Weider

Contemporary Books, Inc.
Chicago

Library of Congress Cataloging in Publication Data

Weider, Joe.
    Bodybuilding : the Weider approach.

    Bibliography: p.
    Includes index.
    1. Bodybuilding.   I. Title.
GV546.5.W44   1981   646.7′5   81-65194
ISBN 0-8092-5909-5   AACR2
ISBN 0-8092-5908-7 (pbk.)

All photos courtesy of the International Federation of Bodybuilders.
Principal Photographers: Bill Reynolds, John Balik, Mike Neveux,
Craig Dietz, Russ Warner, Jimmy Caruso, Pete Brenner, Bill Dobbins.

Principal Models: Arnold Schwarzenegger, Lou Ferrigno, Frank
Zane, Dr. Franco Columbu, Gary Leonard, Chris Dickerson,
Dennis Tinerino, Roy Callender, Tony Pearson, Tony Emmott,
Ken Waller, Mike Katz, Carlos Rodriguez, Casey Viator,
Samir Bannout, Ed Corney, Andreas Cahling, Bill Grant,
Mohamed Makkawy, Larry Scott, Sergio Oliva, David Shaw,
Jim Benjamin, Mike Mentzer, Ray Mentzer, Boyer Coe, Bertil
Fox, Mike Bridges, Steve Davis, Robby Robinson, Roger Walker,
and Bob Birdsong.

Published by Contemporary Books, Inc.
180 North Michigan Avenue, Chicago, Illinois 60601
Manufactured in the United States of America
Library of Congress Catalog Card Number: 81-65194
International Standard Book Number: 0-8092-5909-5 (cloth)
                                    0-8092-5908-7 (paper)

Published simultaneously in Canada by
Beaverbooks, Ltd.
150 Lesmill Road
Don Mills, Ontario M3B 2T5
Canada

Contents

Joe Weider (top) poses with two of his greatest pupils, Lou "The Incredible Hulk" Ferrigno and Arnold "Conan" Schwarzenegger.

Introduction

Who Is Joe Weider?

by Andreas Cahling, IFBB Mr. International and IFBB World's Most Muscular Man

Who is Joe Weider?

That is a question I often asked myself as a teenager in Sweden, having just taken up bodybuilding training and occasionally seeing a copy of *Muscle Builder* (now called *Muscle & Fitness*) magazine. And now that I am a friend of Joe Weider's—and closely associated with him and his brother, Ben Weider, President of the IFBB, in promoting bodybuilding worldwide—I am often asked this identical question. So, who *is* Joe Weider?

He is at once the greatest trainer bodybuilding has ever seen, the sport's biggest fan and one of its most outstanding promoters, and a friend and confidant of virtually all the top bodybuilders. He also is an author, a publisher, an art collector, an antique buff, husband to a beautiful former model, a hilarious raconteur, and a great leader.

Joe Weider was born into poverty in Montreal, Quebec, in Canada during the 1920s. He learned early on that hard work was the only way to overcome his slumlike surroundings, because he worked for five to ten cents per hour at any job he could find, just to help keep bread on the Weider family table. Joe was even forced to quit school in his early teens so he could work longer hours and help his family even more.

In the formal sense, then, Joe Weider is not an educated man, but he carries with him at all times a very inquisitive and analytical mind. He is highly self-educated and deeply imbued with the wisdom of life. Joe is, to put it plainly, a genuine genius and the greatest mind ever to tackle our sport, organize its training principles, and promote bodybuilding to its current high level of public acceptance.

In 1936—while still in his teens—Joe Weider began to train some of his friends, then others across the United States and Canada through a small newsletter that eventually became a magazine called *Your Physique* in 1940. More than 40 years later this magazine is *Muscle & Fitness*, which is read by more than 1.5 million bodybuilders around the world.

Since 1936, Joe Weider has been called the "Trainer of Champions," an appellation with its veracity backed up by more than 7 million successful and happy pupils. Joe has trained every champion bodybuilding has ever produced—Steve Reeves, Reg Park, Arnold Schwarzenegger, Lou Ferrigno, Frank Zane, Sergio Oliva, Franco Columbu, Mike Mentzer, and thousands more. And the "Master Blaster" has always been my personal trainer.

Joe has been a bodybuilder and weight lifter since the age of 13. He was a Provincial Champion weight lifter, strong enough by the age of 17 to Continental Clean and Jerk 310 pounds, while weighing only 155 himself (a double–body weight Overhead Lift). In bodybuilding workouts, he has Bench Pressed 410 pounds for three reps and Curled 180 for ten repetitions in strict form (both of these efforts were at body weights ranging from 200 to 210 pounds).

Even though he was always too busy promoting the sport to train optimally as a bodybuilder, Joe developed an outstanding physique. One year, he placed quite high in the Mr. Universe contest, losing to his own pupil, Reg Park. Even today, Joe Weider is as hard as a rock and sports a 47-inch chest and 17-inch arms.

Because he truly *is* a bodybuilder, Joe Weider was able ultimately to bring order to a training activity that was in total confusion during the 1940s and early 1950s. Gradually, he codified a large number of training principles (now called "Weider Training Principles" in his honor) and made bodybuilding training understandable to everyone. These principles formed the now world-famous Weider System of Training, which allows almost any man or woman to develop an outstanding physique, both quickly and easily. Every bodybuilder—champion and novice alike—for the past 30 years has used the Weider System. It's that simple!

Primarily, Joe Weider promotes bodybuilding through *Muscle & Fitness*, of which he is the publisher. But back in 1947, he and his brother Ben founded the International Federation of Bodybuilders (IFBB), recognizing the fact that bodybuilding would eventually become so popular worldwide that it would need a parent federation to overlook each national federation. In 1947 there were only two member countries to the IFBB, Canada and the United States. Now there are more than 115 member nations, making bodybuilding the sixth most popular sport internationally!

(Left) Andreas Cahling poses proudly with his 1980 IFBB Mr. International trophy. (Below) Andreas does a heavy set of Incline Presses to further thicken his upper chest muscles.

Frank Zane, three-time Mr. Olympia winner, receives some sage training advice from "The Master Blaster," Joe Weider.

Over the years, Joe and Ben Weider selflessly invested thousands of their own dollars to promote the IFBB, which grew rapidly as a result. Finally, the IFBB was accepted for membership in the prestigious General Assembly of International Sports Federations (GAIF) in 1970.

It has long been the goal of Joe and Ben Weider to have bodybuilding accepted as an Olympic sport, and they are progressing rapidly toward that goal. Since 1976, results of IFBB competitions have been featured regularly in the International Olympic Committee's official organ, *Olympic Review*. Bodybuilding has already been included in the Asian Games and Pan American Games, and it soon will be included in the World Games. The Olympics? It's just a matter of time!

In 1965 Joe noticed that most Mr. Universe winners—having nothing more to compete for—retired and quit training as soon as they had won their titles. To forestall this, Joe organized the first Mr. Olympia competition as a Superbowl for former Mr. Universe winners. This contest has grown in prestige until it is now the most coveted of all bodybuilding titles. And prize money has risen from $1,000 in 1965 to more than $50,000 today.

Joe also promoted a large-scale professional bodybuilding movement. And he was the visionary who kicked off the tremendous women's bodybuilding explosion a couple of years ago. Now the women threaten to outstrip the men, in both amateur and pro ranks!

Above all, however, Joe Weider creates bodybuilding superstars. As Boyer Coe (Mr. America and Mr. Universe) has said, "Joe is unquestionably the greatest star maker in the history of bodybuilding." In 1968, for example, he gave a plane ticket from Munich to Los Angeles to Arnold Schwarzenegger, a virtually unknown 20-year-old Austrian. Joe then promoted Arnold into the greatest bodybuilder of all

Ray Mentzer (front) receives position instruction from Joe Weider as his brother Mike looks on. Ray and Mike Mentzer are the only brothers who have both won Mr. America titles.

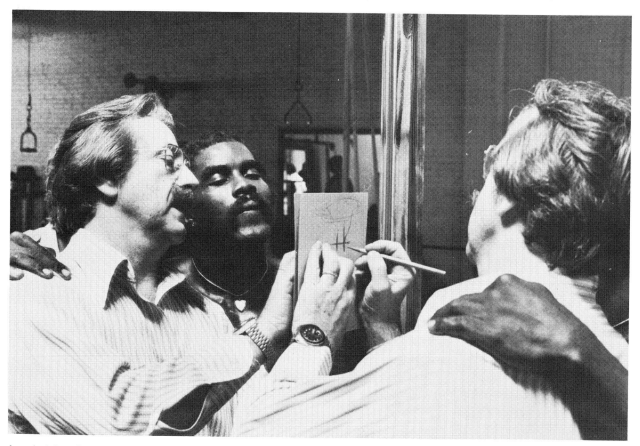

Joe sketches the proper biomechanics of an exercise for the great Robby Robinson, a Mr. America, Mr. World, and Mr. Universe winner.

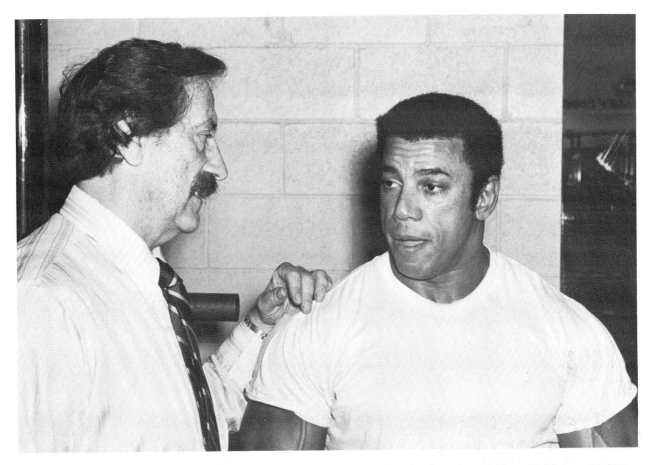

Joe Weider personally advises all of the greatest champion bodybuilders. Here he discusses nutrition with 42-year-old Chris Dickerson, the 1980 and 1981 Overall Pro Bodybuilding Grand Prix Champion.

time, making the man a millionaire in the process.

And Joe has done the same for scores of other stars. Now, with this great book, he will begin to do the same for you. This book epitomizes the best route through which to achieve Joe Weider's personal motto: "Strive for excellence, exceed yourself, love your friends, speak the truth, practice fidelity, and honor your father and mother. These principles will make you master yourself, make you strong, give you hope, and put you on a path to greatness."

As usual, Joe Weider knows what he's talking about, and in this book he will show you exactly how to achieve physical greatness. So, read it carefully. Good luck with your workouts!

Joe Weider helps Lou Ferrigno perfect his front double-biceps pose. Lou played The Incredible Hulk on television for four years. Below, Joe escorts some of his champions from the stage, accompanied at far right by his brother, Ben Weider.

1

Bodybuilder!

Bodybuilding! The word evokes radically different impressions, emotions, and images from almost everyone who hears it. These images are as unique to each person as the individuals themselves are unique.

To one person bodybuilding might mean merely keeping fit and looking trim in clothes. To another man bodybuilding might be gaining a little body weight to play a higher class of football next fall. But to most men and women, bodybuilding is an activity that produces herculean men with mind-blowing muscle size, garden hoses for veins, and a total absence of body fat.

So, why would anyone ever want to look like that?

This is a valid question, and one that has been answered best by seven-time Mr. Olympia winner Arnold Schwarzenegger, the Babe Ruth, Kareem Abdul-Jabbar, and Eric Heiden—all rolled together to form one athlete—of bodybuilding. As Arnold points out, "Once you make the decision to change your body with exercise and diet—even if it's just to add a little muscle to your arms and chest, or to reduce your waist—you *are*

a bodybuilder. Everyone doesn't have to— or even want to—become Mr. America, Mr. Universe, and Mr. Olympia. In fact, of all those men who want one day to win even a state title, like Mr. California, only a small handful have the inherent potential to build a physique competitive enough to win a title. In the entire history of bodybuilding, only five men have won the Mr. Olympia title.

"But, while only one man can win Mr. Olympia each year, hundreds of thousands of men and women can improve their bodies through bodybuilding training and healthy dietary practices. Anyone can improve his health, fitness, and appearance through bodybuilding. And if hard training appeals to him enough to make competitive bodybuilding his sport, he will have every opportunity to maximize his potential through personal effort and self-discipline."

The beauty of bodybuilding is that you succeed spectacularly or fail miserably totally on your own merits. Through strong self-discipline and consistently hard training, you—and virtually anyone else—**can** develop an outstanding physique. You are the only one who can make decisions on how to train and eat, but you are ultimately the product of your own endeavors. **You will literally create yourself!**

It won't be easy to attain the goals you set for yourself in bodybuilding, so if you bought this book thinking it would be a cakewalk to develop a superior physique, you have wasted your money. Bodybuilding training is exceedingly hard work, and it always hurts to some degree. But at the same time, conquering this pain and fatigue can feel absolutely terrific.

When you do an all-out set on any exercise, fatigue toxins are produced so rapidly and in such huge quantities that your body simply can't remove the waste products quickly enough, and as a result you experience a deep burning sensation in the muscles you are working. But even though bodybuilders aren't masochists, they avidly seek such pain and revel in it when they find it, because fatigue toxin pain indicates that you have stressed a muscle group so hard that it has been *forced* to grow larger and stronger.

Because competitive bodybuilding demands total dedication—and because when you want to win badly enough, your life will be filled with pain and sacrifice—the sport often brings out the best in a man. The determination, the ability to sacrifice, the unilateral focus you put on a task, a capacity for hard work, the ability to set and achieve goals, a tremendous degree of tenacity, and the ability to accept both victory and defeat with magnanimity transfer well to everyday life.

As Lou Ferrigno—the champion bodybuilder and successful television actor—has often said, "The lessons learned as a bodybuilder will make you a great success in life, be it as an athlete in another sport, businessman, mechanic, student, or even as an actor like myself. If you're a successful bodybuilder, you should also be a successful person in any other sport or activity, because competitive bodybuilding is such an incredibly difficult sport to succeed at, and any other endeavor will seem like a playground in which you only need to *play*

at working to achieve great success. Compared to hard bodybuilding training and maintaining a disciplined diet, acting is almost like a hobby to me, while the 12-hour days we put in *kill* everyone else on my show!"

Along the path toward your ultimate goal of winning a prestigious bodybuilding title, you will undoubtedly discover that you were not blessed with all the components necessary for you to attain your goal easily. No one has ever been born with perfect bodybuilding potential. Some bodybuilders gain muscle mass more slowly than others, some have skeletal structures far from what they should be, and some men have a muscle group that seems to defy all efforts to develop it. The best bodybuilders inevitably find a way to overcome such obstacles, however, and these men become the superstars of the sport.

SOME WHO HAVE SUCCEEDED

On the next few pages I will report to you several case histories of men who have succeeded magnificently as bodybuilders, often by overcoming what seemed to be insurmountable odds. Three of these men—Lou Ferrigno, Arnold Schwarzenegger, and Dr. Franco Columbu—are among the handful of elite superstars of bodybuilding, while some of the others that I will list in table form a bit farther on are less well known and successful in the sport.

I fervently hope that these brief success stories will inspire you either to begin regular bodybuilding workouts or to redouble the efforts you are currently putting into weight training. I will be especially happy one day to publish the success story you write about yourself for my magazine, *Muscle & Fitness*, because that will be a sure indication that this book has served its purpose.

Lou Ferrigno

As a young boy, Lou Ferrigno was the least likely candidate you could imagine for reaching the incredible physical condition he attained to win the Mr. America, Mr. International, and Mr. Universe titles. If you had seen him as a painfully introverted, pathetically thin boy of 14, you would never have guessed that he would one day become one of the world's best-liked and most easily recognized bodybuilders.

At the age of three, a serious and undetected ear infection destroyed more than 90 percent of Lou's hearing. Then, because he grew up unable to hear people talk, he developed severe difficulties with his speaking ability. Added to his shyness and introversion, Ferrigno's speaking and hearing problems condemned him to a friendless existence at school, where he regularly served as a punching bag for the bullies in his neighborhood.

Faced with such an excruciatingly lonely and painful life, Lou retreated into a fantasy world where he could imagine himself as Superman, Batman, and all his other comic book heroes, save for The Incredible Hulk, whom he was destined one day to play on television, because Lou deemed The Hulk too unbelievable to include in his fantasies.

"The Hulk was like something from outer space, all green-colored, weighing 1,000 pounds, and eight feet in height," Lou remarked. "The Hulk was too unbelievable for even my vivid imagination, so I could never fantasize myself being him and running amok whenever David Banner Hulked out. It was much easier to pretend I was Superman or a pro football hero.

"Even though I was extremely thin, anemic, and weak as a child, I always imagined myself as a very tall, muscular, and strong adult, a hero that everyone could look up to. At 6'5" in height and weighing 275 pounds of solid muscle, I'm now an international folk hero. I would say that I have attained all of my childhood fantasy-goals, and I owe all of this success directly to bodybuilding!"

Lou Ferrigno started weight training in

the basement of his family home in Brooklyn, New York, at the age of 14. Already nearly 5'10" tall, he weighed in at a skinny 135 pounds. "There wasn't a muscle on my entire body," Lou recalls nostalgically. "I was so weak that I couldn't even Press 75 pounds over my head, and I struggled to finish six uncoordinated and clumsy reps with 55 pounds in a Barbell Curl movement."

Lou was so self-conscious about his thin and weak body that he trained in his basement for three full years before finding the courage to venture into Jules Levine's R&J Health Club in Brooklyn. "I finally had to conquer my fears of what other people thought about me," Lou said, "because I had reached the point where I needed to use the greater variety of equipment found in big commercial gyms. I'd simply outgrown my basement and the small barbell-dumbbell set I'd used for three years."

At the age of 18, Ferrigno won the Teenage Mr. America title. And two years later, at only 20 years of age, he placed first

in the Mr. Eastern America, Mr. America, and Mr. Universe contests. At 21, he won the Mr. International competition and another Mr. Universe title, being defeated only by Arnold Schwarzenegger—a much older and more experienced athlete—in the 1974 and 1975 Mr. Olympia competitions.

Following his '75 Mr. Olympia defeat, Ferrigno took a full year off from bodybuilding to excel as an athlete in the ABC Television "Superstars" show. He also nearly made the grade as a pro football player in Canada, despite never having played even a single down of football in high school. Only a torn Achilles tendon kept him off the team.

Ferrigno returned to bodybuilding in late 1976, and by the summer of '77 he was in such tremendous condition that virtually every one of his competitors conceded him the 1977 Mr. Olympia title. But only a couple of weeks before the contest, Lou was given the opportunity to portray in a made-for-television movie the comic book character that was too unbelievable for him to include in his fantasies, The Incredible Hulk. Surprisingly, this pilot film was so popular that a television series evolved from it, starring Lou Ferrigno as The Hulk and Bill Bixby as his alter ego, David Banner.

"The Incredible Hulk" television show has run for several years quite successfully. And when the popular show finally goes off the air, its reruns will be widely syndicated for afternoon showings on a daily basis. The television series has made Lou Ferrigno a wealthy man, a much sought after actor for other film properties, and an international sex symbol.

"I owe everything to bodybuilding," he reaffirms. "The training I did to build my physique taught me how to work toward a goal with great intensity and total dedication. Bodybuilding has also taught me to be persistent, to work hard, to be self-reliant, and to look at myself objectively. And most importantly, bodybuilding drastically improved my self-image, allowing me first to become a normal person after years as a shrinking violet, and later to assert myself

as an actor and an outstanding person.

"Yes, I truly owe everything I've achieved in my life to bodybuilding. Beginning to train hard with weights at 14 was the best thing I ever did for myself. And the beauty of bodybuilding is that **anyone** can improve his strength, health, and appearance by training with weights and maintaining a healthy diet. Everyone should be a bodybuilder!"

Arnold Schwarzenegger

Most bodybuilding fans and authorities in the sport consider Arnold Schwarzenegger the greatest bodybuilder of all time. Certainly, with seven Mr. Olympia titles to his credit (more than twice the number that any other bodybuilder has won), it would be difficult to argue that Arnold isn't *numero uno* in our sport.

Arnold Schwarzenegger is the quintessential fast-gainer, as evidenced by the fact that he won his first of five Mr. Universe titles after only five years of training. This is a rather unprecedented feat in bodybuilding, because most Mr. Universe winners have been training at least twice as long at the time they win their titles.

Arnold had an extensive youth sports background in his native Austria, excelling in soccer, swimming, skiing, curling, and powerlifting at one time or another. But despite his success in sports, Arnold was unhappy and unfulfilled as an athlete.

As Arnold Schwarzenegger has often said, "I knew that I wanted to become the best in the world at some sport, but I'd not felt the right vibrations from any of the sports I'd tried. But the first time I touched a barbell and did a set of Curls, something clicked in my head and I knew that bodybuilding was the sport I had been destined to excel in."

With only five years of heavy training under his belt—some of it using incorrect training principles—the huge Austrian youth (he was only 20 years old at this point, stood 6'1½" in height, and weighed 235 pounds) won his first Mr. Universe title, defeating the current Mr. America,

Dennis Tinerino, in the process. He then followed up this initial international success by winning a total of 15 world championships, including seven Mr. Olympia titles, five Mr. Universes, and a host of lesser titles like Mr. World, Mr. Europe, and Mr. International.

Undefeated in six consecutive Mr. Olympia competitions between 1970 and 1975, Arnold Schwarzenegger announced his retirement from competitive bodybuilding following his sixth Olympia. And for the next five years he built up a successful business, investing widely in real estate holdings. He also began promoting professional bodybuilding shows: he promoted the Mr. Olympia competitions from 1976 through 1979 and is scheduled to promote more Olympias and other top-level pro competitions throughout the 1980s.

One of Arnold's most thriving business enterprises during the late 1970s was his acting career. His superb physique and charismatic personality won him many roles, including that of the mythical and muscular barbarian Conan in mid-1980. While training casually to regain his muscle mass for the Conan role, Arnold was again bitten hard by the competitive bug. Whipping himself into contest condition in only seven weeks, Schwarzenegger surprised the bodybuilding world by entering the Mr. Olympia competition again and winning his seventh Mr. Olympia title! Truly, Arnold Schwarzenegger remains one of the greatest athletes and promoters of the sport with the general public that we have ever seen in bodybuilding.

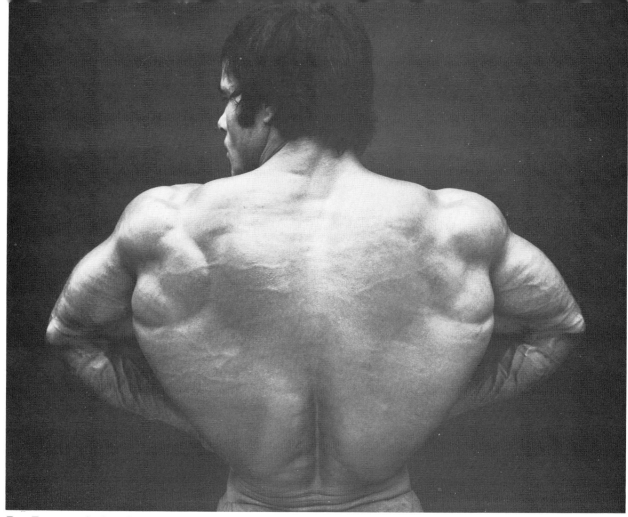

Dr. Franco Columbu

Franco Columbu lived in virtual poverty as a child in his native Sardinia, an island off the coast of Italy. His early choice of a career was to become a shepherd or to join one of his island's famous band of kidnappers. Columbu chose sheep over crime and eventually developed a rare degree of physical fitness running up and down the rocky hillsides of Sardinia chasing errant sheep.

This strength and endurance helped him win a local boxing tournament, which in turn induced him to train for that sport and ultimately win the Italian championship in his weight class. But shortly afterward, Columbu moved to Germany to work in an automobile factory and continue boxing, this time as a professional.

Franco's German trainer insisted that his talented charge train with weights to improve his punching power. But Columbu gained strength so rapidly that he almost killed his next ring opponent. This upset Franco considerably, and since he was already becoming more interested in weight training than in boxing, he decided to become a bodybuilder.

In short order, Franco Columbu won Mr. Italy and Mr. Europe, plus several European powerlifting championships. Seeing greater opportunities to maximize his potential in California, Franco then emigrated to America, continued to train, and won the Mr. World and Mr. Universe titles and finally the Mr. Olympia title.

Along the way, Franco Columbu completed a degree in chiropractic and joined his wife's successful chiropractic practice. He also authored several successful weight training and bodybuilding books (some of these are listed in the annotated bibliography at the end of this book), and became a successful and prosperous businessman. This is not at all bad for a skinny young Italian kid who once had to decide between becoming a kidnapper and becoming a shepherd!

Others Who Succeeded

To give you an even more complete idea of what you can realistically expect to achieve from bodybuilding training, here is a chart of 15 additional champion bodybuilders, complete with their before and after body weights and measurements.

Name (and title won)	Weight: Before/After	Biceps: Before/After
1. Bill Pearl (Mr. Universe)	138/235	12″/20½″
2. Larry Scott (Mr. Olympia)	128/212	10″/20½″
3. Sergio Oliva (Mr. Olympia)	160/242	13″/22″
4. Frank Zane (Mr. Olympia)	130/200	10½″/19″
5. Robby Robinson (Mr. Universe)	150/219	14″/21″
6. Ken Waller (Mr. Universe)	150/235	13″/20″
7. Tom Platz (Mr. Universe)	133/211	11½″/19″
8. Boyer Coe (Mr. Universe)	143/212	11½″/20½″
9. Bill Grant (Mr. World)	127/197	9½″/20″
10. Dennis Tinerino (Mr. Universe)	135/235	10½″/21″
11. Andreas Cahling (Mr. International)	135/195	11½″/19″
12. Steve Davis (Mr. World)	285/200*	16″/19″
13. Gary Leonard (Mr. America)	145/218	14″/20″
14. Rod Koontz (Mr. USA)	150/210	11½″/20″
15. Jusup Wilkosz (Mr. Universe)	148/222	12″/20½″

* *Note:* Steve Davis was grossly overweight to start with, and he normalized his weight while gaining considerable muscle mass through bodybuilding and maintaining a good low-calorie diet.

So, now you know implicitly what you can expect to achieve from persistent, scientifically applied bodybuilding methods. While you may not have the genetic potential to achieve the appearance, muscular body weight, or measurements of the champions listed above, rest assured that you can and *will* make great improvements in your physique!

Larry Scott (above left), Sergio Oliva (left), and Frank Zane (above) have radically different body types, but each has won Mr. Olympia at least two times. Regardless of your body type and native potential, you can become a champion if you train correctly and persistently.

11

Boyer Coe, a Louisiana native now living in southern California, has won nearly 50 bodybuilding titles, including Mr. America and Mr. Universe (five times). While winning the 1981 Professional World Cup Championships he scored a record 307 points.

Robby Robinson, one of the most popular bodybuilders of the 1970s, won four pro titles before retiring from competition. His combination of gargantuan muscle mass and extreme muscularity is unparalleled.

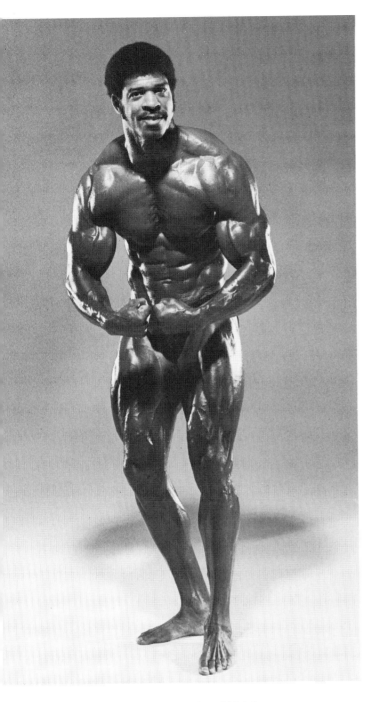

Gary Leonard, the 1980 Mr. America winner, is typical of today's rising champs. With only four years of Weider-style training, he won his Mr. America title. This photo was taken a year before he won.

Bill Grant, Mr. World, has placed high in numerous professional championships. His weak calf development—although constantly improving—has often held him back.

Dennis Tinerino has won every major title except Mr. Olympia. Originally from Brooklyn, New York, he runs a successful gym equipment store in Westwood, California.

Andreas Cahling, who wrote the introduction to this book, moved from Sweden to southern California specifically to train under Joe Weider. A former Swedish Junior National Champion in both wrestling and judo, he is one of today's hottest pro bodybuilding stars.

Steve Davis, a Newhall, California gym owner, typifies the classic Apollo-type of physique. Steve's won the Pro Mr. World title and, with his lovely wife Ellen, has placed high in the World Couples Championships.

Once a skinny 120-pounder, Tom Platz has trained persistently for nearly 15 years to develop his current herculean 210-pound physique. Tom is a former World Light-Heavyweight Bodybuilding Champion.

BODYBUILDING MYTHS AND REALITIES

Until the mid-1970s, when the mass media "discovered" the sport, bodybuilding was considered a sort of closet activity by the general public. Bodybuilders were widely ridiculed, and when this is the case numerous popularly believed misconceptions can evolve. This has definitely been the case with bodybuilding. So that you will know how to handle the few remaining critics of your sport when they pop into your life, let's discuss five of the more popular myths about bodybuilding and reveal the logical truth behind each myth.

1. *"All bodybuilders are muscle-bound."* This is undoubtedly the biggest and most persistent misconception about our sport that you will encounter. In point of fact, however, numerous scientific studies have been conducted since the early 1950s, each of which proved that weight training actually *increases* flexibility. The first of these studies was performed by Professor Edward K. Capen at Iowa State University. (If you're curious enough to look up the complete study, it was published in *Research Quarterly*, Volume 21, Number 1, pages 83–93.)

Professor Capen took a number of college students in the university's physical education activity classes and divided them into two groups—a control group that did only the regular physical education class activities for the course of the experiment and an experimental group that trained on a program of basic weight-training movements for several weeks.

At the end of the experiment, Professor Capen found the following results when he tested the two groups.

a. The students in the experimental group were much stronger than those students in the control group.
b. There wasn't even a hint of muscle or joint tightness in the experimental group subjects. In fact, many experimental group subjects had shown an increase in joint flexibility.
c. In tests of speed, the weight-trained group was markedly superior to the control group.

In numerous other scientific studies during succeeding years, it has been demonstrated that weight training and bodybuilding have had a positive effect on athletic performance, particularly on flexibility. Indeed, it can be truthfully said that those individuals who exercise with weights are far less muscle-bound than those who don't.

You can quite easily prove this fact to any skeptic who is giving you a hard time about being muscle-bound. One very simple test of flexibility that you will probably excel in—particularly if you regularly include Stiff-Leg Deadlifts in your training routine for your lower back muscles—is touching the floor with your hands while keeping your legs straight. Few ordinarily sedentary people will be able to touch the floor with even their fingertips, if they can touch it at all. With only a few weeks of bodybuilding training, you will easily be able to touch both hands flat on the floor. And John C. Grimek, the first AAU Mr. America winner in 1940, could actually touch his elbows to the floor with his feet held together and his legs perfectly straight!

2. *"Bodybuilders aren't athletes."* The answer to this common allegation can take either of two tracks. First of all, bodybuilders are athletes just as much as figure skaters, divers, synchronized swimmers, gymnasts, equestrians, and other exhibition-type athletes. We exhibit our bodies in a posing routine that is far more fatiguing than a one-meter dive, and a two-hour all-out bodybuilding workout is far more demanding than any workout the vast majority of athletes will ever do for their sports, especially since bodybuilders often must train when also dieting very severely prior to competing.

Second, as far as bodybuilders being athletic is concerned, there is a long list of bodybuilders who have been tremendous athletes in the past and who still retain their athletic abilities. Robby Robinson has run 100 yards in 9.4 seconds. In a sprint race he can still beat anyone but a trained sprinter, and if he resumed sprint training for a few weeks, he would no doubt defeat all but the very best sprinters at their own game.

Roger Callard, a former Mr. USA winner, was also a distinguished sprinter as well as a defensive back at Michigan State University. Other very good football players include Mike Katz (Mr. America), who played professionally with the New York Jets, and Lou Ferrigno and Ken Waller (both Mr. Universe winners), who played professionally in the Canadian Football League.

Andreas Cahling (Mr. International) was a Junior National Champion in Sweden in both judo and wrestling. Arnold Schwarzenegger was a European Champion in curling. Bill Pearl was an All-Navy Champion in wrestling before becoming Mr. America and Mr. Universe. And Frank Zane (Mr. Olympia) is a champion archer. The list could go on and on.

Probably the best argument for bodybuilders being good athletes was provided by Lou Ferrigno's sterling performance in the ABC Television "Superstars" competition in 1975. In his preliminary heat Lou easily bested a number of pro athletes for first place, none of whom could believe his overall fitness and athletic ability. And then in the finals he also did extremely well, ending up with more than $20,000 in total prize money for the two competitions.

3. *"It will all turn to fat when you stop working out."* This is a myth that owes its believability to the rotund, beer-guzzling 19th-century strongmen in Europe. In *The Police Gazette* and other magazines of that era these men were occasionally depicted, and the public somehow began to believe that the muscle would turn to fat. And, of course, this has been a tremendously persistent misconception for nearly a century.

The fact is that it is physiologically impossible to turn muscle into fat, except through a very complicated chemical reaction, which happens inside the human body only during periods of starvation, when the body actually runs out of stored fat and is forced to begin consuming its own muscle tissue to survive. Then the tissue to be consumed is drawn from the least vital areas (the brain and spinal column are the last to be used, for example) and the protein is turned into free fatty acids for energy usage.

What usually happens when a bodybuilder stops training—and you must understand that very few do, because most men enjoy bodybuilding enough to continue it for life—is that he gradually reverts back to the somatotype (body type) he had before he began training. If he was skinny, he again becomes skinny; and if he was originally fat, he again becomes fat. This process takes roughly as long to complete as it took to reach the point of muscular development he had attained when he quit working out.

In a few cases, as the overall muscle mass atrophies back to its original size, a bodybuilder *will* get fat. This is caused by failing to cut back on caloric intake after ceasing to use up so many calories in daily workouts. Anyone who has been training very hard as a bodybuilder has been burning up enormous quantities of calories, and if he keeps eating as much as he did when he was training, he will be effectively overeating and will gain fat weight. Reduce the amount of food eaten, however, and you will have no problem with gaining extra fat once you quit training.

4. *"You guys just aren't interested in women. You're all gay."* Whether or not you are personally gay is something that you must decide for yourself. But you should understand that there are no more gay bodybuilders than there are homosexuals in any other segment of society. There are, however, a disproportionately large number of gays around the periphery of the sport, no doubt because bodybuilding emphasizes the male body so prominently.

As far as lack of interest in women among bodybuilders is concerned, I have personally *never* seen a group of heterosexuals more interested in women, nor a group more successful with women.

5. *"Bodybuilders are all stupid. They're all bums."* Anyone who would believe this kind of tripe ought to meet some of the top men in the sport. C. F. Smith, a multi-title winner and Mr. America finalist, is an outstanding physician. Mike Besikoff, a former Mr. California winner, is an attorney.

Franco Columbu, as I mentioned earlier in this chapter, is a Doctor of Chiropractic. Ellington Darden, a Collegiate Mr. America, has a Ph.D. Arnold Schwarzenegger is an extremely successful businessman who got his business degree from UCLA in record time. Again, the list could go on and on.

I would be the first to admit that there are a few gym bums in the sport—guys who don't work unless they absolutely have to—but the majority of bodybuilders are gainfully employed. And bodybuilding takes the place in their lives of a serious hobby, a place where it fits in very well.

HOW IT WORKS

Assuming that you are now convinced that the sport of bodybuilding is what *you* want to do, let's go briefly into a discussion of how bodybuilding training really works inside your body—how the training and food result in big muscles. A full discussion of the physiology of muscle hypertrophy (growth) could fill a very large book, but I can briefly give you a good working knowledge of what goes on inside a growing muscle.

First of all, you need to know that a muscle does not actually grow past a certain point in terms of the total number of fibers and cells it contains. And this growth doesn't occur past the point that your body actually stops growing, which is usually in your late teens. What happens after this is an enlarging (hypertrophy) of the existing muscle cells.

Muscle cells hypertrophy as a response to stress, and they keep expanding in mass as a function of progressively increased overloads. This progressive increase of resistance (stress) being placed on the muscle is the very heart of bodybuilding. This function is called the Weider Overload Principle, which is the basis of the whole Weider System of bodybuilding training.

For decades it was thought that muscle cells were broken down by exercise and then during periods of rest built up larger and stronger than they were before being trained. Recent scientific research has tended to disprove this theory, however. Physiologists now support a theory that involves *inhibition of catabolism*.

To understand this theory, you need to know that your body is in a constant state of building up cells (anabolism) and tearing down cells (catabolism). In most individuals, the rates of anabolism and catabolism are balanced, so the body is in an equilibrium. In other words, it is maintaining its size and body weight at a constant level.

Bodybuilders want to shift this balance toward the anabolic end of the scale, so they can add muscle mass to their bodies. Research now suggests that this is not done by increasing the anabolism, but actually by decreasing the catabolism, which makes the net anabolic rate essentially higher. And physiologists believe that heavy resistance training definitely inhibits the catabolic rate, instead of augmenting the anabolic rate, and *this* is what makes the muscle grow in mass.

Any way you cut it—old theory or new—the application of the Weider Overload Principle is what *causes* muscles to hypertrophy. We will discuss how to overload a muscle progressively in Chapter 2 and continue this discussion intermittently throughout the balance of this book.

THE AGE FACTOR

Up to this point I have assured you that disadvantages of physical structure and slow muscle hypertrophy rate can be overcome, but I have said nothing about the effect of a bodybuilder's age on his ultimate progress in the sport. Unfortunately, age is something you can't change. And after about age 45–50 it is tough to continue building muscle mass.

If you started working out at 15, a very common age to begin, you will have 30–35 years ahead of you in which to improve. Even if you started at 35, you would still have 10 good years ahead of you, and a lot of people have won the Mr. America title with only five or six years of training.

Some very young men have become

Casey Viator was history's youngest Mr. America winner at 19 (above). Today, at 30 (left), he's even more muscular, despite an eight-year layoff between the ages of 20 and 27.

tremendous bodybuilders. One of the best examples of this is Casey Viator, who won his Mr. America title in 1971 at the age of only 19. And he is to this day one of the best men ever to have won that title.

Viator started training during his early teens, and when only 18 he exploded onto the national bodybuilding scene by placing third in the Mr. America competition. Within a year he had won the Mr. USA, Teenage Mr. America, and Mr. America titles. And he is still winning professional titles today.

On the opposite end of the age scale, we have numerous examples of older bodybuilders who have succeeded magnificently. Ed Corney, a Mr. America and Mr. Universe winner, didn't start competitive bodybuilding until he was 33, and 10 years

Competitive bodybuilding recognizes no age barriers. If 19-year-old Casey Viator can win titles, so can 46-year-old Ed Corney (above) and 42-year-old Clarence Bass (right).

later he placed third in the Mr. Olympia show. Vic Downes, an Englishman who had emigrated to Canada, was 32 before he even touched a barbell. Yet four years later he was Mr. Canada. Two years after that he created a sensation by winning the Most Muscular Man award at the Mr. Universe competition. And finally, Bill Pearl, the 1953 Mr. America, was still in his greatest all-time shape at age 50!

So you can see that age has little to do with whether or not you will succeed in bodybuilding, unless you are already in the 45–50 age group. Even then, bodybuilding will greatly increase your health, appearance, and fitness. And if you are in your teens or twenties, and you are dedicated enough, you could be on your way to becoming Mr. Olympia.

DISADVANTAGES OF BODYBUILDING

Here, near the end of Chapter 1, I have hidden away a few disadvantages of bodybuilding. There *are* a few disadvantages, but each one can be minimized quite easily by simply using the brief suggestions I will present with each listed disadvantage of bodybuilding.

To some individuals, the main drawback to bodybuilding will appear to be *boredom*, because by its very nature, the training involves repetitious exercise. The same movement is done over and over for years. If you weren't into it, bodybuilding could be boring, but to an individual who is a *bodybuilder* the training is pure ecstasy. It's a quest for the sometimes elusive muscle pump, an extremely pleasurable physical sensation, likened by Arnold Schwarzenegger in the film *Pumping Iron* to the sensation of a man's sexual orgasm.

The main factor that keeps bodybuilding training interesting is the deep mental involvement and concentration inherent in the sport (these concepts are discussed in greater detail in Chapters 4 and 6). With the mind totally geared to the training, you are constantly monitoring each contracting muscle, your breathing rate, your body's temperature, feelings of comfort and discomfort, sweating, and myriad other training functions and side effects. And the end result of this is a total lack of boredom for a real bodybuilder, as compared to the inevitable boredom of someone just going through the motions of working out and "thinking" he is a bodybuilder.

As much as I hate to say this, if you *think* you're going to be bored, you might as well forget about bodybuilding right now. Psychologists recognize a phenomenon they call *self-fulfilling prophecy* (which I will discuss as a positive factor when teaching you the technique of "visualization" in Chapter 5). This involves a process in which what you deeply believe will happen to you actually comes true, when it would normally not have done so. If you expect to be bored, therefore, you will be, because your brain will subconsciously make the decisions and choices that will fulfill this prophecy.

Another possible drawback to bodybuilding is what some would consider an excessive time expenditure in bodybuilding training. Your training can require anywhere from one to three hours each day, and even up to five just before a major international contest. And you will need to train for anything between three and seven days per week. This *can* be a lot of time to some people, if they fail to consider that this time expenditure is actually an investment in their physical and mental health.

Spending a lot of time in a gym can be valuable in another sense as well. Bill Grant, Mr. America and Mr. World, states, "I grew up in Newark, New Jersey, in a very tough neighborhood. Most of my boyhood friends are either in jail or dead from heroin overdoses, while in contrast I have become successful and well known in my sport and have a good job. The crucial factor between my old friends and me is the sense of purpose in life that bodybuilding gave me and the fact that I was in the gym training while they were out on the street learning how to be criminals and junkies."

A really genuine disadvantage of bodybuilding is that once you reach a certain physical size, clothing is difficult to find. Clothiers simply don't take bodybuilders into consideration when they make up their inventories. A bodybuilder's thighs are so big that when he finds a pair of pants that will fit comfortably over them, the pants come with a 40-inch waistband, not one of 32–34 inches. And our 18- to 19-inch necks are supposed to match up with another 40-inch waist, so shirts hang like Bedouin tents around our waists. Have you ever seen an off-the-rack sport coat that would have sleeves big enough to fit over a 20-inch arm without splitting every seam in the sleeve?

The solution to the clothing problem is to have clothing tailor-made—like Lou Ferrigno does—because you will look really exceptional in it if the tailoring has been well-done. But if you can't afford a tailor's bill, thank God for doubleknits! Casey Viator wears doubleknit pants with a 34-inch waist that fit him well around the middle, while the material of the pants stretches enough to firmly encase his economy-sized, 28½-inch thighs!

Another somewhat legitimate drawback to our sport is that even in this enlightened age, a small percentage of the general public will still laugh at bodybuilders. Despite the fact that the mass media are finally treating us as normal people who just happen to live inside big bodies, this does occur. Unfortunately, there is little defense against this type of abuse, other than maintaining a polite attitude and appearing as normal as possible (no "painted on" short-sleeved shirts or spread lats!) in public. Hopefully, these attitudes will keep changing toward the positive until everyone becomes a little more tolerant, a quality for which the human race has seldom been noted through the ages.

The final disadvantage of being a bodybuilder is the expense. I will caution you right now that bodybuilding can be expensive, and you will be training for an extended period of time before you can begin making enough money from the sport (from exhibitions, seminars, mail-order courses, etc.) to support your training expenses. You will be spending far more on food than our friend Albert Average, especially on food supplements. You will need to buy special pieces of training equipment from time to time, and if you compete, it will cost you quite a bit for travel and lodging expenses.

The only sane solution to this problem is to point out two ways that bodybuilding actually saves you money, perhaps enough to balance out the money you spend on it. First, you are able to regulate personally your bodybuilding expenditures. Only you decide what to spend your money on as well as how much to spend. And even such an eminent authority as Dr. Franco Columbu—who will have his Ph.D. in nutrition science by the time most of you read this—feels that no bodybuilder needs to spend more than $10 to $15 per month on vitamin and mineral supplements, so the costs *can* be held down.

Second, you are at least spending your hard-earned bucks on something healthful instead of on drugs, booze, loose women, cigarettes, and other highly destructive activities. There are so many drug addicts around that society doesn't need any more of the dudes. It's far better to spend your money on building your health than on destroying it. If you're prone to an addiction, get **positively addicted** to the bodybuilding lifestyle. Such an addiction will enhance, rather than destroy, your life.

ADVANTAGES OF BODYBUILDING

For every disadvantage listed above there is a very good advantage that bodybuilding can give you. The first of these has already been hinted at earlier in this chapter. It is simply that you can *sculpt* your body into almost any shape you want.

At the risk of quoting Arnold Schwarzenegger too much, he is fond of saying, "Being a bodybuilder is like being a sculptor, except that we mold our own bodies instead of working on a lump of clay. If a sculptor notices that his statue's shoulders are too narrow, he slaps on a couple of new slabs of clay and works them into shape until he has the statue's shoulders looking as wide as he wants them to look. We bodybuilders take a little longer to do the same thing, because we work with Presses and Lateral Raises instead of clay, but we still end up with wider and thicker-looking shoulders."

Operating within our skeletal limitations, we can indeed sculpt our bodies. We can reduce the waist here and add to the arms there, which leads to a corollary advantage of bodybuilding. This is the selectivity with which we can add to or subtract from various areas of the body.

The deltoid muscle, for example, is composed of three distinct lobes, called *heads*. Numerous exercises exist for each head, allowing you to stress whichever head you choose to train hardest in reasonable isolation from the rest of your deltoid. So if any muscle area lags behind the rest of the body, it can be attacked selectively even harder to bring it back in line with your other muscles.

ʹAll of our bodybuilding exercise ultimately leads to good health as well, because it stimulates the cardiorespiratory system (although to a lesser degree than does aerobic exercise) and courses life-giving oxygen in increased amounts to all parts of the body.

Since bodybuilders pay special attention to their diets—especially in eliminating such poisonous refined foods as white sugar and white flour (both of which Arnold Schwarzenegger refers to as "white death")—an even greater degree of health can be attained, then maintained for a lifetime. Indeed, few bodybuilders ever become seriously ill, and many of the old-timers of our sport are still alive and kicking quite lustily in their seventies and eighties.

Along with good health, we have the advantage resulting directly from bodybuilding training and nutrition of good appearance. Nothing can beat a slim waist and narrow hips, combined with wide shoulders, for setting the image of a healthy and masculine appearance. While some women may be turned off by bigger-than-usual muscles, our personal observations have indicated that a large proportion of women are driven absolutely whacko by big, hard-looking muscles!

Continuing with the good appearance advantage, I am sure that many readers will be bodybuilding to develop only a slim and muscular body, not a contest-winning physique. In this case, bodybuilding is still quite a valid activity, and the type of body these men develop is often more appealing to women than that of a large-muscled bodybuilder. And it is far easier to develop a Richard Gere or John Travolta body than a Boyer Coe physique!

While it may not seem like such an important factor right now, the advantage of having reserve strength should not be overlooked, and it is another normal by-product of weight training. As Bill Reynolds, editor-in-chief of *Muscle & Fitness* magazine and a former title-winning body-builder, once told me, "During my younger and more foolish days, when I was in the Navy in Norfolk, Virginia, and owned a 650cc Triumph Bonneville motorcycle, I became intimately acquainted with the value of having reserve strength when I was involved in a serious bike accident.

"I was training quite hard at the time—intending to enter the Mr. Chesapeake Bay contest—doing exercises for every part of my body, including for my neck. One morning, a friend and I took our bikes down into North Carolina, near Kittyhawk, to do some speed runs up and down the beach.

"On my third run, I was edging past the 100 mph point on my speedometer—or perhaps even faster, since it's a little scary to look down long enough at such a speed to tell how fast you're actually going—when I saw a white flash in front of my cycle as a large sea bird flew into the front wheel spokes, which in turn launched me over the bike's handlebars.

"Later, my friend George told me I had landed directly on my head and then Evel Knieveled end over end down the beach, then slid on my back feet first for almost a quarter mile down the beach. I am very sure that anyone else would have been killed in such an accident, but my only damage was a few slight abrasions from the sand, and moderately sore neck muscles for the next couple of days. Thank God that my neck was so strongly developed!"

As an additional example of the advantages of having greater-than-normal strength, Franco Columbu once told me that he had to defend his wife and two friends when they were accosted by a group of thugs one evening. The first one came at Franco with a short length of chain, which he never got to use, because a short right to the man's jaw shattered it so badly that the others fled in total fear of the same thing happening to them. Because Franco was so strong, he easily handled a potentially disastrous situation.

To many, the carry-over value of bodybuilding lessons to everyday life would be the most important reason to take up the activity on a regular basis. Bodybuilding demands great discipline in both training and diet for maximum success, but because of the gradually intensifying nature of the training, this discipline is built slowly and painlessly.

Many bodybuilders have discovered that the discipline they have built through bodybuilding's rigors has generalized to everything they did in the rest of their lives. Arnold Schwarzenegger got through the UCLA Business School in record time. Franco Columbu graduated from one of the world's toughest chiropractic schools, and now he is nearing a Ph.D. in Nutrition Science. Frank Zane has a Master's degree and is closing in on a Ph.D. in psychology. Steve Davis has a Master's and is working on a Ph.D., too.

If you have ever had trouble sitting down to study, just imagine the discipline it takes to do it while holding down a full-time job, working out hard, and taking college classes, like all these men did. It won't be so difficult to study then!

I have just given scholastically oriented examples of the carry-over value of bodybuilding in everyday life, but there are numerous other good examples in various facets of life, particularly in life-or-death situations. The old *Your Physique* magazine, the father of *Muscle & Fitness*, used to feature monthly stories of bodybuilders who survived shipwrecks and other natural catastrophies in which everyone else involved perished. And superior conditioning and mental discipline saved these men's lives.

The final advantage of bodybuilding is that it brings with it—at the higher levels—what Joel Grey sang in the film *Cabaret* was "What makes the world go around." There is money in it, or at least there *is* a pot of gold at the end of the training rainbow for the sport's superstars. Here is a concise listing of the numerous sources of income now available to professional bodybuilders:

1. Contest prize money
2. Endorsements and commercials
3. Revenues from issuing mail-order training courses and related equipment
4. Personal appearances (at gym openings, etc.)
5. Guest posing fees (ranging from $1,000 up to the $7,500 Lou Ferrigno is reputed to currently receive for two to three minutes on stage)
6. Training and nutrition seminars
7. Film and television work
8. Special competitions (like "The Superstars")
9. Sales of a personal line of food supplements and training equipment
10. Contracts for personal services (with magazines, as bodyguards, etc.)
11. Modeling fees (for painters, photographers, sculptors, etc.)
12. Fees and royalties for writing articles and books
13. Contest promotion
14. Revenues from writing or recording on a cassette tape personalized training instruction for individual bodybuilders living in areas too remote to have personal contact with a champion bodybuilder.

At the time of writing this book, a number of bodybuilders are fully supporting themselves with the money they make directly from the sport or from sources tangential to the sport (e.g., television roles, working as a bodyguard, etc.). There are probably 20–30 top bodybuilders who fall into this category. And at the upper end of the scale, a small handful (four or five) of the true superstars of bodybuilding are making in excess of $100,000 per year from their bodybuilding-related enterprises. Surely, by the time some of you read this book, that select fraternity will have multiplied in number by several times.

Before you charge into the gym with visions of the millions of dollars you will make with your bodybuilding, keep in mind that only an elite few make *any* money from the sport. You will have to win at least one big title to hit the dollar trail, and I even know of a man who has won the reasonably prestigious Junior Mr. America title (an equal second with Mr. USA as the second most prestigious title, behind only the Mr. America title itself) who hasn't been able to draw even one query about his services for training seminars and posing exhibitions.

The crux of all of this talk about money is that if you aren't willing to put out the effort it takes to win a Mr. Universe title, don't even think about making a living from the sport. Don't quit your job in Pittsburgh and move out to southern California with only $500 in your pocket, thinking you can train at Gold's Gym or the World Gym for a few months, maybe with a part-time job on the side, and end up making big money from the sport in less than a year. It just doesn't happen that way, because jobs in Santa Monica and Venice are hard to come by, and your $500 will buy only a one-month gym membership. In addition, if you are really careful with your money and sleep on the beach, what's left after you pay your gym dues might keep you alive for a month.

You're better off training at home, wherever that might be, until you have won a Mr. USA or Mr. America title. Then you can go to southern California with $2,000–$3,000 to settle in and make enough of a name for yourself to begin making a few bucks from the sport.

THE FINAL SET

In the next five chapters, we will explore the actual techniques of bodybuilding, from the total beginner's level to that of an athlete training for competition. It is difficult to assign a specific length of time that will pass before your first contest, but it will probably be at least two years, and more like three or four, unless you want to embarrass yourself on stage the first time out.

To lead you to a point at which you can compete successfully, I have established five levels of training ability, each of which correspond to one of the next five chapters.

They are:

Level One—Total beginners
Level Two—From two to about six months of steady training
Level Three—From about six months to about one year of training
Level Four—A precompetitive phase lasting for one to two years, during which you are steadily building up the muscle mass and density you will need to have before you decide it is time to compete, and enter Level Five, the competitive phase
Level Five—The actual precontest training phase, featuring the exact training, dietary and mental preparation, and recuperation philosophies of Chris Dickerson—Mr. America, Mr. Universe, and one of the greatest professional champions of the late 1970s and early 1980s

These five levels cover plenty of ground, from rank beginners' training tips and workouts through intermediate and advanced training levels, and finally to the point where you will be built well enough to win bodybuilding contests. Numerous training programs are presented at each level, which will cover a variety of individual training philosophies. Read over each chapter of this book carefully at first, and then jump in with one of the training programs at the experience level that you have finally concluded is the correct one for you.

What do you have to lose? I'll be your training partner, so let's go pump some heavy iron together in Chapter 2!

Gold's Gym in Venice, California, is the Mecca of bodybuilding. Owned by Pete Grymkowski (Mr. World), Gold's has been the training headquarters of virtually every champion bodybuilder since 1970.

2

Beginning Bodybuilding

This will be a fairly schizophrenic chapter for beginners, because it will cover so much ground and deal with many seemingly unrelated concepts. As you get further into bodybuilding—or if you are already past the beginners' stage—these basic concepts will begin to take on logical relationships for you.

If you completely assimilate the information in this chapter, you will be taking a vital shortcut to the top of the bodybuilding ladder of success. Let me give you an example of how valuable sound training advice can be to you.

Manuel Perry, Lou Ferrigno's stuntman on the "Incredible Hulk" television show, stands 6'2" and weighs a very muscular 235 pounds. His arms stretch a tape measure to the limit at a huge and cut-up 22 inches. When Manny won the Mr. USA title a few years ago, it was after only four years of bodybuilding workouts, an unprecedented feat in a sport that usually requires that much training just to win a novice title.

Perry told me how he did it. "I began bodybuilding under a coach who knew all the right ways to build muscle," he said. "That gave me a headstart, which was accentuated when I moved from Boston to southern California to train at the world-famous Gold's Gym.

"At Gold's, several established stars felt I had good potential and took me under their collective wings. I learned all the latest training and dietary techniques from the superstars of the sport, which allowed me to make fantastically quick gains. In only four years of hard and steady training, I accomplished what less fortunate—but equally talented—bodybuilders have needed eight to ten years to achieve."

When Manuel Perry told me his story, I simply *knew* that I had to write this book. The information gap at the basic and intermediate training levels was too great, and there was no adequate treatment of advanced and contest-level training. Potentially successful bodybuilders needed help, so in this and succeeding chapters I have distilled the knowledge of my vast experience as the Trainer of Champions, as well as some of the inside tips I have gleaned from my workouts with most of the world's best bodybuilders. So, as sequentially as possible, let's try to fill in the gaps.

WHERE TO WORK OUT

For the most part, bodybuilding has moved into modern and well-equipped gyms from "the privacy of your own bedroom," the typical place that old Charles Atlas ads said you could train. The main reason for this is probably that a whole generation of mothers has gotten fed up with the holes their sons made in those bedroom floors by dropping weights. So bodybuilders have moved into basements, garages, health spas, Nautilus facilities, schools, YMCAs, and especially commercial bodybuilding gyms.

The traditional place to begin bodybuilding training is at home—if not in your bedroom, at least in a basement or garage. Most of the better bodybuilders I have talked to got their first taste of pumping ye olde iron either at home or at school.

There are several advantages and disadvantages to training in a home gym. The first advantage of home workouts is that you can do them at any time of the day, and even on holidays when schools, YMCAs, and commercial exercise establishments are traditionally closed.

Another advantage is the privacy home gym training affords. If you happen to be skinny (and you won't be much longer!) and are self-conscious about training in front of people, your first stumbling efforts should definitely be made at home. Even the legendary Lou Ferrigno was terribly introverted and skinny when he began bodybuilding; he trained in his basement for three years before joining a public gym.

A number of champion bodybuilders have trained at home for the privacy it affords and because this privacy leads to fewer distractions and, consequently, deeper mental involvement in a workout. Dr. Franco Columbu actually won a Mr. Olympia title while training solely in a well-equipped home gym he set up in an unused garage.

A third advantage of home gym training over training in a commercial gym is cost. The gyms extract a fee to train, and gym dues must be paid every year. But once you buy your home gym equipment it is yours for life, and unless you decide to add to your equipment inventory on a regular basis, you won't have to pay additional gym fees.

The primary disadvantage to training at home is equipment limitation. Unless you want to spend an engineer's yearly net salary on your equipment, you will never hope to equal (save for a couple of cost-saving techniques I will outline in a minute) the variety and convenience of the equipment the champs train on at Gold's Gym and the various World Gyms in southern California.

There are three basic ways to build up a good equipment inventory with minimum expense. You can buy your weights and benches cheaply, make most of your equipment yourself, or pool equipment with one or more friends.

Buying equipment cheaply is most easily done by putting an advertisement in one of the weekly shopping papers you find in most supermarkets or, if you live in a rural area, in the closest town newspaper. You can advertise for used equipment, and a lot of people less motivated than you will have the benches and weights they once bought rusting in an attic or basement. They will be overjoyed to get rid of their used equipment for a few bucks, and a little wire brushing and paint will make the weights and benches as good as new.

You can also haunt lawn sales, but stay away from flea markets, because everything there seems to be an expensive antique if it's more than five years old. Always drive a hard bargain. New weights cost about 60–70 cents per pound, but you should be able to buy used plates for 10–20 cents a pound. Other equipment should be discounted by 50–75 percent. Everyone will screech about how you are ripping them off, but they will invariably sell you what you want at your price.

When you buy used weights, you can

make your best deals if you buy the metal plates instead of the ones that are covered with vinyl. The vinyl plates are filled with concrete, which makes them so bulky that you would need a 10-foot bar to use respectable poundages in your basic exercises. Still, if you buy a new weight set, the vinyl plates are cheaper than metal ones.

Pooling is usually as good or as bad as the people involved in it. A trustworthy group of friends can pool the weights, benches, and other equipment they have and find a vacant garage to train in (check with parents, landlords, etc.), ending up with a well-equipped and congenial gym. On the other hand, however, an awful arrangement can result if you are not eminently careful about who you choose to be in your gym pool.

The main disadvantage of home gym training is its inherent lack of supervision. Regardless of how well I describe and illustrate the exercises in this book, you can use poor form and injure yourself if you don't have somebody who knows what he is doing to be on hand to monitor your exercise form for a few workouts. This problem can be surmounted, however, at the following exercise establishments, which I have listed in order of my personal preference.

Schools, YMCAs, health spas, and Nautilus clubs rate about equally for bodybuilders. They are only open at certain hours, but they offer a vastly superior array of equipment—especially in the variety of exercise machines available—when compared to home gyms. YMCAs tend not to offer much supervision, but there are usually some excellent bodybuilders training at well-equipped YMCAs, and they will keep an eye on you.

High school and college gyms can be good, especially if the instructor is knowledgeable enough to be able to coach you. The only problem with school gyms is the usually crowded conditions. High schools and colleges are hard-pressed for funds, so physical education classes tend to be

In addition to having a wide variety of equipment, a commercial gym like Gold's offers the stimulation of other athletes and the supervision of experienced bodybuilders.

The atmosphere of Gold's Gym—or others like it—is essential for competitive bodybuilders. Such gyms are as quiet as this only at meal times.

jammed with students. As a result, the people who get the most out of classes are those who ask the most questions. If you are in such a crowded class, keep this in mind.

Health spas are high-dollar-volume businesses, which are interested primarily in people who can pay to do relatively piddling workouts to "get fit." Health spas are geared to fitness training, so the weights in these establishments usually won't be very heavy. You will soon outgrow a spa and have to move to better training quarters. And there is always a problem of getting too radical with your training at a spa. Work out too hard and you will be taken aside to be discouraged by the instructor or manager. You are scaring off paying customers, you see.

Nautilus clubs are generally poor places for a serious bodybuilder to train. Because they are selling the Nautilus concept, such facilities seldom have free weights available. Bodybuilders do not live by Nautilus alone, because everyone will need to do at least a few free-weight movements with his Nautilus exercises if he hopes to become a champion.

This brings us to—if you have one available—the best place for a hard-training bodybuilder to work out, a bodybuilding gym. Invariably, the best bodybuilders in any area of the country train at these bodybuilding gyms, and if you show them that you are genuinely concerned about your training, they will gladly help you. As huge as they may seem, they are usually sensitive to a beginner's needs, and it is an ego boost for them to be asked for advice.

The feature that most sets off bodybuilding gyms—over and above the people who train there—is the wide variety of heavy-duty equipment they contain. Most even have some Nautilus and Universal Gym machines in addition to free weights. You will need all this equipment eventually, because in two to three years you will easily be capable of doing Incline Presses with a pair of 100-pound dumbbells, when the things usually stop at 60 pounds in health spas. Ultimately, you may even use a pair of 150s like Ken Waller does, or even the legendary 180s that former Mr. America Clarence Ross used to handle for 10 repetitions.

Your next question will probably be about how to find a gym that caters to bodybuilders. You will first need to check out each gym in your area. Look them up in your telephone book and take an introductory workout at every one on your list. Almost every gym I have ever been in gives you the first workout free.

Once you have been to every accessible gym, you will probably already know the one you will want to join. It will have mostly fixed barbells and dumbbells (the kind that are preset for a particular poundage and don't need to be changed from one weight to another as with a home gym adjustable weight set), and there will be two or three big adjustable Olympic barbell sets, squat racks, chinning and dipping bars, leg tables, hack machines, calf machines, a wide variety of pulleys, and numerous other pieces of equipment. But I'm getting ahead of myself, because the next section of this chapter is where you will learn what these pieces of equipment look like and what they can do for you.

EQUIPMENT ORIENTATION

During your involvement with bodybuilding, you will encounter numerous pieces of training apparatus. On the next few pages are depicted most of the pieces you will be using in your workouts, as well as a brief statement of the function of each.

Barbell

A barbell is the most basic piece of bodybuilding equipment. In its simplest form it consists of a long steel bar (usually four to six feet in length) on which a variety of metal discs called *plates* are fastened to add graded resistance. Many barbell bars are encased in a hollow revolving metal tube called a *sleeve*, which makes it easier for the bar to turn in a bodybuilder's hands

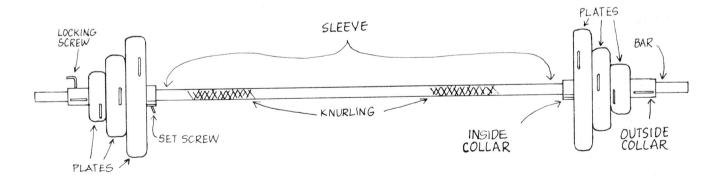

as he exercises. For a more secure grip on this sleeve it is usually scored with shallow grooves called *knurlings*.

On all barbells, plates are kept from sliding along the bar by cylindrical clamps called *collars*. The inner collar on each side is usually fixed into position with a set screw, while the outer collars are easily removable to facilitate adding or subtracting from the weight on the barbell. In large gyms barbells (and dumbbells) are welded into a wide range of *fixed weights* to facilitate training by removing the need for weight changes from exercise to exercise.

Exercise bars with collars weigh approximately five pounds per foot of length. This base weight of the bar should be taken into consideration whenever you make up a certain exercise poundage.

Barbells can be used to exercise almost every skeletal muscle in the body, so an adjustable barbell set will be the first piece of equipment you should buy for a home gym.

Olympic Barbell

For the heaviest loads—such as those used when Squatting or Bench Pressing—an Olympic barbell is usually used. This specialized form of barbell is so finely machined that it balances and revolves much better in the hands than does an exercise bar.

Completely unloaded, an Olympic bar weighs 45 pounds (20 kilograms, or 44 pounds, internationally). The collars weigh five pounds each, and they should always be in place when you use heavy weights in an exercise. Without collars, plates can slide off one end and then quickly off the other, which has caused many training injuries in the past.

An Olympic barbell is used primarily to develop the larger muscle groups of the body, such as those of the legs, back, and chest.

Dumbbells

Dumbbells are simply shorter versions of a barbell that are usually used in pairs, one in each hand. While fixed dumbbells are the rule in large, well-equipped gyms (where the weight of each dumbbell will be clearly marked), you can calculate the weight of an adjustable set by figuring the bar, sleeve, and collars as a base weight of five pounds.

Dumbbells are often preferred by champion bodybuilders to work the body's major muscle groups, since using dumbbells gives one a longer range of motion in each exercise and consequently more complete muscular development.

Universal Gym

These unique multifunctional machines can incorporate exercises for every muscle group, as well as allow six to ten athletes to train simultaneously on one machine. Universal Gym machines are rather expensive, however, and the variety of movements you can do for each body part is restricted. Weight changes from movement to movement can be made by moving an adjustable pin up and down along a clearly marked weight stack.

You can work every major muscle group of your body with a Universal Gym machine. The machines complement barbell and dumbbell training quite effectively.

Here are three types of cambered barbell bars. These are often called "EZ-curl bars."

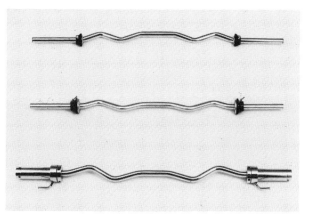

Selectorized pulley apparatus is commonly available in large gyms. Here massive Ken Waller, a two-time Mr. Universe winner, does Pulley Pushdowns for his triceps.

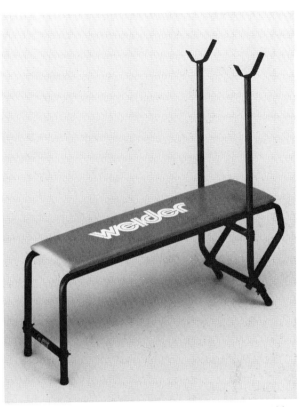

A typical bench-pressing bench has vertical supports with cups at the top to support a heavily loaded barbell. This is a lightweight home gym model.

Nautilus Machines

These relatively new machines offer high-intensity resistance training for every skeletal muscle group. But Nautilus machines are extremely expensive, and it would be prohibitive for any private individual to buy enough machines to equip a home gym adequately. Additionally—as with Universal Gym machines—only a small number of exercises can be done for each muscle group on Nautilus machines.

You can stress all the major muscle groups of your body with Nautilus machines. And as a supplement to barbell and dumbbell training, Nautilus machines can be very helpful.

Bench Press Rack

Initially, you will easily be able to lift a barbell into position by yourself for a chest exercise called the Bench Press. But once your strength becomes sufficient to use heavier weights, it will be easier to use a Bench Press rack to get the barbell into position for the exercise. This rack consists of a flat exercise bench with two cupped uprights attached to one end. A barbell can be placed in the cups and loaded to whatever exercise poundage is desired. Then the barbell can easily be lifted from the rack to the correct starting position and, after the exercise has been finished, replaced. The flat bench can also be used without the rack for a variety of other exercises covering the whole upper body.

Squat Rack

As with Bench Pressing, you will very quickly be able to Squat with exceedingly heavy weights, much heavier than what you will be able to lift up to rest behind or in front of your neck. As with the Bench Press rack, you can load up your bar on the Squat rack, step under the weight, and lift it off the supports for your exercise. Then you can replace the barbell on the rack once you have finished training your thighs to the limit with heavy Squats.

Standing Calf Machine

To avoid having to lift a heavy weight to your shoulders and precariously balance it there for Toe Raises, a yoked weight machine has been developed for you to work the calves with the fullest possible resistance and comfort. You will find this machine ideal for training the large two-headed gastrocnemius muscles at the backs of your lower legs.

Seated Calf Machine

Lying under the gastrocnemius is a wide and flat muscle called the soleus. For full calf development each muscle group in your lower legs must be exercised, but the soleus can be fully stimulated only when stress is put on the calves with the knees bent. So we have evolved the seated calf machine, an apparatus with which you can conveniently rest heavy poundages across your knees for Toe Raises while your legs are bent at a 90-degree angle.

Incline Bench

Incline benches come in various degrees of incline, from about 30 degrees up to 75–80 degrees. The most commonly used incline bench angle is 45 degrees. This bench was developed during the late 1940s by Steve Reeves' trainer, Ed Yarick, so Steve could put stress on his upper pectorals by doing Presses with a barbell or two dumb-

This standing calf machine (left) applies direct stress to the gastrocnemius and soleus muscles of the calves. A bench-pressing bench (below) with weight supports and an adjustable incline board is an essential piece of home gym training equipment.

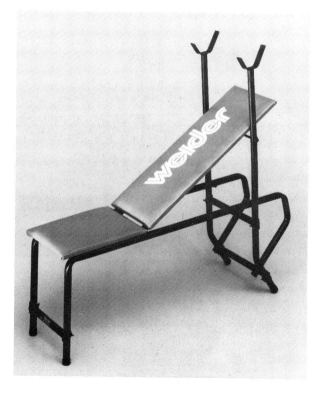

bells while lying back on an angle. Later Steve Reeves modified the bench for biceps work as well, and today we can use an incline bench to do exercises for all the upper body's muscle groups.

Decline Bench

A few years after the incline bench was developed to exercise the upper pectorals, a decline bench was evolved to put the head down instead of up for Presses and Flyes. This brought into play the powerful lower pectoral muscles, which give a sharp outline around the bottom and outer edges of your pecs. Decline benches are also an excellent tool for doing various triceps exercises.

Leg Table

This incongruous-looking machine allows a bodybuilder to train both the fronts and backs of his thighs in a very direct manner. By sitting and placing your toes under one padded roller, you can work the fronts of your thighs. And by lying face down and placing your heels under another roller pad, you can bend and extend your legs to stress directly the biceps femoris muscles (hamstrings) on the backs of your thighs.

Scott Bench

Larry Scott, the first Mr. Olympia winner, used this bench (often called a *preacher bench*) extensively to develop a phenomenal set of biceps muscles. Because of its angled pad, this bench completely restrains your upper arms when you do barbell and dumbbell Curls, almost totally isolating resistance on your biceps. A Scott bench is particularly valuable for building up the lower part of the biceps.

Curl Machine

A curling machine has been developed in an effort to keep pressure on the biceps muscles through a full range of movement. Regular Barbell Curls become easy to do at the finish position, because there is no effective way to harness gravity at that point of the movement. The curling machine solves this problem effectively with a large pulley, affording the biceps greater-than-usual stimulation.

A leg table allows any bodybuilder (in this case, Dr. Franco Columbu) to do Leg Curls and Leg Extensions for the thigh muscles.

Chinning Bar

The old playground standby is in almost all gyms, because it is an effective tool for building the upper back muscles with Chins. Various attachments that go with a chinning bar allow you to do an even more effective back workout than merely with regular Chins.

Dipping Bars

One of the most effective upper body exercises is Dipping on parallel bars. It is primarily for the pectoral muscles of the chest, but it also develops the deltoids and triceps. Two types of dipping bars exist— one with actual parallel bars and one with the bars wider apart on one end than they are on the other. Both types of dipping bars are excellent pieces of equipment for chest, shoulder, and triceps stimulation, and even for an abdominal exercise or two.

Dipping bars, an old playground standby, are essential for complete shoulder, chest, and triceps development.

Leg Press Machine

As an alternative to the Squat for thigh development, a Leg Press machine was developed. The primary exercise is done while lying on the back and pushing a sliding weight platform up and down along parallel rails. A very effective calf movement can also be done on the Leg Press Machine.

Hack Machine

Another frontal thigh movement can be done on a hack machine, in which the back is placed on a different type of sliding platform and Squats are done against the platform's resistance. Hack Squats build up the quadriceps muscles, especially in the area just above the knees. As with the Leg Press machine, an effective calf exercise can also be done on the hack machine.

This vertical leg press machine (used here by Damien Poole, Mr. Universe) provides intense stimulation for the quadriceps and buttocks muscles.

Lat Machine

This apparatus consists of a bar attached to a cable running through an overhead pulley and then back down to a weight stack. Lat machines exercise the body similarly to Chins, except that the bar is pulled down to the neck rather than the body pulled up to the bar. Lat machines are used to develop the large latissimus dorsi muscles of the upper back.

Abdominal Bench

Because regular Situps and Leg Raises soon become ridiculously easy for advanced bodybuilders to do, a bench was developed to add resistance to both exercises. As the end of the bench is raised progressively up its ladder, both movements become more and more difficult to do. This bench works the frontal abdominal muscles.

Roman Chair

The Roman chair is another type of abdominal bench, in which a bodybuilder sits and does partial Situps to develop the frontal abdominal muscles. The Roman chair is very popular with the superstar bodybuilders in California.

Neck Strap

To provide direct work on the neck muscles, a head harness called a neck strap was evolved. This apparatus effectively adds resistance to side-to-side and front-to-back movements of the head. With continued practice very heavy weights can be used with a neck strap, and the neck muscles will expand in size quite rapidly.

Pulleys

Various pulley arrangements have been developed to exercise most of the muscles

An abdominal board with an adjustable incline can be used for both Situps and Leg Raises. The higher the degree of incline on such a board, the more intense a movement done on it becomes.

of the upper body. There are so many of these pulley apparatuses that it would be difficult to explain all of them in detail. Suffice it to say that all are effective pieces of equipment for bodybuilding, and each piece will become more familiar to you as it is used in the workouts in this book.

Wrist Roller

Numerous forearm exercises exist. One of the best can be done with an easily constructed forearm developer called a wrist roller. This apparatus consists of a thick wooden dowel about 18 inches long with a cord run through a hole drilled in the center. A weight can be attached to the free end of the cord, which is then rolled up both forward and backward to stimulate all the forearm muscles.

INFORMATION AND INSTRUCTION SOURCES

If you live in an area where it is difficult to find an experienced bodybuilder to help you with your initial training efforts, this book will be your best source of information. I planned the book for a full year before writing it, and the instructions I give should be very clear, particularly when coupled with multipositioned exercises photos and perhaps with other readings. But as much as my ego rebels at the thought, even what I consider to be exceptionally clear instructions can be misinterpreted. So, you would do well to try to find someone with bodybuilding experience to check out your exercise form when you are starting out.

Numerous weight-training and bodybuilding books are listed in the bibliography at the back of this volume. They will all help you to some degree, but three books are especially valuable. *Arnold—The Education of a Bodybuilder,* by Arnold Schwarzenegger, will give you not only training instructions but also a unique glimpse at the lifestyle of the world's greatest bodybuilder. *Winning Bodybuilding,* by Franco Columbu, is similar. And Bill Reyn-

olds' *Complete Weight Training Book* is a good companion volume for this particular book.

A variety of bodybuilding magazines are also listed in the bibliography, and all are available on large newsstands. I especially recommend my own *Muscle & Fitness* magazine, the bible of bodybuilding.

The only word of caution I can give you about using bodybuilding magazines as information sources is that they are primarily geared toward advanced bodybuilders, and to select and use one of the routines listed would be a disaster. You would very quickly overtrain, so I suggest that you do modified versions of these training programs, cutting back on the total number of sets you do for each body part until the program is appropriate for your training level. The workouts listed in the magazines are invariably well thought out, but you will probably be able to gain only on one or two sets of each movement. (Bodybuilding jargon is covered later in this chapter.)

Gym instructors are excellent sources of information, but they usually have a whole gymnasium to cover and you will need to seek them out for advice. Because they are so busy, they will tend to lose interest in you very quickly. On the other hand, however, gym instructors usually know bodybuilding inside and out, or they wouldn't have their jobs.

The number one source of training information is definitely the bodybuilding champions. The vast majority of good bodybuilders will answer your questions in an eminently authoritative manner, *if* you approach them correctly. Never ask a question of a bodybuilding champion when he is training, even if he is resting between sets. There is a tremendous amount of mental involvement in training at the high level he occupies, and you will break his concentration with your question. It will be far more congenial to wait until after his workout, because the champions usually stay around the gym for a few minutes to shoot the breeze. That's the best time to ask questions.

If you don't have direct access to a champion, you can still learn his training secrets by either buying his training courses (advertised in *Muscle & Fitness* magazine) or attending one of his training seminars around the country. Some of the courses are excellent, and everyone's seminars will be worth the investment of $10–$20 for a three-hour session. If you get a chance to attend a seminar, grab it!

BASIC BODYBUILDING TERMINOLOGY

If you run across a term that you don't understand while reading this book, it will probably be defined in the glossary at the end of the book. Still, there are a few terms so basic that they need to be defined now.

Each individual movement in a training program is usually called an *exercise*. A knee bending movement is an exercise, whether it is done freehand or with a 500-pound barbell held across your shoulders. In your exercise *routine* you may do a series of 10–20 of these squatting movements. Each individual, complete, up-and-down movement is called a *repetition* (often abbreviated to *rep*). The whole series of 10–20 reps is called a *set*. And one or more sets of each exercise can be done in the *workout*.

FREE WEIGHTS VERSUS MACHINES

Other than home gyms, virtually every weight room you visit will have both free weights (barbells and dumbbells) and a variety of exercise machines. Both types of equipment have advantages and disadvantages.

For the most part, machines are far more expensive than the barbells, dumbbells, and benches that they replace. And all the machines offer you only a handful of exercises for each body part, as contrasted with literally hundreds of movements that can be done for each body part with free weights.

On the positive side of the coin, machines are usually safer and more convenient to use than barbells and dumbbells. And even more important, those machines—like

Nautilus—that put resistance on a muscle in the contracted position are superior to any other form of resistance exercise, except for certain free-weight movements that also involve such a peak contraction. It is only in the fully contracted position that the maximum number of muscle fibers are working, and if the weight is still heavy in this position, the muscles benefit more from the exercise (this is called the Weider Peak Contraction Principle).

So which is best—free weights or machines? In my opinion, the answer to this question is "both." For the most complete workouts you should utilize every form of resistance equipment available to you— Nautilus, Universal Gym, free-apparatus machines, and free weights.

PROGRESSION

As I mentioned in Chapter 1, progression of resistance is the foundation of bodybuilding. If a muscle is stressed more and more in each succeeding workout, it is forced to hypertrophy (increase in mass) to accommodate the additional work load put on it. This is the basis of the Weider Overload Principle of training, which is used universally in bodybuilding.

Resistance can be increased in three ways. The least important of these for beginning bodybuilders—yet one of the most important for advanced men—is to reduce the rest periods between sets while maintaining the same sets, reps, and training poundages from workout to workout. For our purposes, however, the rest intervals between sets will consistently remain at about 60 seconds. Some contest bodybuilders will rest as little as 10–15 seconds between sets when peaking for a competition.

The variables we will be playing with to augment intensity will be increased repetitions and increased weight on the bar or machine being used. It is common practice to add to the number of repetitions until an upper limit *guide number* is reached. Then five to ten pounds are added to the bar or machine and the number of reps is decreased to a lower guide number.

Since the number of repetitions to be done is cut considerably when weight is added to a movement, the new exercise poundage should not be too difficult to handle. From the lower guide number, add a rep or two at each workout until you are again at the top guide number. Add weight, drop the reps, and build up again and again.

Just so you understand fully what I am talking about, let's say your Bench Press workout calls for one set of eight to twelve reps. Eight is the bottom guide number and twelve is the top guide number. On successive workout days you might progress like this over four weeks of three-times-weekly workouts (75 x 8 means to do 75 pounds for eight repetitions).

Day 1	Day 2	Day 3
75 × 8	75 × 10	75 × 11

Day 4	Day 5	Day 6
75 × 12	80 × 8	80 × 9

Day 7	Day 8	Day 9
80 × 11	80 × 12	90 × 8

Day 10	Day 11	Day 12
90 × 9	90 × 10	90 × 11, etc.

This process becomes a little more complicated when you are dealing with multiple sets of each exercise. Let's follow another four weeks of Bench Press workouts, this time for three sets of eight to twelve reps.

Day 1	Day 2	Day 3
75 × 8	75 × 10	75 × 11
75 × 8	75 × 9	75 × 10
75 × 8	75 × 8	75 × 10

Day 4	Day 5	Day 6
75 × 12	80 × 8	80 × 9
75 × 12	80 × 8	80 × 9
75 × 12	80 × 8	80 × 8

Day 7	Day 8	Day 9
80 × 11	80 × 12	80 × 12
80 × 9	80 × 10	80 × 11
80 × 9	80 × 10	80 × 11

Day 10	Day 11	Day 12
80 × 12	85 × 8	85 × 10, etc.
80 × 12	85 × 8	85 × 9, etc.
80 × 12	85 × 8	85 × 9, etc.

You have undoubtedly noticed in the above example that you should be trying to increase the number of reps in *each* set. Never increase the weight until you have reached the upper guide number for all three (or whatever number you are doing) sets.

NUMBER OF REPS

Research has pretty well established that for most individuals the correct rep range for muscle building is from about six reps to twelve or fifteen. With fewer than six reps you will build more power than muscle mass; with more than fifteen reps the emphasis shifts to enhancing endurance.

As you have undoubtedly been told, there are exceptions to most rules. Reg Park, Mr. Universe, used sets of single reps for his pectorals at one time and achieved great results. And Casey Viator won the Mr. America title at the age of 19 while doing predominantly 20-rep sets.

REPETITION SCHEMES

Typically, beginning bodybuilders do one to three sets of eight to twelve repetitions for each exercise (although more reps—up to 20—will be done for the calves, and even more for the abdominals). For some who are lacking in endurance, the three sets will not be 12–12–12 reps, but probably 12–10–8. If this is all you can do, great! Don't worry about it. Also, you can increase resistance when you have reached a level of 12–11–10 reps rather than 12–12–12.

Another type of repetition scheme you may want to try eventually is one of descending weights on each set with the same repetitions for every set. Instead of doing three sets of Curls at 70 x 12 x 12 x 12, you might want to do 75 x 10, 70 x 10, and 65 x 10. This scheme is every bit as effective as using the same poundage for every set.

A final repetition scheme can be used when trying to build power. It is one of ascending poundages and descending reps on succeeding sets, which is called *pyramiding*. Using the Curl example from the preceding paragraph, this could consist of something like 60 x 12, 70 x 9, and 80 x 6. In this case, the first set is a warmup, the second is a muscle-builder, and the third one a power-builder.

TIME FACTORS

There are five temporal factors that should be considered in bodybuilding—frequency of workouts, when to train, how long to train each session, training tempo, and when to change exercise schedules.

Frequency of Workouts

At this training level and for most of the next one we will be training three nonconsecutive days each week, e.g., Monday–Wednesday–Friday, Tuesday–Thursday–Saturday, etc. This allows the body to rest and recuperate fully between training sessions. At Level Three, or perhaps at the end of Level Two, you will be able to do what is called a *split routine*, which involves training half your body one day and the other half the next day. This allows you to train four or more days per week and also shortens the length of each daily workout.

For now, however, let's consider training only three nonconsecutive days per week. So that your weekends can be free, let's try Mondays, Wednesdays, and Fridays.

When to Train

I personally prefer training at the same time each day, probably because I work all day, and after dinner is the only time I consistently have available to do my workouts. Many champion bodybuilders with whom I have worked out prefer getting up early and training before work, however. Bill Pearl—one of the greatest champions our sport has ever produced—has trained at 5:00 or 5:30 A.M. for nearly 30 years, and he has obviously thrived on it. So, if you are a morning person, try training before you go to school or work.

Champion bodybuilders train at all times of the day, so it makes little difference when you actually do your workouts. The crucial factor is merely choosing a time of the day when you can find one to two hours totally free from distractions.

The champions used to subscribe to the theory that working out at the same time each day was a way to make your body peak its energies for that regular hour or two. But, in actuality, muscles will often grow faster if trained with different workouts on each training day, and even when trained at different times every day. This involves the Weider Muscle Confusion Principle, which advocates doing radically different types of training each day to keep the muscles from adapting to a particular stress and halting their growth.

How Long to Train

None of the programs in this chapter should take you more than 30–45 minutes to complete, unless you are doing more talking in the gym than training. And unless it is just before a competition when you will be training two to three hours per day, you will probably never need to spend more than 1½ hours in the gym.

Training Tempo

As mentioned earlier, we will be resting for about a minute between sets. Be careful not to rest too much longer, because training too slowly will cause the body to cool off, which is courting injury.

The speed of actually moving the bar during an exercise should be moderately slow, especially on the first two or three reps, after which the speed can be accelerated. In the next chapter we will cover more on this by discussing a concept called *negative emphasis*.

Changing Training Schedules

To prevent boredom, I suggest that you switch to a totally new workout program each four to six weeks. Some bodybuilders—such as Lou Ferrigno—use a "nonroutine routine" in which they utilize muscle confusion by never doing the same workout twice. Arnold Schwarzenegger, on the other hand, uses the same workouts for some body parts for years, believing that once he has found a supereffective program he would be foolish to change it. Either of these techniques may one day be found to work best for you, but for now train on a program for only four to six weeks before changing to another one.

WHAT TO WEAR

Your training attire depends largely on the temperature. In hot weather you will need to wear no more than a pair of shorts and a tank top, while a hard winter will require a full sweat suit, or perhaps even two. I always recommend wearing clothing that is either loose fitting or very stretchy, because you will need complete freedom of movement when bodybuilding.

Training shoes with good arch supports are essential for several reasons. First, they protect your feet from some of the pain of a plate accidentally dropped on them. Second, it's good to have the arch support for foot health when using very heavy weights, which can compress your arches when your feet are bare. And finally, when doing calf exercises, it is essential to have a good tread on the soles so your feet won't slip while doing Toe Raises.

On occasion, you will need a few other miscellaneous pieces of training attire/equipment. One of these is a leather weight-lifting belt, which is used by many individuals for lower back support when training with heavy weights in standing exercises. Most of the bodybuilding magazines carry ads for these belts, and many sporting goods stores sell them.

Some bodybuilders also use rubber waist and knee bands to keep the lower back and knees warm and free from injury when training heavily. These are available through ads in most bodybuilding magazines or at sporting goods stores.

STRICT FORM

While cheating a weight up definitely has its merits and will be discussed in a later chapter, for now we will be doing all of our exercises in the strictest possible form. Toward the end of this chapter we will present a number of exercises to be combined into a beginners' program. When using strict form it is essential that each movement be done over its complete range of motion and without any assistance from the parts of the body not actually being exercised by the movement. Feel the weight the whole way up and then lower it under full control. There's a lot of research that lowering a weight slowly (lowering is called the negative phase of a movement) has great potential for muscle growth and strength increase.

Another facet of training with strict form is to move only the working parts of the body, keeping the rest of the body stiff and supporting the movement. Loosening everything up is an invitation to cheating up the weight, which negates much of the value of the resistance of the barbell, dumbbells, or machine over part of the range of movement on an exercise.

BREATHING

Most gym instructors and college weight-training teachers say that the most common questions asked by beginning bodybuilders concern how to breathe properly while exercising with weights. There are basically three schools of thought on the subject. One involves inhaling as you exert, while another calls for inhaling as the weight is lowered and exhaling as you exert. The Weider Research Clinic recommends breathing naturally and whenever it is convenient during a movement. Thinking too much about breathing detracts from your concentration on the working muscles, and as long as you are taking in enough air to avoid passing out, you're doing a great job.

MUSCLE SORENESS

An inevitable consequence of applying a much-heavier-than-usual load to a muscle is stiffness and soreness. The muscle just isn't used to heavy stress, and nature responds by making it sore. This soreness can be avoided, or at least reduced in severity, in several ways:

1. Hot baths and hot showers will increase blood circulation and relax the muscles.

2. Massage will alleviate soreness, but sometimes the pain of manipulating sore muscles can be worse than the original pain.

3. Repeating the previous day's workout usually will hurt a little, but it will cut the overall pain considerably.

4. Break in slowly when you begin to train. Use light weights and only one to two sets per exercise until your body grows accustomed to the stress.

SAFETY FACTORS

Because of the very heavy weights you will eventually be using, it is a good idea to adopt appropriate safety practices starting with your first workout.

Always use collars on the bar when doing heavy exercises. I once injured my back doing Squats without collars. Half the plates fell off one side in the middle of a rep, and then the heavy side dipped and dumped all of its plates. Finally the first side snapped downward and shed the rest of its plates. I was left with an empty Olympic bar across my shoulders and a painfully twisted lower back.

Another safety precaution is to use spotters when attempting limit efforts in the Squat and especially in the Bench Press. There are records of bodybuilders who died from training alone and being strangled by a bar that fell across a neck. Having a spotter standing at the head of the bench will prevent any problems like this when you are Bench Pressing.

SETTING GOALS

Unless you have a road map, it's tough to locate a place that you have never visited. In bodybuilding this road map will be the goals you set and your ultimate physique will be the place you visit. Without the first of these factors you will not find the second.

Goals are a means for striving, and they come in two types: major and minor. Let's say you have a 16-inch arm and you want to push it up to 18 inches. The 18-inch measurement is your major goal. Between 16 and 18 inches you can have any number of minor goals. You can make 16½ inches a minor goal, then 17, then 17½, until you reach the major goal. Or, you can proceed in even smaller increments of a quarter or an eighth of an inch.

The key to achieving major goals lies in making the smaller, minor goals eminently achievable. When you reach each minor goal, the major goal becomes less formidable. This is clearly illustrated by one of Confucius's major aphorisms: "The journey of a thousand miles is started with a single step."

Hero Images

A part of goal setting is having a hero image, a person you can strive to emulate. This can be a single bodybuilder like Arnold Schwarzenegger or a composite of Robby Robinson's back, Roy Callender's chest, Ken Waller's calves, and so forth. In the next section I will talk about record keeping, and you might like to cut a picture of your hero image from *Muscle & Fitness* and paste it in the back of your record notebook for constant inspiration.

When adopting a hero image, be sure to pick one with a skeletal structure similar to yours. If you are light-boned like Frank Zane and pick a larger-boned hero like Franco Columbu, you will never achieve Columbu's muscle size. You would be better off shooting for a Zane-like body—and you still might ultimately find it difficult to come close to your idol's development, because everyone has unique muscle shape and development potentials. Use your hero only as a guide and develop the best physique you can. Then somebody else seven or eight years from now will be cutting your picture out of a magazine and pasting it into his diary.

Record Keeping

Accurately kept records of each workout, your daily diet, and a monthly progress log are deemed beneficial by many champion bodybuilders, including Frank Zane, three-time Mr. Olympia. As I will discuss in the next chapter, the essence of bodybuilding is the "Great Experiment." It is using your body as a big chemistry lab and trying different things on it, seeing what works, keeping it and discarding what has proved worthless. And a training log is one of the best ways to see graphically what is doing you the most good in your workouts. As such, it is invaluable.

The best kind of record book is a bound ledger that can be found in most dime stores. Also, get a fine-point ballpoint pen while you are there. Most other types of pens have water-soluble ink that will run all over if you sweat on the page you are writing on, so I would advise against them.

Work out some sort of page format and abbreviate the weights and repetitions as I did earlier in this chapter. While some peo-

ple like to get accurate records down while they are doing the actual workout, many find that this spoils their concentration. Most of the champs remember very accurately what they have done in a training session, and after a workout they can make their entire entry.

Here are a few of the miscellaneous things you can also include in your record book: what you have eaten, including supplements and amounts of foods; daily body weight; monthly measurements; how much sleep you got and how deeply you slept; your mood and energy levels prior to and after the workout; your thoughts during training; and your recovery rate after the workout.

Measurements

I have talked a lot about measurements in this book, so perhaps we should touch on their value to a bodybuilder. In general, they are good for beginners and bad for more advanced men.

One sure way to increase enthusiasm for training is to see progress, and one way to see progress at first is to note that an arm, leg, or chest measurement has increased by a half inch or your waist size has been reduced a little. So, for beginners, whose measurements almost invariably go up quickly, this is a great tool.

But, if you are familiar with geometry, you will understand that the bigger a muscle gets, the more added tissue it is going to take to increase the muscle an additional inch in girth. Therefore, actual circumference gains seem to occur very slowly in advanced trainees, which can be discouraging. And even more discouraging is going on a precontest diet and seeing the measurements actually go *down* from fat loss, even though you invariably begin to look better.

As a result of the above situation, very few champion bodybuilders actually take measurements, though many quote them. Be wary of these quotes—including all that I have already mentioned—because they are often inflated claims.

Should you intend to take measurements—and I encourage beginners to do so—try to take them at about the same time each day and definitely do so prior to your workout. After training, the muscles will be pumped up a little and will show an impressive, but unreliable, measurement. This muscle pump is caused by an augmented flow of blood through the tissues to flush out fatigue products and replace them with new fuel and oxygen supplies. So, this pump is very temporary and results in false measurements.

Inspiration and Enthusiasm

Due to natural body fluctuations of energy and enthusiasm, there will be days when you will prefer not to train, or at least you will feel like working out would be a chore. The fact is that regularity of training is essential to success, so the only excuse for missing a workout is death or at least being sick enough to be in bed. You must take your regular workout, even if it is only an abbreviated version of the one you usually do.

Inspiration is the way to build enthusiasm for workouts and there are a number of ways to become inspired. One is to get a new issue of *Muscle & Fitness* in the mail or at a newsstand. Or, you can catch a Steve Reeves movie on a television late show. Talk to your hero at a gym; go to a bodybuilding competition; watch an inspiring movie like *Rocky*; or make love to your lady (it's a good warmup anyway).

If all else fails, start leafing through your training diary. Check out your measurements and exercise poundages of six months or a year ago. You will see an incredible degree of improvement that just isn't noticeable day to day. And that's guaranteed to fire you up for at least half a workout.

BASIC DIET

No matter how hard you train, your progress can grind to a shuddering halt if you don't eat right. Indeed, most top body

builders credit good diet for 50 percent or more of their success. Here is a list of basic "do" and "don't" maxims that will improve your diet and result in faster muscle gains.

Do

1. Eat a little protein at each meal. Eat beef, fish, poultry, eggs, and milk products. Your body can digest and assimilate only 30 grams of protein per feeding, so you needn't eat huge protein meals.
2. Eat fresh fruits and vegetables, all as close to being raw as possible.
3. Eat a little vegetable fat in the form of seeds and nuts for skin and nerve health.
4. Eat a chelated multiple-mineral and multiple-vitamin supplement with each meal.
5. Eat with as much variety as possible.
6. Eat at least three meals per day. Small meals are digested and utilized more efficiently by the body.
7. Drink plenty of pure water.

Don't

1. Eat junk foods, which are highly processed, fried, or full of sugar and white flour.
2. Eat excessive animal fats. (Trim fat from all of your meat.)
3. Drink soft drinks or alcoholic beverages.
4. Use too much salt or other seasonings.

This is an excellent overall dietary philosophy for the beginning bodybuilder, but we will have to go into some refinements

Christine Zane provides her husband Frank with nutritious, high-protein meals such as this one of baked trout, salad, and iced tea.

for specific bodybuilding purposes later, in the intermediate and advanced sections. In the meantime, don't be surprised if your appetite increases once you are training hard, because you will be burning up plenty of extra calories in your workouts.

Should you be a vegetarian, you can still make good muscle gains. Two former Mr. Americas—Bill Pearl and Roy Hilligen—and Mr. International, Andreas Cahling, are lacto-ovo-vegetarians and have retained superb condition. Just concentrate more on protein foods like milk products, nuts, and seeds.

REST AND SLEEP

Innumerable bodybuilders have used their bodies as laboratories over the years, and all of them have concluded that maximum growth occurs only with adequate sleep and rest. What is "adequate," however, is difficult to predict for each individual. Eight hours of sleep has become a fairly widely accepted average, and during that eight hours your muscles will recuperate from a hard workout and expand in size.

In addition to getting eight or nine hours of sleep, it is an excellent practice to take a short nap in the late afternoon. This added half hour or so of sleep will refresh you considerably and make your training day even more productive.

If you cannot sleep a full eight hours or if you need more than that amount of sleep, it should be clear to you that you have discovered something else about your working body. Also, keep in mind that there are natural fluctuations from day to day in the amount of sleep you require. Seven hours may be enough one day, nine the next, and eight the third. It all balances out over the long run, so don't worry about such fluctuations.

PROPORTION

Even before you touch a weight, get it solidly into your head that you will be exercising all parts of your body equally

hard. The common result of lack of guidance in the first year or two of training is to discover a favorite body part and overdevelop it at the expense of overall body proportions. Usually this means concentrating on the showy upper body muscles and neglecting the legs, which results in a badly proportioned physique.

At a bodybuilding contest, the judges look first for proper proportion among all the body parts. Any underdeveloped area is something that will kill your standing in the contest, so make developing good proportions your primary goal in bodybuilding beginning with your first workout. Exercise each body part with the same intensity, and once you discover lagging areas, work them even harder.

FEELING IT OUT

We are almost ready to start working out now, but there is one last word of caution I want to throw out to you. Your first few weeks of training are a feeling-out and learning process, so please do *not* get carried away with piling extra weights on your barbell too soon. For at least the first five workouts you will be learning how to do the movements themselves, and adding weight too soon could encourage the development of bad exercise performance habits. It could also make your muscles very sore.

In a few pages you will find a number of beginning programs. For the first workout day, be content to do one set of each exercise with the suggested poundages. During each subsequent session you can add three or four new total sets to your workout until you have slowly worked up to the full program. *Then* you can start adding weight to each movement.

WARMUP

Extensive athletic research has confirmed the value of a warmup prior to doing any type of heavy training. It loosens the joints and muscles, which is a primary factor in preventing injuries. Warmups also will allow you to use heavier training poundages than you could ever use going into a workout cold.

There are numerous types of warmups you can use, and they involve jogging, stretching, and, for all I know, jacuzzi dips. The warmup most commonly used by champion bodybuilders, however, involves simply starting out a workout by doing one or two sets each of two or three basic exercises with a light weight. Then, if they are using heavy weights—which you aren't using yet but will be using a few months from now—they might do a set with a medium-heavy intermediate poundage on a basic exercise for each body part as an additional warmup. Otherwise, it is mostly a matter of keeping a steady pace in your training so your body doesn't cool off during your workout.

LEVEL ONE EXERCISES

In this section, I will give you a pool of basic exercises that can be used in the beginning programs at the end of this chap-

ter as well as in all the training routines in the balance of the book. Be sure to refer to the photos with each exercise description as you read the directions.

Thighs

Universal Gym Leg Press. Sit in the seat as illustrated and place the arches of your feet on the pedals in front of you. There are two silver handles at the sides of the seat, which you can grasp with your hands to keep your body from popping out of the seat as you exercise. Straighten your torso. From this starting position, simply push out the pedals until your legs are straight and then return them to the starting position. Be careful not to bang the plates of the machine together at the bottom of the movement, because they are somewhat brittle and break easily. For a longer range of movement on these Leg Presses, you can move the machine's adjustable seat closer to the pedals.

Universal Gym Leg Press—start (left) and finish (right).

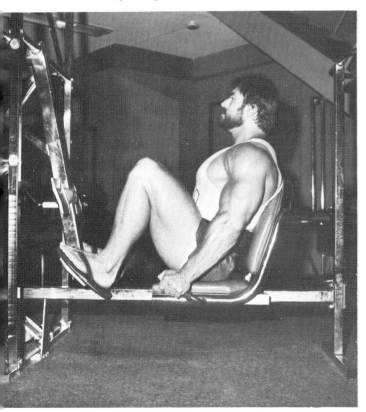

Vertical Leg Press. Under this machine will be a padded board with one end higher than the other. Lie on it with your head at the lower end and your hips directly under the board above you. Place your feet at about shoulder width on the center of that foot board. Attached to the uprights at your sides are two stop bars that you can rotate outward to free the weight carriage. Push up on the board, rotate the stops,

Angled Leg Press—start (above) and finish (below).

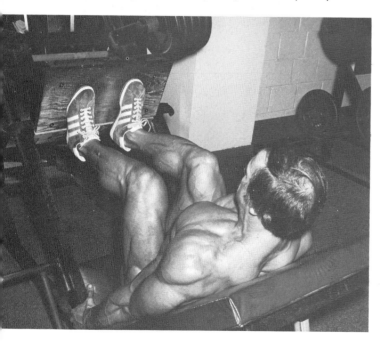

Vertical Leg Press—start (above) and finish (below).

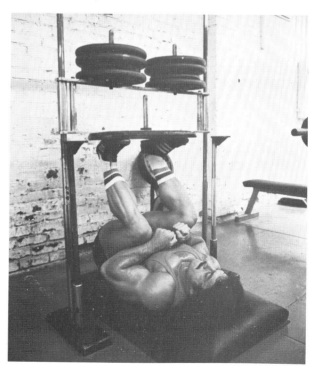

bend and straighten your legs for the required number of repetitions, and then replace the stops when you are finished. If the weight proves to be too heavy to complete a rep, don't worry, because safety stops to catch it are built into the uprights of the machine.

Squat. This is a Deep Knee Bend with a barbell held across your shoulders. It is also one of the single best weight-training and bodybuilding movements in existence, since it works not only the frontal thighs but also the hamstrings, lower and upper back, and abdominal muscles.

You have probably heard that Squats will ruin your knees. I could write several pages about why this is not true, but take my word for it, there is *no* chance of damage unless you bounce at the bottom of the movement. Only then would it be remotely possible to damage your knee ligaments and cartilage.

To start a Squat, put a barbell behind your neck, balancing it in position with your hands. Stand erect with your feet set at about shoulder width and your toes pointed slightly outward. Keeping your head up and your torso as upright as possible, squat down as deeply as you can and then return to the starting position. If you are having trouble with your balance while Squatting, put a two-by-four-inch board under your heels.

Squat—start (left) and finish (below).

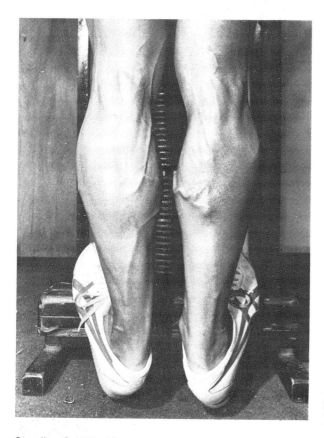

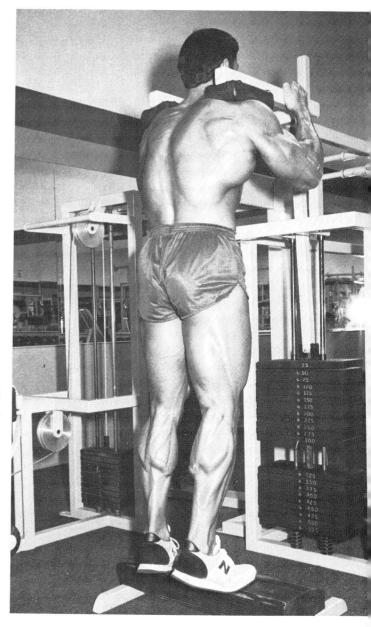

Standing Calf Machine—start/detail (above) and finish (right).

Calves

Calf Machine. Doing Toe Raises on a calf machine is fairly simple, but it is nonetheless an effective movement for the gastrocnemius muscles at the backs of your lower legs. Start by putting your shoulders under the yoke of a calf machine. Place your toes and the balls of your feet on a four-inch block (on some machines this block is built in). Keeping your body straight, stretch your heels as low as possible so they are at least two or three inches below the level of your toes. Then rise up on your toes as high as you can. Return to the stretched position and repeat for the required number of repetitions.

There are three toe positions you can use for this and all other calf movements: toes pointed inward, toes pointed outward, and toes pointed straight ahead. Alternating among these three toe positions is the best way to achieve full calf development, because each toe position stresses the calves from a slightly different angle.

If a calf machine isn't available, you can hold a barbell behind your neck and rise up and down on your toes. The inherent problem with doing Toe Raises with a barbell is in the balance; hence the popularity of calf machines. Still, if you do the movement slowly, you will be able to keep your balance fairly easily.

Seated Calf Machine—near start (left) and finish (above).

Seated Calf Machine. As mentioned earlier in this chapter, this machine is used primarily to develop the soleus muscles of your calves. Sit in the seat and wedge your knees under the weight pads. Your toes and the balls of your feet should be on the toe board. Release the weight by rising slightly on your toes and swinging the machine's stop bar forward. Rise up and down on your toes to complete your set and then replace the stop bar to its original position. Use all three toe positions on the Seated Calf Raise.

Calf Press. On either the lying or seated Leg Press machine, get into the same position as you would to finish a Leg Press—your legs will be straight—except that only your toes and the balls of your feet are kept in contact with the board or pedals of the machine. From this basic starting position you can stretch your calves and then extend your feet in the standard three toe positions.

Calf Press—midpoint (left) and finish (below).

Back

Lat Machine Pulldown. This is analogous to doing Chins, but instead of pulling your body up to the bar, you will be pulling the bar down to your body. This will be especially effective if you can't do many Chins. Kneel or sit under the pulley and grasp the bar with a grip slightly wider than your shoulders and with your palms facing away from your body. From there, pull the bar down alternately to your upper chest and then to your upper back behind your neck. Emphasize pulling your elbows down and back during the movement, and you will be working the powerful latissimus dorsi muscles of your upper back.

Lat Machine Pulldown—start (right) and finish, behind neck (below).

Seated Pulley Rowing—start (above) and finish (right).

Seated Pulley Rowing. This exercise is very similar to rowing a boat, and it affects the latissimus dorsi muscles as well as the biceps. Take a narrow grip on the machine's bar or handle, brace your feet on the foot bar, and sit back. Keep your back muscles tensed throughout the movement. Lean forward and stretch your arms out as far as possible. Try to feel a stretching sensation in your upper back muscles. Lean backward slowly as you pull the handle in to touch your lower chest. At this finish point of the movement your torso should be upright. Slowly return to the stretched position and repeat the movement for the required number of repetitions.

Bent Rowing. This is the barbell version of the preceding exercise. With your feet set at about shoulder width, bend over until your back is parallel to the floor. Your knees should be bent slightly throughout the movement to reduce the strain on your lower back. With either a wide grip or a narrow grip, palms facing your legs, pull the barbell from a dead hang upward until it touches your lower chest. Pause for a second in the top position and return the barbell to the starting point. Repeat for the required number of repetitions.

Bent Rowing—start (above) and finish (below).

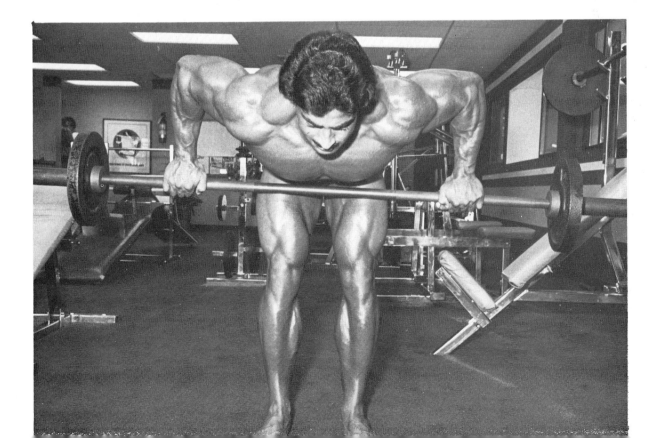

Shoulder Shrug. To develop the trapezius muscles of your upper back, hold a barbell across your thighs with your palms facing your legs. You should be standing erect, and your grip should be set at about shoulder width. From this basic starting position, sag your shoulders downward as far as they will go and then shrug them up as high as possible. Try to touch your shoulders to your ears before lowering the weight back to the starting point. Shrugs can also be done with dumbbells or on the Universal Gym Bench Pressing station.

Shoulder Shrug—start (right), finish (below), and finish, dumbbell variation (below right).

Stiff-Leg Deadlift. For your lower back muscles you can do Stiff-Leg Deadlifts. It is best to stand on a bench as you do them, because this will allow you to stretch your spinal erectors and hamstrings more by lowering the weight farther than you could while standing on the floor. Use the same grip and starting position as you did for the Shrug. Keeping your legs straight, bend over slowly as far as you can, or until the barbell handle touches the bench, and then return to the starting position. Repeat the movement for the required number of repetitions.

Stiff-Leg Deadlift—start (below left) and finish (below right).

Chest

Bench Press. Many bodybuilders consider this pectoral muscle builder to be the king of upper body movements. Lie back on the bench and take a grip with your hands about six inches wider on each side than the width of your shoulders. Your palms should be facing your feet. Lift the bar off the rack and start the movement by supporting it at arm's length directly above your chest. Then lower the barbell under control to your chest so that it touches at the bottom edge of your pecs. Push the barbell back up to the starting position and repeat the movement.

Bench Press—start (above) and finish (below).

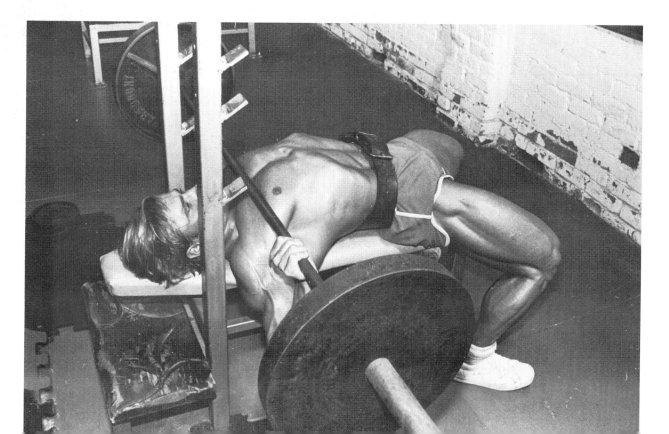

Incline Press. This movement stresses the upper pectorals and is the same as a Bench Press, except that it is done lying back on a 45-degree incline bench. This time lower the bar to the base of your neck before pressing it back up. Inclines take a little time to get used to, and at first the bar will want to go every which way but up. Keep at it, though, and you will be doing them like a Mr. America soon.

Incline Press—start (below left) and finish (below right).

Parallel Bar Dips. A lot of readers have done this exercise in a physical education class at one time or another as part of a physical fitness test. Champion bodybuilders use Dips primarily to work the lower and outer parts of their pectorals. Start by jumping up on the bars and supporting yourself with straight arms. Some bodybuilders like to bend their legs for balance; others prefer their legs held straight. From the supported position, bend your arms and sink down as far into the movement as you can. Then press back up to the starting point.

Parallel Bar Dips—start.

Parallel Bar Dips—finish.

Military Press—start (above) and finish (right).

Shoulders

Military Press. This is a sort of silly old name for a great shoulder, upper back, and triceps movement, but the name shouldn't detract from the effectiveness of the exercise. Take a shoulder-width over-grip (palms facing your legs when the bar is lying on the floor) on a barbell and bring it to your shoulders. Your feet should be set a comfortable distance apart, and your torso must remain strictly upright during the movement. Press the weight overhead close to your face until it is at extended arm's length directly above your head. Lower and repeat. Some bodybuilders have to be pretty careful with this movement, because if they have large noses they might hit them with the bar as it is pressed upward!

Upright Rowing—start.

Upright Rowing. This is genuinely one of the best upper body exercises ever invented. It stresses the shoulder muscles quite hard, as well as the trapezius, biceps, and forearms. Take a narrow over-grip (six inches between your hands) in the middle of a barbell. Start the movement standing erect with the bar, your hands resting on your upper thighs and your arms held straight. Steadily pull the bar up to your chin, emphasizing getting your elbows up at the top of the movement. Hold the bar at your chin for a second or two and lower it slowly back to the starting point. Repeat the movement for the required number of repetitions.

Upright Rowing—finish.

Side Laterals. This is a dumbbell movement that will do much to broaden your shoulders. Grasp a pair of dumbbells and start with them resting on the fronts of your thighs, your palms facing each other and your arms slightly bent. Keep your palms down as you raise the bells up in semicircles directly to the sides until they are at shoulder height. At the top of the movement, rotate your thumbs slightly downward. This twist of the wrists at the top of the movement is essential if you want to isolate stress primarily on the sides of your deltoids. Lower the dumbbells back to the starting point and repeat the movement for the required number of repetitions.

Side Laterals—start (right) and finish (below).

Arms

Barbell Curl. Begin to work your biceps and forearms by taking a shoulder-width under-grip (palms facing away from your body) on a barbell. Start by standing erect with the bar across your thighs. Your arms should be straight, and your upper arms should be pinned to the sides of your torso, where they must remain throughout the movement. From this basic starting position, curl the bar in a semicircle from your thighs to your chin. Return the barbell along the same arc to the starting point. Be very sure to keep your body still while doing Curls, moving just your forearms. You should also try to cock your wrists as the bar is being raised.

Barbell Curl—start (left) and near finish (below).

Dumbbell Curl. This is almost exactly like the Barbell Curl, except that it is done with two dumbbells instead of a barbell. The main difference in doing Dumbbell Curls is that some people find the Barbell Curl an unnatural movement for their wrist structure, causing wrist pain. Doing Curls with two dumbbells allows your wrists to move more naturally. As you curl up the dumbbells, your thumbs should be pointing straight forward at the start of the movement. Then they are rotated outward as far as possible during the actual movement. This hand rotation is called *supination*.

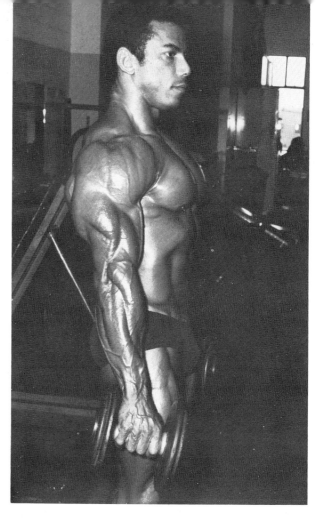

Dumbbell Curl—start (right) and finish (below).

Lying Triceps Extension. This is a very direct triceps stressing exercise. Start by lying back on a flat exercise bench with a narrow over-grip on a barbell (there should be four or five inches between your index fingers). For the starting position the bar should be above your chest and your arms should be straight, much the same as in the finish position of a Bench Press. From there, unlock your elbows and lower the bar in a semicircle to the bridge of your nose. Return it to the starting position and repeat the movement for the required number of repetitions. For maximum triceps stress, it is essential to hold your upper arms in the same position (straight up and down) throughout the movement.

Lying Triceps Extension—start (above) and finish (below).

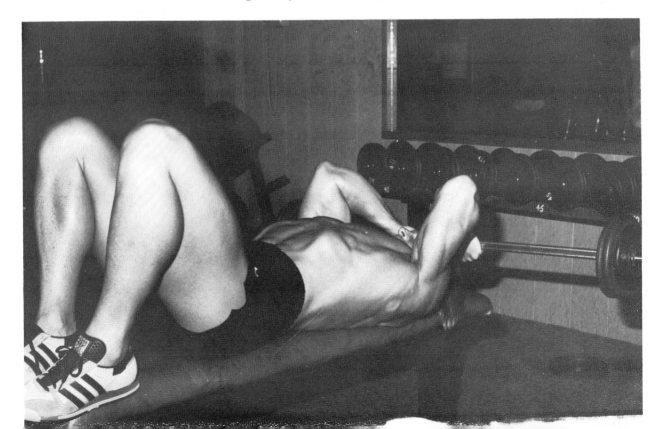

Lat Machine Pushdown. This movement is very similar to the Lying Triceps Extension in that the upper arms must be kept motionless at all times while the arms are being bent and straightened. Start with a narrow over-grip on the lat machine pulley bar. The starting position calls for your upper arms to be held straight down at your sides and the bar across your thighs. Unlock your elbows and let the bar travel in a semicircle to your chin. Then press it back along the same arc with triceps strength to the starting point. Repeat for the required number of repetitions.

Lat Machine Pushdown—start (above) and finish (right).

Abdominals

Situps. Certainly, anyone who is reading this book must have a pretty good idea of how to do this movement, but there is one important thing you need to pay attention to when doing Situps. Be sure to keep your knees *bent* slightly during the exercise, even though many misinformed people will tell you to keep them straight. Keeping your legs straight when doing Situps will eventually injure your lower back! For added resistance on Situps you can raise the angle of incline of your abdominal board.

Situps—start (above) and finish (below).

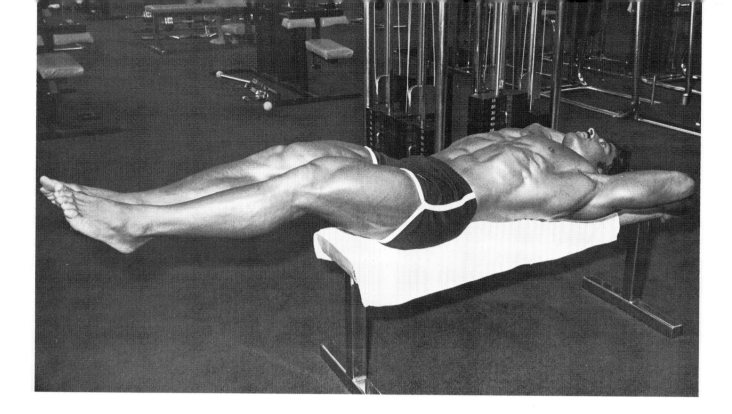

Leg Raises. Again, keep your knees bent slightly during the movement to prevent strain on your lower back. Start your Leg Raises by anchoring your hands behind your head on the strap or roller of an abdominal board or on a heavy piece of furniture. This will keep your upper body restrained while you raise your legs in a semicircle from a straight body position until they are at right angles to your torso. Again, you can raise the head end of your abdominal bench to add resistance to the movement.

Leg Raise—start (above) and finish (below).

LEVEL ONE TRAINING PROGRAMS

Now that you know all the basics about bodybuilding training, we arrive at the workout programs you will use at the beginning level of training. The tables list several such routines. Again, keep in mind that you need to break in slowly with each routine to lessen the chance of developing muscle soreness. In each program, % indicates the percentage of your body weight that you should use for a starting poundage in each exercise.

Universal Gym Program (first six weeks)

Exercise	Sets	Reps	%
1. Leg Press	3	10–15	60
2. Calf Press	3	15–20	60
3. Bench Press	3	8–12	35
4. Lat Pulldown	3	10–15	40
5. Military Press	2	6–10	30
6. Shrug	1	15–20	40
7. Pulley Curl	3	8–12	30
8. Lat Pushdown	2	8–12	25
9. Situps	1	25–50	—

Barbell-Dumbbell Program (first six weeks)

Exercise	Sets	Reps	%
1. Seated Calf Machine	3	15–20	60
2. Squat	3	10–15	60
3. Stiff-Leg Deadlift	1	10–15	40
4. Bent Rowing	3	10–15	40
5. Bench Press	3	8–12	35
6. Upright Rowing	2	8–12	30
7. Lying Triceps Extension	2	8–12	20
8. Dumbbell Curl	3	8–12	30
9. Leg Raises	1	25–50	—

Mixed-Equipment Program (first six weeks)

Exercise	Sets	Reps	%
1. Standing Calf Machine	3	15–20	60
2. Leg Press	3	10–15	60
3. Stiff-Leg Deadlift	1	10–15	40
4. Seated Pulley Row	3	8–12	35
5. Incline Press	3	8–12	30
6. Side Laterals	3	8–12	5*
7. Lat Pushdown	2	8–12	25
8. Barbell Curls	3	8–12	30
9. Situps	1	25–50	—

* (each dumbell)
Note: In each of these programs, you should be gradually working up to the number of suggested sets. Be careful to start out with only one set of each movement and then slowly add sets to your routine.

Barbell-Dumbbell Program (second month)

Exercise	Sets	Reps
1. Standing Calf Machine	3–5	15–20
2. Squat	3–5	10–15
3. Stiff-Leg Deadlift	1–2	10–15
4. Upright Rowing	3	8–12
5. Bent Rowing	3	8–12
6. Bench Press	3	8–12
7. Incline Press	2	8–12
8. Lying Triceps Extension	3–4	8–12
9. Dumbbell Curl	3–4	8–12
10. Side Laterals	3–4	8–12
11. Leg Raises	1–2	25–50
12. Situps	1–2	25–50

Mixed-Equipment Program (second month)

Exercise	Sets	Reps
1. Calf Press	3	15–20
2. Seated Calf Machine	2	15–20
3. Leg Press	3–5	10–15
4. Stiff-leg Deadlift	1	10–15
5. Lat Pulldown	3	8–12
6. Seated Pulley Row	2	8–12
7. Bench Press	3	8–12
8. Incline Press	2	8–12
9. Side Laterals	3–4	8–12
10. Lying Triceps Extension	3–4	8–12
11. Dumbbell Curl	3–4	8–12
12. Situps	2–3	25–50

Note: These two programs are a logical progression from the first three workouts. They will soon lead to the routines at the end of the next chapter, Level Two Training. You have my apologies for not giving you a second Universal Gym program, but there are so few exercises that you can do on the machine that it would be impossible to come up with one that has any variation from the basic program, other than merely doing a greater number of sets for each exercise.

PUMPING OUT

In the next chapter I will give you a wide variety of intermediate-level training tips, nutrition programs, exercises, and workout routines that you can use for the next six months of your bodybuilding training. If you follow this upcoming advice well, you should be able to add 6–10 pounds of solid muscle mass to your body and increase all of your training poundages by at least 50%. And by the time you have concluded your Level Two training, your physique will have improved so much that you'll begin to receive compliments on your build.

Mike (left) and Ray Mentzer (right) are the most successful team of bodybuilding brothers in history. Both have won Mr. America titles. Mike, who is two years older, has also won Mr. Universe. Ray placed second to Germany's amazing Jusup Wilkosz in the 1979 Universe.

3

Level Two—Up to Six Months of Training

Don't let the *six months* in the title of this chapter enslave you, because that time period is merely an educated prediction of how quickly Albert Average will progress in his bodybuilding training. It is *not* the Eleventh Commandment, given by God to Joe Weider because Moses didn't happen to be around at the time.

As you have no doubt already discovered, no one is really "average." Every bodybuilder is as unique as a snowflake, and you might very well progress significantly faster—or perhaps even a little more slowly—than our friend Albert Average. Thus, you might be able to pass through Level Two in as few as three months. Or you can dawdle enough to waste a year or more getting from Level One through Level Two and to Level Three.

If you are progressing more slowly than the pace I have set in this book, there is no cause for alarm. You are just as "normal" (a word akin to *average*) as the supermacho bodybuilder who is progressing through his workouts twice as fast as you and building muscle at a rate three times faster than yours. Believe me, there is nothing to worry about.

You may well be one of those bodybuilders—like Ed Corney, a Mr. America and Mr. Universe winner who trained for nearly 15 years before he even entered a competition—who bloom as champion bodybuilders later than everyone else. If you *are* a late bloomer, you'll end up on top over the long haul, *if* you are persistent and train regularly, despite the lack of apparent results from years of steady training. Occasionally, it is safer to be progressing fairly slowly. Let me tell you why.

The primary problem with gaining muscle mass and fat weight too quickly over the first few months of training is that some guys get carried away with this quick progress. They become obsessed with making even faster and greater gains, so they either train their strong points too hard (throwing their bodies even more out of balance, because those muscle groups grow in size much more quickly than other body parts) or they begin to do even more training than they originally were doing to make such impressive gains.

Unfortunately, adding more exercises, more sets, and greater intensity to a workout can lead to disaster instead of success.

A week or two after adding all the new exercises and sets, our size-obsessed bodybuilders are horrified to see their bodybuilding progress—i.e., their muscle growth rate—grind to a shuddering halt. The reason? Because their bodies could not handle the drastically increased volume of work, our friends have *overtrained.*

Life and bodybuilding are both filled with commonly accepted fallacies, and one of them in our sport is, "If three sets are enough to make good muscle mass gains, then 12 sets will make me gain four times as fast." In actual practice, doing 12 sets instead of three often results in *one-fourth* of the progress rate originally experienced!

We will discuss overtraining in much greater detail in Chapter 4, but for now you must understand that when the body's energy stores are expended, they can only be replenished at a fixed rate. And if you are using up energy faster than you are replacing it, and you do this for a long enough period of time, you will literally run out of gas (fuel) and become overtrained.

To put this more simply, when you use up more energy than your body can replace, you go into energy debt, the same as you would go into debt financially if you spent more money than you could earn for the next five years. Gradually, your energy reserves are used up, just as your checking account is used up over time if you keep spending money faster than you can earn it.

Just as a bank sends you a letter advising you that your checking account has been closed, your body signals you that its energy account is bankrupt by telling the muscles that they can't continue growing. To conclude our analogy, an overtrained condition in your body is exactly like an overdrawn checking account with your bank. Either way, you're in big trouble!

The logical solution to an overtraining problem is to keep your total number of sets for each body part within the tolerances I have already recommended or will recommend in future chapters. You should also be careful to increase progressively

the weights you are using for each movement, as well as to begin using the intensity techniques—like cheating, forced reps, and negative emphasis—that I will explain in the rest of this book.

The key to avoiding overtraining, then, is not to do more work, but to continue with the total number of sets you have been doing and just train much harder within each set. That's the way Mr. America and Mr. Universe Mike Mentzer does it in his uniquely personalized Heavy Duty Training System. He gains faster on four or five sets per body part than most bodybuilders do on 20–30 sets per muscle group, because he trains very intensely and scrupulously avoids overtraining.

A NATURAL?

Perhaps only one out of 100,000 men could be called a "natural bodybuilder," the type of man who has been blessed with the potential to become the next Arnold Schwarzenegger, Sergio Oliva, or Mike Mentzer. If you happen to be that one gifted man in 100,000, you will become a truly incredible bodybuilder within the next five or ten years. You *may* be that one man in 100,000, but how can you tell if you have the potential—both physically and mentally—to become a champion bodybuilder?

As I mentioned in Chapter 1, there is a continuum of ability to gain muscle mass, and that continuum ranges from gaining very slowly to gaining incredibly quickly. If you are a naturally talented bodybuilder, you will be at the fastest-gaining end of the continuum. You will blow up with muscle tissue like a balloon expands with added air. You may gain 10–15 pounds of solid body weight in your first month of training. And you could easily put on 30–40 pounds in your first full year of steady training.

There are also skeletal advantages that a truly talented bodybuilder must have, but it will be difficult for you to identify them by yourself. Any experienced bodybuilder can evaluate your skeletal structure in two or three minutes and accurately tell you if

Sergio Oliva, a Cuban currently living in Chicago, had the greatest natural potential of any bodybuilder. He won three successive Mr. Olympia titles.

Larry Scott, two-time Mr. Olympia, had abysmal potential, but with perseverance and dedication he finally succeeded as a champion bodybuilder.

you have the bone structure to be great. But even without a perfect skeletal structure, you can succeed magnificently as a bodybuilder.

Larry Scott, the first Mr. Olympia winner, had a narrower-than-normal shoulder structure and fairly wide hips, but by dint of total dedication to bodybuilding, unswerving perseverance, and faithful adherence to the Weider System of Training, Larry did a magnificent job correcting and otherwise compensating for these weaknesses in his body. He obviously did a good job of it, because Larry Scott has won two Mr. Olympia titles.

The third quality a potential champion must have is intelligence. At first glance it might seem like a bodybuilder could succeed with only the intelligence of a toad, but bodybuilding has become a complex science in recent years, and a bodybuilder must be intelligent enough to understand the scientific concepts behind his training. If he is unable to grasp the essentials of kinesiology, anatomy, biochemistry, exercise physiology, psychology, and numerous other scientific disciplines, he will never reach his ultimate potential as a bodybuilder.

The final quality all champion bodybuilders must possess ties into the last factor. You must make a total mental commitment to bodybuilding, which involves much more than just having intelligence. If, as happened to Arnold Schwarzenegger in his youth, you just "click" onto bodybuilding, you will automatically have a strong mental commitment to training for the sport.

You will know when you have this type of mental commitment, because you will feel much like you did when you first fell in love with a foxy lady. You won't be able to think of anything but bodybuilding, just as you couldn't think of anything but your girlfriend back in junior high school. The bodybuilding bug will have taken such a big bite out of your arm that you will be infected with iron fever for the rest of your life.

If you can soon develop such an all-consuming love for the sport, you are in luck, because your training will always be a joy to you and never a burden, as it is for some bodybuilders. Still, because you are blessed with such a great love for the sport I also love, you must be careful that you don't let your enthusiasm get out of hand, because that will lead you to train so hard and so long that you will soon be over-trained. Then you can train for months without making an iota of progress, and you may even lose ground occasionally.

TRAINING PARTNERS

By now you may have already started training with someone in the gym where you work out. If not, let's discuss the advantages and disadvantages of utilizing a training partner so you can decide if you need one.

There are two minor drawbacks to working out with a training partner. The first is a slight loss of concentration when pumping iron, because it is difficult to concentrate deeply on the working muscle when you are training at someone else's pace. This leads to, or perhaps is even part of, the second disadvantage of partner training. You will constantly be at someone's mercy. If he is sick, has to work late, or is just plain lazy, you are stuck by yourself, often waiting fruitlessly at the gym for him to show up.

Both training partners must compromise on their workout programs and the length and frequency of their training sessions, because there is little room for individuality when using a training partner. And that

is the main reason that many superstars, like Frank Zane, balk at using a training partner.

The main advantages of training with a partner are the assurance of always having a fast and consistent workout pace, a degree of general inspiration emanating from your partner, and an ever-present spotter for your forced reps.

To get deeply into the Weider Quality Training Principle before a contest, you must rest very little between sets and yet still use reasonably heavy weights in all your exercises. This is a brutal way to train, and it is much easier to use Quality Training when you have a partner to urge you on and to take turns on the bar or machine with you. And it becomes easier to exceed all your previous training efforts when someone is constantly urging you to go far past your reps and poundages from

Ray and Mike Mentzer are super-effective training partners. Here Ray helps Mike complete a set of forced reps in the Pulley Curl.

the previous workout. A training partner can also inspire you through example, just as you inspire him with your own fast and heavy workouts.

Two of the most enthusiastic proponents of partner training are Lou Ferrigno and Andreas Cahling. Both of these great champions are convinced that they can get in much better workouts using a training partner than when pumping iron on their own.

To conclude this discussion of partner training, I must mention the growing incidence of male-female training partnerships. This has become a very popular concept, because the men feel that they usually end up showing off by using heavier poundages when training with a woman. And if a woman is in good physical condition, she can really push her male training partner to his limit in a workout. Obviously, she won't be able to handle his training poundages, but she will almost invariably have greater endurance, which allows her to set a much-faster-than-usual workout pace.

NEGATIVE EMPHASIS

Physiologists have scientifically determined that the negative (lowering) phase of a movement actually has more potential for muscle growth and strength increase when it is trained hard than does the positive (lifting) phase. This is why I developed the Weider Retro-Gravity Principle, which stresses the use of negative reps in a workout.

For two or three years during the early 1970s, it was "in" to do a lot of pure negatives in every workout. This involves having a training partner help you lift a very heavy weight to the finish position of a movement, so you can mightily resist the downward momentum of the barbell or machine as it is lowered. This was obviously as hard on the training partners as it was on the bodybuilders doing the negative reps, which is probably the main reason pure negative training soon waned in popularity.

A much more convenient method of utilizing negative reps in a workout was evolved by the great bodybuilder/intellectual, Mike Mentzer. He calls this training method *negative emphasis*. In its most basic form it consists of raising the weight normally and then lowering it half as fast as you raised it, thus emphasizing the negative portion of the movement. This, of course, puts greater-than-normal resistance on the negative half of an exercise, which makes your muscles grow a little faster.

An incidental advantage of using negative emphasis is that it obviates any chance of letting the momentum of the barbell help you complete the movement. Ordinarily, as you move a weight from the starting point to the finish of its range of motion, a significant degree of momentum is developed, effectively making the barbell significantly lighter than it really is at the end of the movement. You have no doubt experienced this phenomenon with Military Presses and other movements.

By lowering the weight slowly from the finish position back to the starting point of the movement you are using, you eliminate the chance of momentum helping you lift the weight. And because there is a full quota of heavy resistance along the entire range of motion of the exercise, your muscles are stressed more and consequently are forced to grow larger and stronger at a faster rate than they would hypertrophy if momentum aided them in lifting the barbell.

Herculean Mike Mentzer has taken his concept of negative emphasis much further than merely slowing the movement of his exercise apparatus during the negative phase of an exercise. On some movements, such as Leg Extensions, he will do the positive half of the exercise using both legs to get the weight to the finish position. Then he removes one leg from contact with the machine, which forces the other leg to bear twice as much resistance for its negative phase than it had to lift in the positive phase of the movement. Mike alternates the leg that bears the resistance in the negative part of the exercise with each repetition.

When training to total muscle failure with forced reps and negative reps, a training partner is essential. Here Kent Keuhn, Past-40 Mr. America, helps Mike Mentzer blitz his lats on a Nautilus pullover machine.

And he has obviously built incredible muscle mass and density using this technique.

Obviously, you can only use this form of negative emphasis on exercise machines, where removing an arm or a leg from the apparatus will not destroy the balance of the exercise. You could, for example, easily remove one hand from the gripping handle of a curling machine, but it would be impossible to do the same thing when performing a set of Barbell Curls.

Mike Mentzer has also developed a method of including pure negative reps along with positive repetitions and forced reps in a single set of any exercise. Forced reps will be discussed in detail in Chapter 4, but for now I will tell you briefly that they involve having a training partner pull up just enough on a barbell or machine to assist you to *force* out two or three reps more than you could have completed on your own.

To achieve nearly maximum intensity in his training, Mike does a set consisting of four to six full-range (no cheating or short-range movements) to failure. Then, when he cannot complete another full rep on his own, he has his brother Ray assist him in completing two or three forced reps. Finally, when Ray has come to the point where he is lifting most of the weight instead of Mike—because Mike's working muscles have become almost completely fatigued from the positive and forced reps—he lifts the weight up to the finishing position for Mike, who then resists it as best he can as it is lowered back to the movement's starting point for two or three pure negative reps.

This type of training is extremely intense, and Mike and Ray are both in obvious pain at the completion of a set of positive, forced, and negative reps. But they grow much more quickly using this type of training on one or two exercises per muscle group than they can with any other technique except rest-pause training, an almost inhumanly brutal training method that will be fully discussed in Chapter 5. This is such a painful way to train that at times I'm almost ashamed that I conceptu-

alized rest-pause training. But then again, Ray and Mike Mentzer swear that their muscle mass increases much faster using the Weider Rest-Pause Principle than when training in any other manner.

CHEATING

Cheating was one of the first training principles I developed for the Weider System of Training, and I publicized this effective training method in my bodybuilding magazines as long ago as the early 1950s. It's a very stressful training method but still a much more mild way to work out than is rest-pause training.

In its original form, the Weider Cheating Principle consisted of kicking or swinging a weight up to the finish position of a movement by using the legs or some other part of the body in conjunction with the muscles that would ordinarily supply impetus to the movement. The amount of cheat used to get the weight to the finish position of an exercise varied from a little bit to a lot, depending on how fatigued the muscles being worked had become.

After the barbell had been cheated up, it was lowered back to the starting point with the bodybuilder mightily resisting its downward momentum, the same way you do it when you are performing a negative rep. This last part of the cheating movement is almost pure negative work, so cheating worked quite well in building bigger muscles, even though I didn't understand negative-rep training at the time. I had merely stumbled upon negative reps, and several years elapsed before I discovered why and how they worked and codified the Retro-Gravity Principle.

Obviously it is best to use the Cheating Principle only on the lighter type of movements, e.g., Barbell Curls, Dumbbell Side Laterals, and Dumbbell Bent Rowing. You have been using heavier and heavier poundages for your Squats and Bench Presses on each workout, so you are probably fairly strong in these movements at this point. I'm sure that you can imagine how difficult it would be to cheat on a set of 300-

pound Squats. And if you did try to cheat on such a heavy exercise, you would be risking serious injury.

In a bodybuilding workout, the Weider Cheating Principle is best used at the end of a set of strict reps, so you can push past the point of normal muscle failure and receive greater muscle-building stimulation from a set. Using Barbell Curls as an example of how to cheat correctly, you might have done six strict reps before failing to complete the seventh repetition. But instead of terminating your set—as many bodybuilders would—you should cheat just enough to get the weight up for that seventh rep and then lower the barbell in a negative movement. Do this for two or three extra result-producing reps at the end of any heavy set of the exercises you are doing in your workout routine.

LAYOFFS

The human mind and body just weren't constructed to endure many consecutive years of hard year-round training. As a result, minor injuries begin to crop up if you have been training continuously for too long, or you can become mentally sick of training. It is perfectly normal to experience these symptoms of having become worn out both physically and mentally. When this happens to you, it's time to take a one- or two-week layoff. If you are totally worn out, you may even need to stop training for as long as four to six weeks before your enthusiasm for lifting heavy iron returns.

During your layoff, stay totally away from the gym. You can—and should—keep physically active by swimming, hiking, bicycling, running, playing basketball, or kicking a soccer ball, but *stay away from the gym.* And while you are taking a layoff, don't use it as an excuse to junk out on hot dogs and ice cream. Maintain a good diet and avoid all junk foods, because junking out will make it much more difficult to regain your prelayoff condition once you resume training.

A week or two of laying off training will totally rejuvenate both your mind and your body. The little injuries that used to make a few exercises somewhat painful will have totally healed, and you will be mentally eager to jump back into a regular training routine. Once you are back in the gym working out, you will notice that your training energy is twice what it was before you took your layoff, and your workouts will have the momentum and power of a runaway locomotive screaming down a 10-percent grade.

It is inevitable to lose a little muscle mass and quality during your short layoff, but don't worry about that, because only two or three workouts after getting back into training, you will actually be looking better than you did just prior to laying off!

As you get further into serious bodybuilding training, it won't hurt to take a full month off every year. Dr. Franco Columbu, Mr. Olympia of 1976, regularly takes a month completely off training following his major competition each year. And Frank Zane, a three-time Mr. Olympia, trains only recreationally for three or four months after a competition and sometimes takes six to eight weeks totally off weight workouts to practice archery and other recreational activities. Then, in January, when he buckles down to train seriously for the Mr. Olympia competition in the fall, he's all business and makes great year-to-year gains, largely because he does rest his body for so long each year.

HANDLING TRAINING INJURIES

You will probably recall from the preceding discussion that taking a short layoff is one way to heal training injuries. These injuries are seldom serious, and when they are manifested merely as a bothersome minor pain, I suggest that you take a layoff to heal them.

The real secret to handling training injuries is to *prevent* them from occurring. This can easily be done by being sure that you are thoroughly warmed up before using any heavy poundages in your workouts. And once you are fully warmed up, be sure to stay warm for the entire workout by resting no more than 60–90 seconds between sets, regardless of how heavy your training poundages might be. By warming up correctly and staying warm during your workouts, you will avoid at least 80 percent of all potential training injuries.

If you do suffer a muscle pull or a tearing of tissue in any joint or muscle, start home treatment with a first aid procedure consisting of icing the injured area for 10 minutes each hour for the first 24 hours (except, of course, while you are sleeping). This will prevent—or at least limit—swelling and hemorrhaging at the injury site, which in turn will allow the injury to heal much more quickly.

After 24 hours of periodic icing of the injury and another 12–24 hours of rest, you can speed up the healing process by applying heat to the injured area for a few minutes several times a day. Damp heat is best, because it is more efficiently conducted into the body's internal tissues, so use a hot water bottle wrapped in a rather moist towel to apply heat to the injured joint or muscle.

While you are recuperating from an injury, you can continue to train with weights for the rest of the body, as long as you avoid all movements that might stress the injured area even slightly. After a week has passed—and if your injury was not so severe that you had to see a physician about it—you can begin putting light stress on the injured body part during your workouts for the rest of your body.

By gradually increasing the resistance used in exercises stressing the injured area, you can quickly restore it to full strength. Occasionally you can make a muscle or joint even stronger than it was prior to being injured, merely by training it hard and consistently with weights and being cautious enough to reduce the resistance and training intensity for the injured area whenever you feel any pain at the site of the injury.

Should you suffer a severe training injury—which is less common in weight training and bodybuilding than in most other sports, including such innocuous activities as running and playing tennis—you should immediately ice the area and seek transportation to a hospital emergency room for an examination. You should also consult a physician about an injury if it does not respond positively to the foregoing at-home rehabilitation procedures. I'm definitely not a medical doctor, and I don't presume to practice medicine. So, if the injury is serious, see a physician as quickly as possible.

NAUTILUS MACHINES

Sooner or later, somebody will tell you about the wonders of training on Nautilus machines. A sales representative at one of the numerous Nautilus facilities that have sprung up like mushrooms around the country will tell you how you can develop an outstanding physique, optimum strength, and a distance runner's level of aerobic conditioning by doing only one set on each of their Nautilus machines (a total of about 20 sets for your whole body) three times a week. He will also tell you that your entire workout will take as few as 20 minutes and will certainly not last longer than 30 minutes. One popular advertising slogan that I have seen claims that Nautilus workouts are torture but that they definitely work in building maximum strength and endurance.

Each week I receive scores of letters at the offices of *Muscle & Fitness* magazine from bodybuilders who have heard all of these claims and who want to know if the claims are true. Up to a certain level—and keep in mind that at one point I trained exclusively on Nautilus machines for three months—the machines are marvelous inventions. I know Arthur Jones, the inventor, personally, and he has designed machines that apply a balanced resistance to each muscle over its full range of motion, including at the fully contracted position of each movement. This feature incorporates the Weider Peak Contraction Principle (discussed in detail in Chapter 5). Actually, the main reason that Nautilus machines are

Mike Mentzer, again shown using a Nautilus pullover machine, is one of a handful of champion bodybuilders sold on the benefits of using Naultilus machines. Most champs prefer training with free weights and associated machines.

able to provide such intense resistance to working muscles is that they have incorporated in their design features most of the time-tested Weider training principles, which have been in existence for almost 30 years.

Mike Mentzer and other bodybuilders can get a thorough workout doing only three to five sets per body part on Nautilus machines, but there are (as mentioned briefly in Chapter 2) several drawbacks to Nautilus machines.

It would easily cost $35,000–$40,000 to outfit your home gym with enough of the machines to work your body fully. A year's membership at most Nautilus clubs costs between $300 and $400. So, the first disadvantage of Nautilus training is its relatively high cost. You could buy enough equipment to give yourself workouts just as intense as—and often more intense than—Nautilus for far fewer bucks by investing in barbells, dumbbells, and a variety of weight-supporting racks, benches, and pulley arrangements.

Another major problem, even though the most recently developed Nautilus machines are trying to cope with it, is that some people—individuals like 6'5" Lou Ferrigno and 5'2" Danny Padilla—are bigger or smaller than average and just don't fit into most of the machines.

A few of the machines fit my own body like a white glove fits a beautiful woman's hand, but many other machines don't conform to my body proportions at all. The leg machines are excellent for me, as are the deltoid unit, the behind-neck lat machine, the two neck units, the overhead biceps curling machine, and the lat rowing machine. The lat pulldown station and pullover unit, however, are depressingly mismatched to my body. I get zero muscle growth stimulation from both types of their triceps machines and zero plus perhaps a half point from the shoulder shrugging machine. All the shrug machine does is put painful pressure on my forearm muscles.

The final drawback to Nautilus machines is the most depressing of all the problems they present to a hard-training body-

builder. This is boredom. Compared to the myriad movements evolved over the years for use with barbells, dumbbells, benches, pulleys, racks, and exercise machines developed for use with free weights, there are depressingly few Nautilus exercises to choose from for each muscle group. And this leads to boredom quite quickly, which in turn results in an aversion to training and a consequential abandonment of regular progressive resistance training.

To eliminate boredom in your workouts you need merely do 25–30 of the 50 or 100 exercises for your chest that you can think up, putting them in some sort of sequential rotation, so you needn't do the same one more than once or twice a month. This is an extreme case, of course, but simply using 10–12 chest movements with free weights will eliminate the boredom of training your chest with the *two* Nautilus exercises available for pectoral training.

INTERMEDIATE DIET TIPS

Except for a few food supplements I will recommend in the next section of this chapter, you really won't be eating much differently than the diet I suggested in Chapter 2. You should still be consuming plenty of protein. Taking into consideration the average American daily diet, let's clarify how an intermediate bodybuilder's diet should differ. Here is a sample menu for one day of beginning-intermediate bodybuilding nutrition:

Breakfast

1. Three to five eggs with cheddar cheese in an omelette.
2. A hamburger patty (stay away from bacon and sausage, because they are both almost pure fat, which is more than twice as high in calories as protein and carbohydrates); as an alternative to the hamburger patty, you can occasionally eat a broiled or baked fish fillet.
3. One piece of fruit (e.g., a grapefruit, a basket of strawberries, a cantaloupe, a honeydew melon, an orange, etc); canta-

loupe and strawberries are lower in calories than any other fruits.

4. One glass of nonfat milk (use raw milk if it is available); the milk is much better for you if it has had its fat content removed than if it is still a full-fat milk, and your body can digest and assimilate the protein and other nutrients in raw milk much more efficiently than it can use pasteurized milk.

Mid-Morning Snack

1. Nuts or seeds (sunflower, etc.—all nuts and seeds should be eaten raw, not roasted and salted); or cold cuts or meat; or a cup or two of naturally flavored low-fat yogurt.

Lunch

1. Broiled fish; or tuna salad; or broiled meat, poultry, or lamb (avoid pork, because it is high in fat and hence overloaded with calories).
2. One vegetable dish (green beans and spinach are much lower in caloric content than oil-bearing vegetables like corn and soybeans; never eat avocados, which contain huge amounts of fat).
3. A green salad (unless you opted for the tuna salad as your main course).
4. An apple or one piece of some other kind of fruit.
5. Another glass of nonfat raw milk.

Preworkout Snack

1. Two or three pieces of fruit, preferably with each one different from the others (this is a good method for building up a greater reserve of energy for your workout).

Dinner

1. Broiled meat, fish, or poultry.
2. One or two vegetable dishes, including one high-starch food like potatoes, rice, or yams.

3. A large green salad (use only oil and vinegar dressing and a little black pepper on your salads; most commercial salad dressings are loaded with unnecessary fats and are therefore excessively high in caloric content).
4. Another glass of nonfat raw milk.

Evening Snack

1. Two or three ounces of your favorite type of hard cheese or a small serving of cottage cheese.
2. Alternatively, you can eat a few ounces of cold cuts and a piece of fruit (preferably a low-calorie fruit like strawberries).
3. A final glass of nonfat raw milk.

This diet is very heavy in milk products, because milk and its by-products promote muscle growth quite readily. Unfortunately, a number of individuals are unable to digest milk. This inability to digest milk is called galactose intolerance, and this digestive problem is two or three times more common among blacks and Orientals. And galactose intolerance is much more common among men than women and among adults than children.

There are varying degrees of the severity of galactose intolerance, but they all manifest themselves as digestive discomforts like gas bloating and often as a strange, giddy, almost drugged or intoxicated sensation.

One well-known bodybuilder—whose name must go unmentioned—has a galactose intolerance so severe that every time he eats even a single scoop of ice cream, he almost immediately begins acting like he has drunk a fifth of Scotch. He staggers around and giggles like a drunk for an hour or so, and then he falls asleep like a baby for 10–12 hours.

Naturally, this champion bodybuilder usually avoids eating ice cream and other milk products, but he has a weakness for the unbelievably delicious Häagen-Dazs version of chocolate chip/chocolate ice cream, and even his tremendous willpower crumbles like a stale cookie whenever he "accidentally" drives past the Häagen-Dazs ice cream shop in his neighborhood, with such accidents tending to occur two or three times per week.

Should you suspect that you might have galactose intolerance, I suggest that you immediately stop consuming milk. You can still eat hard cheeses, however, because the enzyme that causes this problem is leached in the manufacture of cheese. For milk itself, you can substitute iced tea, diet sodas, water, or fruit and vegetable juices.

After ceasing milk consumption, make an appointment with your family physician, who will probably just advise you to abstain from consuming milk and then send you a bill for the office call! But, at least you will have positively identified the root cause of the excessive gas buildup in your stomach as well as your frequent and uncontrollable bursts of flatulence, which were periodically emptying your house or apartment—and, embarrassingly, even public restaurants—of all living organisms, save plants, for 15–20 minutes at a time.

Bodybuilders always seem to want to know exactly what quantities of foods they should be eating. The body individuality factor we discussed earlier again makes it impossible to answer this question in a way that will specifically help everyone who has asked it. People vary so much in their biochemical makeup that it would be impossible to provide more than the following three general rules to govern your eating habits:

1. Your body will naturally determine how much you should be eating, as long as you don't eat so quickly that you can't even taste your food. A primary cause of overeating is eating too fast, because your body isn't able to keep up with your eating pace and is delayed by several minutes in signaling that you have eaten enough. During that four or five minutes you could have consumed at least 750 calories more than what your body actually needed. Listen to what your body tells you and then follow

its instructions in planning and following your nutrition schedule each day.

2. Eat until you are comfortably full, but don't stuff yourself. It's a waste of money to eat excessive amounts of food at one meal, because your body can only efficiently process and use moderate amounts of each food (i.e., about 30–35 grams of protein at each feeding). If you always overeat, you will have the most expensive urine and bowel movements in your neighborhood!

3. Eat at regular times during the day, but eat frequently (four to six smaller meals per day) instead of consuming the traditional three large meals each day. Eating smaller quantities of food more frequently during the day will ensure maximum utilization of the nutrients you take into your body, which is a blessing if your food budget is limited.

Buy yourself a good book on nutrition and study it carefully. After you have mastered the knowledge contained in that book, buy another and another, until you become somewhat of an expert on nutrition. I recommend buying the *Nutrition Almanac*, a fantastically detailed and complete book on the subject.

Begin to form an accurate knowledge of the food values contained in everything you eat. Tables showing exact quantities of every vitamin, mineral, protein, fat, carbohydrate, and numerous other nutrients for an incredible variety of foods are listed in the *Nutrition Almanac*. Once you can easily calculate the amounts of protein, fat, and carbohydrate in everything you eat, it might even be a good idea to record your daily food intake and its protein, fat, carbohydrate, and caloric content in your training diary, if you aren't already doing so.

During the year I was planning and researching the contents of this book, I polled approximately 50 of the greatest bodybuilders in America and around the world about their diets. This survey produced a consensus of the amounts of major food elements they believe a growing young bodybuilder should include in his daily diet. (Assume that he weighs 180 pounds.) Here are the daily figures for major nutrients that have been recommended by 50 of the world's greatest bodybuilding champions.

Protein	200–250 grams
Fat	100–250 grams (primarily from vegetable sources)
Carbohydrate	200–250 grams
Total Calories	3,500–4,000
Water and Other Fluids	2–3 quarts

Note: Several bodybuilders said they regularly drink two or more gallons of water and other fluids per day!

This table covers the major food elements you will eat every day, which leaves the minor food elements—the vitamins and minerals as well as the trace elements—that you should also include in your nutritional program each day.

VITAMINS, MINERALS, AND TRACE ELEMENTS

As you become more technically and intellectually sophisticated as a bodybuilder, you will slowly develop a personalized vitamin and mineral supplementation program. For now, however, you should take only a couple of these food supplements. This will help you avoid becoming confused about the large number of other vitamins, minerals, and trace elements that you read about in *Muscle & Fitness* and various health and nutrition journals. These two supplements are the only ones that are absolutely essential for all bodybuilders. And you should definitely be taking each one daily for the rest of your life, if you intend to remain healthy and physically active as a senior citizen.

Go to a health food store and ask for a high quality multiple-vitamin capsule and a good chelated multiple-mineral supplement that also includes the trace elements that your body needs in infinitesimal quantities to remain optimally healthy. Or you can conveniently supplement your diet effectively with my own Weider Olympian

Dynamic Body Factors tablets, each of which contains 15 vitamins, 10 essential minerals, and all the trace elements your body needs to maintain its good health.

When you are selecting a mineral supplement—be it a multiple-mineral tablet or one of the many individual minerals available in tablet form at all health food stores—be sure that it is chelated (a chemical process that bonds an amino acid molecule to each molecule of the mineral), because your body won't be able to use nonchelated minerals as efficiently as their chelated brothers.

As far as the "right" dosages of each multiple-vitamin and multiple-mineral supplement are concerned, take twice what the bottle labels recommend. An increased dosage can be justified, because these recommended dosages are intended for sedentary individuals. When you train very hard in your workouts, however, you will build up a need for greater amounts of all food elements, especially for the various minerals—potassium, calcium, and magnesium in particular.

Bodybuilders commonly rely too heavily on food supplements, using them as a *substitute* for—rather than as a *supplement* to—a healthy and well-balanced diet of fresh foods. At maximum, all you will ever really need to take is one or two Weider Good Life Megapacks—each of which contains seven vitamin and mineral tablets—every day, except for four to six weeks prior to a competition. Then your diet will be so severely restricted in order to bring out maximum muscularity that it will lack most of the vitamins and minerals found naturally in fresh fruit and vegetables. So for the last four to six weeks of a severe diet, you will probably need to take two or three times the amount of supplements you normally consume in the off season, just to compensate for the nutritional deficiencies caused by a definition diet. And you will undoubtedly have discovered several individual vitamins, minerals, and dessicated animal organ tablets that help you peak perfectly if you take them for several weeks before competing.

THE ESSENCE OF BODYBUILDING

At last we arrive at the biggest secret of bodybuilding, the essence of the entire sport. I hinted at this secret in Chapter 2, but now I'll hit you right between the eyes with it. The essence of serious bodybuilding is the **EXPERIMENT.**

Bodybuilding is a continually ongoing group of experiments, in which you try technique after technique in your body-lab, to determine what will work best to build muscle on your own unique body. Since everyone is different, you will soon discover that what works for Chris Dickerson will not necessarily work for you or that it will not work at all on your body. Still, one of Dennis Tinerino's or Frank Zane's routines might work as well for you as it does for these champions. You will never know for sure, however, until you try out a routine or training technique for four to six weeks.

Once you have discarded all the unproductive routines and training techniques, and have discovered the gems of training knowledge that provide your best gains, you will be close to formulating an ideal training philosophy for your unique body. But even then, your experiments will probably never end.

Ed Corney reached his lifetime peak condition and placed third in the 1977 Mr. Olympia competition at the advanced (for bodybuilding) age of 44. Immediately after that show he told me that he was *still* experimenting with different training techniques and still learning as much about how his body reacts to various stimuli as he had 25 years earlier, when he was a beginning bodybuilder who knew *nothing* about training with weights. With this exemplary attitude, Eddie will probably still be conducting experiments in his body-lab when the morticians are measuring him for a casket!

Even though you are only at the intermediate bodybuilding stage, you should already be conducting experiments in your own body-lab, tuning into your body's reactions to various foods, exercises, and training techniques. You will be able to tell what is working for you and what isn't, simply by monitoring the growth rate of your muscles.

I have developed a technique for evaluating bodybuilding progress called the Weider Instinctive Training Principle. Essentially, this principle involves gradually learning how to interpret your body's biofeedback signals until you develop an intuitive sense—an instinct—of what is or isn't producing good results in your body. It takes a year or more to become adept at instinctive training, but once mastered, this technique will dramatically accelerate your progress rate.

As you experiment with various bodybuilding techniques, exercises, and routines, replace what isn't working in the routines included in this book with the exercises, body part routines, and techniques that you have discovered to work best for you. The essence of bodybuilding—

Ed Corney, who placed third in the Olympia at 43 years of age, checks his pump by posing before a mirror. Such biofeedback as muscle pump is an essential prerequisite to developing instinctive training ability.

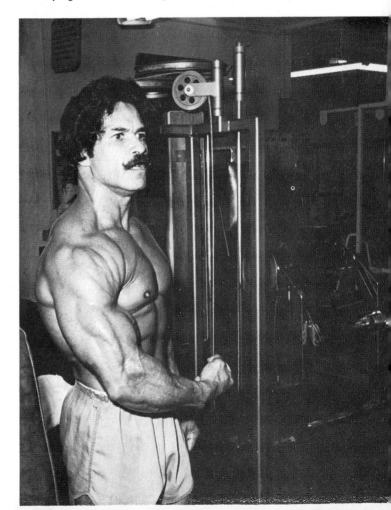

the experiment—is that simple, and I have no great ego investment in the training programs outlined in this book. Feel free to change them whenever you feel you can do so and begin experiencing better results from your training.

Only **you** can tell what works and doesn't work in your body. No one can climb into your body and do this for you. As I've said, **you** ultimately have sole responsibility for making all of your body-building decisions and then living with them. All I can do is advise you about how various workout philosophies might work for you, after which **you** must take appropriate action to find the right training philosophy for your unique body. But once you have developed a championship physique, only **you** can take credit for your success and bask in the adulation everyone will give you.

AGAIN, TAKE IT EASY

Again, I must warn you about the dangers of breaking in a new training program too quickly. Every time you make a training schedule change, you must go easy in the workout for the first two or three training sessions, especially if your new routine includes a few more total sets or much greater training intensity than the old one. Even merely switching to different exercises for the same muscle group can cause muscle soreness, because no two movements stress a muscle in the same manner or from the same angle.

LEVEL TWO EXERCISES

In this section are a number of new exercises you can add to the pool of basic movements developed in Chapter 2. Combined with that first group of exercises, these new movements will give you an acceptably wide variety of exercises from which to choose when formulating your own routines or modifying an existing training program.

Thighs

Hack Machine Squats. A little earlier I briefly discussed the effects of this movement on the frontal thigh muscles. You should also recall that your upper body will move up and down with the sliding platform on the machine as you bend and straighten your legs. Keeping these facts in mind, start this exercise by placing your feet about 12 inches apart in the middle of the foot platform, with your toes angled outward at a 45-degree angle on each side. Bend your legs enough to enable you to place your back against the movable platform and grasp the handles at the side of the platform. Once you are in this position, merely straighten and bend your legs for the required number of repetitions in your training program.

Hack Machine Squats—midpoint.

Leg Extensions. This movement is excellent for carving deep cuts down the fronts of your thighs, which is an essential quality on stage at a bodybuilding contest. Begin by sitting at the end of the leg table with the backs of your knees against the edge of the padded horizontal surface of the machine on the end to which the machine's movement arm is attached. Hook the insteps of your feet under the lower set of padded rollers, and grasp the handles at the sides of your hips or the edges of the table if there are no handles. From this starting position, slowly straighten your legs and hold them straight for a slow count or two before returning to the starting point. Repeat this movement for the required number of repetitions.

Leg Extension—start (right) and finish (below).

Leg Curls. The Leg Curl is the only exercise that directly stresses the biceps femoris muscles on the backs of your thighs. The movement is done on the same apparatus as Leg Extensions. Lie face down on the padded bench, with your head facing away from the end with the movement arm and your knees set on the padded bench two or three inches from the edge of the bench. Hook your heels under the top set of padded rollers and grasp the handles or sides of the bench for upper body stability during the movement. From this basic starting position, bend your legs as far as you can and then return to the starting point. Repeat the movement for the required number of repetitions.

Leg Curl—start (above) and finish (below).

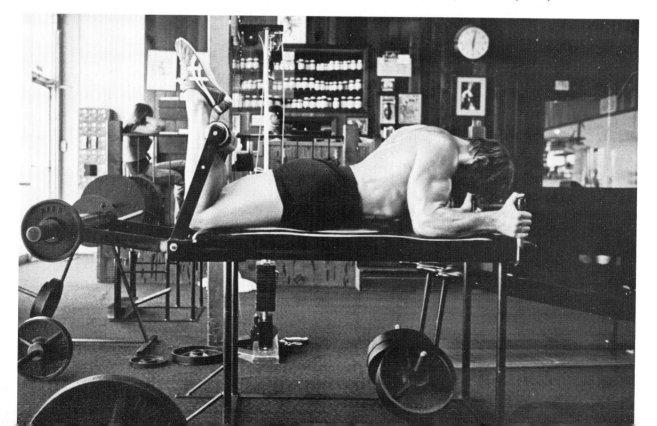

One-Leg Toe Raise—midpoint.

Hack Machine Toe Raise—finish.

Calves

One-Leg Toe Raise. Occasionally you should exercise one arm or leg at a time, because this technique allows you to focus your concentration more intently on the working muscles than when working on both limbs simultaneously, which splits the focus of your concentration and makes it weaker for each leg. Obviously, greater training intensity results in greater muscle gains. With this movement you can train one calf at a time, alternating legs on every set. Start these Toe Raises with your left calf. Place the ball and toes of your left foot on a four-by-four-inch block of wood, bend your right leg so it is out of the way during the entire set, and grasp some stable object with your right hand to balance your body. Holding a light dumbbell in your left hand, simply rise up and down on your toes over the fullest possible range of movement. Be sure to accentuate the stretched position of your calf at the bottom position by forcing your heel far below the level of your toes on every repetition of this exercise.

Hack Machine Toe Raise. For this movement you will lie face down on the machine's sliding platform. Start by placing your toes and the balls of your feet on the top edge of the foot board, with your feet about 12 inches apart. You will seem to be a little clumsy when trying to grasp the handles—which are set very low on the machine—and pull the sliding platform up so you can rest your chest on it. However, once you manage this comfortably, you will feel a tremendous growth burn in your calves as you rise up and down on your toes against the resistance provided by the hack machine. And, just in case you have forgotten it, you should **always** use the three toe positions I discussed earlier when doing this and all other calf exercises.

Hyperextension—start (above) and finish (right).

Back

Hyperextensions. Most bodybuilding gyms, like Gold's and the World gyms, have a special bench for this exercise. So all you need to do is stand inside the bench, facing the larger of the two pads on the bench. Then lean forward while simultaneously swinging your legs backward, so you can hook your heels under the rear pad and position your hips over the larger front pad while lying facedown. Place your hands behind your head and then merely do a Reverse Situp, moving your torso from a position hanging straight down to one in which it is slightly above an imaginary line drawn parallel to the floor. Going much higher than this parallel position makes it remotely possible for Hyperextensions to injure your lower back. Once this movement becomes easy to do, you can add resistance to it by holding a barbell plate behind your head.

If you don't have access to a Hyterextension bench, you can still do this movement simply by lying facedown across a leg table or any horizontal surface that is more than 2½–3 feet higher than the floor, which allows you to hang your toes straight downward without having your head bang against the floor. Have someone lay his torso across your legs to restrain them dur-

Rotating Dumbbell Shrug—top position.

ing the exercise and then simply do the Reverse Situp I mentioned.

This exercise is excellent for developing the powerful erector spinae muscles of your lower back, and you can even do it when your back is slightly injured, because it is the only lower back exercise that stretches your spine. All the other lower back movements in existence have a mildly compressing effect on your spine, which can increase pain in an injured back.

Rotating Dumbbell Shrugs. This exercise is similar to Barbell Shrugs, except that it is done with dumbbells, which allows you to rotate your shoulders forward, backward, upward, and downward, to achieve a greater range of motion during the move-

ment. Start by grasping a pair of heavy dumbbells, standing erect, and sagging your shoulders downward and forward as much as possible. Then simply shrug your shoulders upward to the limit and then move them backward as far as you can. Finally, lower your shoulders while still holding them back, until they return to the starting point by moving forward at the bottom of the movement. For greater clarity, visualize this type of Shrug as a square pattern of shoulder movement when viewed from the side, with the square's corners slightly rounded, and then simply trace the square's outline with the movement of your shoulders as you shrug up the two dumbbells. You can also rotate your shoulders in the opposite direction.

One-Arm Bent Rowing. As with One-Leg Toe Raises, you can usually place a greater intensity of stress on your back muscles by doing Bent Rows with one arm at a time. Start with your left side by holding a moderately heavy dumbbell in your left hand, with your palm turned toward the rear of your body. Bend over and place your right hand on a flat exercise bench to support your upper body in the same position during the movement. Your left leg should be extended to the rear, which allows you to stretch your latissimus dorsi muscles more completely when you have the weight at the bottom of the movement. Your right leg should be bent about 30 degrees and placed a little forward of your body. Begin the rowing movement with your exercising arm straight, which completely stretches your lats. Then pull the dumbbell up as high as you can at the side of your torso, being sure your upper arm travels upward and backward, staying at about a 45-degree angle from your torso. Lower the dumbbell back to the starting point and repeat the movement for the required number of repetitions. All rowing movements primarily build muscle thickness in the middle and upper sections of your back and only do a little to add width to your lats.

One-Arm Bent Row—start (left) and finish (above).

Bent-Arm Pullovers. While many body-builders consider Bent-Arm Pullovers a chest exercise, I have always felt that they primarily stimulate the latissimus dorsi muscles of your upper back. Begin by lying on your back along a flat exercise bench. Grasp a barbell with a narrow over-grip (about six inches between your index fingers). Be sure that you are positioned on the bench so your head hangs off the edge of it. The barbell should be resting on your chest—almost as in the bottom position of a Bench Press—at the start of the movement. From there, move the weight in a semicircle over your face and backward behind your head as far as it will comfortably go, being sure to hold your elbows as close to each other as possible throughout the entire exercise. Pull the barbell back along the same arc to the starting point and repeat the movement for the required number of repetitions. This is one of the best exercises for all of your torso muscles, because it stresses your lats very strongly, your pectorals and deltoids to a slightly lesser degree, and even your rib cage to a small degree.

Bent-Arm Pullover—finish.

Dumbbell Flyes—start.

Chest

Dumbbell Flyes. Grasp two dumbbells and lie back on a flat exercise bench or on an incline or decline bench, both of which will place stress on different sections of your pectorals. Start with your arms bent about 10 degrees and hold them bent slightly at this angle throughout the exercise. The dumbbells should be touching each other directly above your chest. From this starting point, lower the dumbbells directly out to the sides in semicircles to a position as far below the level of your chest as possible. Return the dumbbells to the starting point and repeat the movement for the required number of repetitions. Flyes build both muscle mass and shape in your pectorals, so you should always do one or more variations of this Flye in your chest workouts.

Dumbbell Flyes—finish.

Pulley Crossovers—start (above) and finish (right).

Pulley Crossovers. One of the best ways to keep continuous tension (I will discuss the result-producing Weider Continuous Tension Principle in greater detail in Chapter 5) on your pectoral muscles over their complete range of motion is to do Flyes with pulleys. Start by standing between two high pulleys, grasping the pulley handles and extending your arms upward at about a 130-degree angle from the sides of your torso. Bend forward at the waist so your torso is inclined at about a 45-degree angle and then do your Flyes in this position. Be sure to keep pulling down on the cables until your hands either touch in front of your hips or cross over each other.

Pec Deck Flyes—start.

Pec Deck Flyes. The curious-looking pec deck machine has recently become quite popular on the West Coast, because it also allows you to keep continuous tension on your chest muscles through their full range of motion. Pec Deck Flyes are actually superior to Cable Crossovers in this respect, because the machine is designed to place heavy stress on the pectorals at all times, while you feel a lessening of resistance near the bottom finishing point of Pulley Crossovers.

Start your set of Pec Deck Flyes by adjusting the machine's seat height so your shoulders are about two or three inches below the tops of the vertical pads in front of you when you sit on the machine's seat. Place your forearms on the pads so they run down the full length of the pads with your elbows an inch or two above the bottom edges of the pads.

From this basic starting position, stretch your pecs fully by allowing the pads to move backward as far as possible. Then, slowly and with deep concentration on the working muscles, move the pads forward with pectoral strength until they are crunched together in front of your torso. Hold this contracted position for two or three seconds and then return slowly to the

Press Behind Neck—above start.

stretched position, being careful to always keep your pectoral muscles tensed. Repeat the movement for the required number of repetitions.

Shoulders

Press Behind Neck. This movement is very similar to Military Presses, except that your grip on the barbell should be two or three inches wider on each side, and you will lower the bar down behind your head on each repetition until it lightly touches your trapezius muscles. Once the barbell handle has touched your traps, press it

back up to straight arm's length directly over your head, being sure that your elbows are directly under the bar throughout the movement. Presses Behind Neck are excellent for all three heads (lobes) of your deltoids—anterior, or frontal head; medial, or side head; and posterior, or rear head—but especially for the anterior heads of your deltoids. You can do this and all other variations of Overhead Presses seated at the end of a bench as well as standing erect. Done seated, Presses can't be pushed up with leg strength, so you should expect to use 10–15 percent less weight than the poundage you can easily handle for a set of any form of Standing Overhead Presses.

Bent Laterals. To place direct stress on the posterior heads of your deltoids you must do Bent-Over Lateral Raises (usually shortened to *Bent Laterals*) with two dumbbells. Begin the movement by placing your feet at about shoulder width. Bend over until your back is parallel to the floor and unlock your knees slightly. Grasp a pair of light dumbbells and let them hang directly below your chest. Your elbows should be bent slightly and held in that position throughout the movement. From this basic starting position, raise the dumbbells directly out to the sides in semicircles until they are above an imaginary line drawn parallel to the floor. Lower the weights back to the starting point and repeat for the required number of repetitions. Some bodybuilders do this movement seated at the end of a flat exercise bench with their chest resting on their thighs, a position that minimizes cheating during the movement. Arnold Schwarzenegger particularly favored this variation of Bent Laterals when he was training hard.

Bent Laterals—start (right) and finish (below).

Front Laterals—barbell variation start (left) and finish (right).

Front Laterals—dumbbell variation done alternately.

Front Laterals. To stress the anterior heads of your deltoids directly, you can do Front Laterals with a barbell, with two dumbbells, or with one dumbbell held in both hands. I will explain how to perform the version using two dumbbells and then you can refer to the photos accompanying this exercise description for correct positioning on the other two versions.

Start the movement by standing erect with a dumbbell in each hand and your arms held slightly bent and along the front of your body, so the dumbbells rest on the tops of your thighs with your palms facing your body. From this starting position, raise one arm directly forward in a semicircle until it reaches shoulder height. As you begin to lower that dumbbell back to the starting point, start raising the other dumbbell to shoulder height. Doing Front Laterals (sometimes called "Forward Laterals") with alternate arms like this will keep you from cheating by swinging the dumbbells up instead of raising them slowly with your shoulder strength, which in turn stimulates your deltoids much more intensely.

Arms

Machine Curls. This is probably the most easily learned biceps movement of all. Just sit on the machine's horizontal bench, drape your upper arms over the angled pad so they are resting on the pad parallel to each other, grasp the curling handle, and do your Machine Curls over a complete range of motion for the required number of repetitions. The advantage of this form of curling, as I hinted in Chapter 2, is that resistance is still heavily concentrated on your biceps when that muscle group is fully contracted. In contrast, there is little or no resistance on your biceps for the final third of a Barbell Curl's range of motion. Thus, Machine Curls are actually a better exercise than Barbell Curls. But you should still do both exercises—plus numerous other biceps movements—in your arms routine, because complete biceps development comes only when a large variety of exercises have been done for the biceps over a long period of hard and steady training.

Concentration Curl. For peaking your biceps muscles, I suggest that you do several sets of Concentration Curls, one arm at a time with a moderately heavy dumbbell, during every biceps workout. Start the movement by sitting at the end of a flat exercise bench with a dumbbell held in your left hand. Bend forward and brace the back of your left upper arm against the inside of your left thigh near the knee. Fully straighten your arm and then curl the dumbbell up to your shoulder. At the top of the movement it is important that you twist the outside (the side with the little finger) of your left hand **clockwise** as far as possible. Do an equal number of sets and reps for your right biceps, being sure to move your right hand **counterclockwise** at the top of the movement. This twisting of the wrist is called *supination,* and it allows you to contract your biceps muscles completely.

Machine Curls—start.

Concentration Curl—midpoint.

Dumbbell Triceps Extension. You can either stand erect or sit at the end of a flat exercise bench while doing this exercise. Hold a reasonably heavy dumbbell in your hands so the handle of it passes between the base of your thumb and the index finger on each hand when your fingers are interlaced and your thumbs are crossed. When you have the correct grip on the dumbbell your palms will be resting flush against the inside plate on one end of the dumbbell, and the dumbbell handle will be hanging down vertically during the entire movement.

Begin the exercise with your arms fully extended and your upper arms held verti-cally beside your head. Your upper arms will be an inch or two from the sides of your head, and they should be kept strictly in this position for the whole movement. From this starting point, bend your arms and lower the dumbbell in a semicircle as far downward and backward as possible, trying to touch the back of your neck when the weight reaches the bottom position of the movement. Return the dumbbell along the same arc to the starting point and repeat the movement for the required number of repetitions. You will find this movement excellent for stimulating the large inner head of your triceps.

Dumbbell Triceps Extension—start (above left) and finish (above right).

One-Arm Triceps Extension—midpoint.

One-Arm Triceps Extension. You can do this exercise exactly like Dumbbell Triceps Extensions but with one arm at a time. The arc of the dumbbell will be a little different in this movement, however, because your hand is not forced to remain along the middle plane of your body, as it is when using a dumbbell with both hands. At any rate, you needn't worry about the arc of the movement, because your arm will automatically seek the correct biomechanical groove for the movement. One-Arm Triceps Extensions stress the middle and outer heads of your triceps.

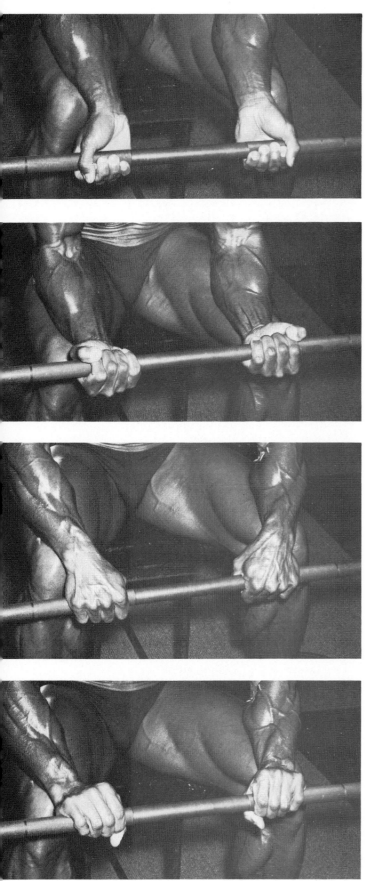

Wrist Curl. I didn't include any forearm exercises at Level One, because as a beginning bodybuilder, merely gripping a barbell or two dumbbells in your hands for all of your upper body exercises stimulated your forearm muscles sufficiently. But now those muscles will be strong enough to require being stressed directly with Wrist Curls.

Start this exercise by sitting at the end of a flat exercise bench with your forearms running down your thighs, your palms facing upward, and your wrists just off the edge of your knees. Hold a moderately heavy barbell in your hands with your grip set at about shoulder width. From this basic starting position, sag your fists downward as far as you can and then curl the barbell up in a small semicircle as high as possible. Doing Wrist Curls with your palms facing upward stresses the muscles on the insides of your forearms. To stimulate the muscles on the outsides of your forearms, you should do Reverse Wrist Curls with your palms facing downward.

Wrist Curls (counterclockwise from top):
  Barbell, Palms Up—start.
  Barbell, Palms Up—finish.
  Barbell, Palms Down—start.
  Barbell, Palms Down—finish.
  Dumbbells variation.

Abdominals

Roman Chair Situps. This movement is essentially a partial Situp, but when it is done correctly it places high-intensity stress on your frontal abdominal muscles, particularly on your upper abs. Sit on the padded seat of a Roman chair and hook your toes under the toe bar. Cross your arms on your chest and sit back about three-fourths of the way to where you would be if your torso were parallel to the floor. As you move your torso backward, be sure to keep your abdominal muscles tensed. Then sit back up until tension begins to lessen on your abs, which will be at a point about a foot short of that in which your torso is perpendicular to the floor. Rock back and forth between these two positions until you feel a strong burning sensation in your abdominal muscles. Roman Chair Situps have become the most popular abdominal exercise among most of the champions in southern California, so they come highly recommended.

Roman Chair Situps—midpoint.

Bench Leg Raises. This is the most effective movement for the lower half of your frontal abdominals. Begin the exercise by lying on your back on a flat exercise bench so that your hips are at the edge of the bench and your legs are hanging off the bench. Grasp the sides of the bench above your head to restrain your torso during the entire movement. Then bend your legs at about a 20-degree angle and do a set of Leg Raises, being sure that your feet are well below the level of the bench at the bottom position of the movement and your thighs are almost touching your chest in the contracted position of the exercise. You will immediately discover that lying on a bench like this allows you to do Leg Raises over a much fuller range of motion than you can achieve by doing them while lying on the floor or on an abdominal board. And this greater range of motion puts significantly more stress on your abdominal muscles.

Bench Leg Raises—near finish.

Seated Twisting—start (above) and finish (below right).

Seated Twisting. This movement has only a tangential relationship with Chubby Checker. Place an unloaded barbell or a broomstick behind your neck and entwine your arms along it on each side. Sit on a Roman chair and anchor your feet under the toe bar or sit on a flat bench and wrap your legs around it securely. Either way, you must anchor your legs securely enough to keep your hips from rotating with the movement as you are twisting from side to side. Moving your hips like this robs you of much of the effect this exercise can have on the sides of your waist.

Once you have gotten yourself into the correct starting position, twist rhythmically from side to side as far each way as possible. Seated Twisting will tone all the muscles at the sides of your waist, which will make your waist look narrower. And that quality certainly can come in handy when you are standing in front of the judges at your first bodybuilding competition.

LEVEL TWO TRAINING ROUTINES

At Level Two you should be trying gradually to increase both the volume and the intensity of exercise in your workouts. You will spend approximately four months training at this level, so I will offer two different workouts to choose between at each of three sublevels in Level Two. This way you can reach the six-month point in your training using the greater of three more training programs, rather than just one, like some trainers recommend. Just train with the Level II-A workout of your choice for four to six weeks, with the Level II-B routine you like most for the next four to six weeks, and finally with your favorite Level II-C program for the last four to six weeks you spend at Level Two.

Note that I have stopped suggesting starting poundages for each exercise at this level, because by now you will know better than I do how strong you are in each muscle group and what your physical capabilities are. You should still do each Level Two training routine three nonconsecutive days per week, even though they are fairly long and energy draining. This will teach you the disciplined approach to training that will eventually make you into a champion bodybuilder, however.

These Level II-C training programs will be quite fatiguing when done three times per week. They will require as much energy to complete as a bodybuilder can be expected to expend. Still, you should attempt to do the entire program for four to six weeks as an exercise in building mental discipline. If you can't complete the entire workout in 1½ hours or less, however, you should cut your routine back by a set or two for each body part. If a workout program is too extensive for a bodybuilder's endurance and energy levels, he usually tends to rest more than 60 seconds between sets, which—as I've already pointed out—can make him susceptible to injuries. Any bodybuilder who rests 60 seconds or less between sets should be able to complete this workout in less than 1½ hours.

Because these Level II-C programs are so fatiguing to complete on every workout day, you should be happy to know that in the next chapter I will show you a training method in which you split your body parts

LEVEL II-A (Choice #1)

Exercise	Sets	Reps
1. One-Leg Toe Raise	3	15–20
2. Calf Press	3	15–20
3. Squat	4	10–15
4. Leg Curl	3	10–15
5. Hyperextension	2–3	10–15
6. Seated Pulley Rowing	3	8–12
7. Bent-Arm Pullover	3	8–12
8. Shrug	2	10–15
9. Incline Press	3	6–10
10. Flyes	3	8–12
11. Press Behind Neck	3	6–10
12. Bent Laterals	2	8–12
13. Machine Curls	3	8–12
14. Barbell Curls	2	8–12
15. Lat Pushdown	3	8–12
16. Dumbbell Triceps Extension	2	8–12
17. Wrist Curl	3	15–20
18. Reverse Wrist Curl	3	15–20
19. Roman Chair Situps	2–3	25–50
20. Seated Twisting	2–3	50–100*

LEVEL II-A (Choice #2)

Exercise	Set	Reps
1. Standing Calf Machine	3	15–20
2. Seated Calf Machine	3	15–20
3. Hack Machine Squats	4	10–15
4. Leg Curl	3	10–15
5. Stiff-Leg Deadlift	2–3	10–15
6. Dumbbell Bent Rowing	3	8–12
7. Lat Machine Pulldown	2	8–12
8. Upright Rowing	2–3	8–12
9. Bench Press	3	6–10
10. Pec Deck Flyes	2	8–12
11. Military Press	3	6–10
12. Side Laterals	2	8–10
13. Barbell Curls	3	8–10
14. Concentration Curls	2	8–10
15. Lying Triceps Extensions	3	8–10
16. One-Arm Triceps Extensions	2	8–10
17. Wrist Curls	3	15–20
18. Reverse Wrist Curls	3	15–20
19. Bench Leg Raises	2–3	15–25
20. Seated Twisting	2–3	50–100

* (to each side)

into halves or thirds and work on only one of these parts of the body on each training day. This will involve training more often than three days per week, but splitting up your routine compensates for more frequent workouts by allowing each session to be much shorter in length. So, instead of training 1½ hours a day and being exhausted at the end of your workout, you will be able to complete a training session in 45–60 minutes and without undue fatigue at Level Three.

LEVEL II-B (Choice #1)

Exercise	Sets	Reps
1. Seated Calf Machine	5	15–20
2. Hack Machine Toe Raise	3	15–20
3. Leg Press	4	10–15
4. Leg Extensions	3	10–15
5. Leg Curl	3–4	10–15
6. Stiff-Leg Deadlift	3	10–15
7. Seated Pulley Rowing	3–4	8–12
8. Lat Machine Pulldown	3	8–12
9. Incline Press	4–5	6–10
10. Pulley Crossovers	3	10–15
11. Press Behind Neck	3–4	6–10
12. Side Laterals	3	8–12
13. Bent Laterals	3	8–12
14. Machine Curls	3–4	8–12
15. Concentration Curls	3–4	8–12
16. Seated Dumbbell Triceps Extension	3–4	8–12
17. Lat Pushdown	3–4	8–12
18. Wrist Curl	3–4	15–20
19. Reverse Wrist Curl	3–4	15–20
20. Incline Situps	3	15–25
21. Seated Twisting	2–3	50–100

LEVEL II-B (Choice #2)

Exercise	Sets	Reps
1. Standing Calf Machine	4–5	15–20
2. Calf Press	4–5	15–20
3. Squat	4–5	10–15
4. Leg Extension	3	10–15
5. Leg Curl	3–4	10–15
6. Hyperextension	3	10–15
7. Bent-Arm Pullover	4–5	8–12
8. One-Arm Bent Rowing	3–4	8–12
9. Dumbbell Rotating Shrug	3	10–15
10. Bench Press	4–5	6–10
11. Parallel Bar Dips	3	8–12
12. Press Behind Neck	4–5	6–10
13. Bent Laterals	3	8–12
14. Side Laterals	3	8–12
15. Dumbbell Curls	3–4	8–12
16. Machine Curls	3–4	8–12
17. Dumbbell Triceps Extension	3–4	8–12
18. Lat Machine Pushdown	3–4	8–12
19. Wrist Curls	3–4	15–20
20. Reverse Wrist Curls	3–4	15–20
21. Incline Leg Raises	3	15–25
22. Seated Twisting	3	50–100

LEVEL II-C (Choice #1)

Exercise	Sets	Reps
1. Calf Press	5	15–20
2. Hack Machine Toe Raise	5	20–30
3. Hack Machine Squats	5	10–15
4. Leg Extensions	4	10–15
5. Leg Curls	4–5	10–15
6. Hyperextensions	3	10–15
7. Seated Pulley Rowing	5	8–12
8. One-Arm Bent Rowing	4–5	8–12
9. Barbell Shrugs	3–4	10–15
10. Incline Press	5	6–10
11. Parallel Bar Dips	4–5	8–12
12. Front Laterals	3	8–12
13. Side Laterals	3	8–12
14. Bent Laterals	3	8–12
15. Dumbbell Curls	4	8–12
16. Concentration Curls	4	10–15
17. Lat Machine Pushdown	4	8–12
18. One-Arm Triceps Extension	4	8–12
19. Wrist Curl	4–5	15–20
20. Reverse Wrist Curl	4–5	15–20
21. Roman Chair Situps	3–5	25–50
22. Seated Twisting	3–5	50–100

LEVEL II-C (Choice #2)

Exercise	Sets	Reps
1. Seated Calf Machine	5	15–20
2. Calf Press	5	20–30
3. Squat	5	10–15
4. Leg Extensions	4	10–15
5. Leg Curls	4–5	10–15
6. Stiff-Leg Deadlift	3	10–15
7. Barbell Bent Rowing	5	8–12
8. Bent-Arm Pullover	4–5	8–12
9. Upright Rowing	3	8–12
10. Incline Presses	5	6–10
11. Pec Deck Flyes	4–5	8–12
12. Press Behind Neck (Seated)	4–5	6–10
13. Side Laterals	3	8–12
14. Bent Laterals	3	8–12
15. Barbell Curls	4	8–12
16. Seated Dumbbell Curls	4	8–12
17. Dumbbell Triceps Extension	4	8–12
18. Wrist Curls	4–5	15–20
19. Reverse Wrist Curls	4–5	15–20
20. Bench Leg Raises	3–5	20–30
21. Seated Twisting	3–5	20–30

Bodybuilding and powerlifting are very compatible with each other. Just look at the herculean development of David Shaw as he strains to complete a World Record Deadlift of 810 pounds (275-pound weight class) at the 1980 Hawaii International Championships!

4

Level Three—
Advanced Bodybuilding

If by chance you are reading these chapters sequentially, and you are reading each chapter only after you have completed the workouts in the preceding one, by now you should have built a fairly large amount of muscle mass around your body. If not, you will be building it soon, so it's time for a minilecture on bodybuilding public relations.

You must first understand that the general public is usually intimidated by a large and/or muscular body, and they will strike out at you if you give them a chance. So what you need to do is know how to avoid giving them this chance to tell you that you are stupid, muscle-bound, or sexually impotent.

There are two main types of bodybuilders—the show-offs and the true champions. And this is a statement that could probably be made about any sport. A show-off walks around with a T-shirt that looks like it was spray-painted onto his body. He will even wear this T-shirt (without a coat) in subfreezing weather. On top

of this, he is continually walking around with every muscle flexed up and with his lats spread so wide he looks like a bat. He's the one who is laughed at by the general public, and he's the one who gives our sport a bad name.

A true champion has enough confidence in his appearance that he doesn't need to try to project it, looking like an orangutan in the process. What he tries to project instead is his personality. And as a result he comes off to the general public as a *person*, not as a hunk of inanimate—and probably brainless—muscle.

Even the best mannered bodybuilders might have a little trouble at the beach, because an outstanding physique sticks out like the Rock of Gibraltar in a swimsuit. This is where all the dudes who are bodybuilding's jerks really strut, so you should be sure to act as naturally as possible. Swim, body surf, throw a football, and catch a Frisbee. Be cool. And soon people will begin to look past your body and see the person who lives inside of it!

WEIGHT LIFTING OR POWERLIFTING?

At about the point you have now reached, some bodybuilders decide to give competitive weight lifting or powerlifting a try. I personally encourage this, because even if you decide you don't like lifting and end up returning to bodybuilding, the heavy training you did will have a beneficial effect on your physique.

Your back and legs will be vastly improved after a few months of weight lifting and powerlifting. And if you've been powerlifting, your chest and shoulders will have benefited enormously from the heavy Bench Presses you did during virtually every workout.

The key thing with trying one of these sports, I think, is that you objectively judge your potential for each one. You should be gaining strength more quickly and easily than other bodybuilders who started out with you, or you will have a hard time making adequate gains in these two sports. How much you can lift is the name of the game in both weight lifting and powerlifting, not how good you look while you are doing it.

(Above) Weightlifting also blends well with bodybuilding. Jim Benjamin, a former American Lightweight Champion, is the lifter. (Below) World Record holder Mike Bridges is just one of many powerlifters who does bodybuilding movements to aid his powerlifting.

SPLIT ROUTINES

As I mentioned at the end of the last chapter, split routines are a way to cut down on the length of your daily training routines. And when you make your workouts shorter, you can increase the intensity of each workout (make them more difficult). In bodybuilding, especially at the competitive level, this is a supreme advantage. This is called the Weider Split-System Training Principle.

At this point I think you could benefit quite a bit from a split routine done four days per week; that is, do half the body on Mondays and Thursdays and the other half on Tuesdays and Fridays. Later, as you get deeper into your training, you can blend into a five-day and then a six-day split routine.

The traditional split routine consists of working on the upper body one day and the lower body the next. This ends up giving you a lot to do on the upper body day and quite a bit less for your legs, so bodybuilders have devised some more equitable splits. Here are a few types of splits you can try.

Monday – Thursday	*Tuesday – Friday*
Chest	Thighs
Shoulders	Back
Triceps	Biceps
Calves, Abs,	Calves, Abs,
Forearms	Forearms

Monday – Thursday	*Tuesday – Friday*
Chest	Thighs
Back	Biceps
Shoulders	Triceps
Calves, Abs,	Calves, Abs,
Forearms	Forearms

Monday – Thursday	*Tuesday – Friday*
Thighs	Chest
Back	Shoulders
Calves, Abs,	Arms
Forearms	Calves, Abs,
	Forearms

Some bodybuilders have further intensified their routines by splitting their bodies into three segments and training each twice per week for a total of six weekly workouts. Here is a typical split routine formulated along those lines, the one Dennis Tinerino used prior to winning both Mr. America and Mr. Universe.

Monday – Thursday
Chest
Back
Calves, Abs

Tuesday – Friday
Shoulders
Arms
Calves, Abs

Wednesday – Saturday
Thighs
Forearms
Calves, Abs

The final type of split routine you can try is the Weider Double-Split System, which I developed several years ago. I don't recommend that you think about actually using this yet, however, since it is an extremely advanced training principle that even some of the Olympians would find too taxing. Here is an example of a type of Double-Split that Arnold Schwarzenegger used to use.

Monday – Wednesday – Friday (am)
Chest
Back
Calves

Monday – Wednesday – Friday (pm)
Thighs
Triceps
Abdominals

Tuesday – Thursday – Saturday
Shoulders
Biceps
Calves, Abs

Note how Arnold used a Double-Split three days per week and a single workout each day on the other three days each week. This allowed him to train every body part three times a week but with much greater than normal training intensity, since the workouts were shorter and more frequent. Some bodybuilders even train on a Double-Split six days a week for short periods of time.

CONCENTRATION

Concentration is the ability to focus all of your mental energy on one point, the muscle being worked, during each repetition in a training session. If you can eventually succeed at this, your workouts will be many times more productive than if you do your sets and reps with no mental involvement whatsoever.

It's tough to describe how to concentrate perfectly, but here is a little scenario that might help you understand how it's done. You are in the middle of a set of Concentration Curls. You can't feel the weight in your hand, but you can concentrate on the biceps contracting and extending under its resistance. You can feel a growth burn coming on; you can see it with your mind's eye swelling the biceps tissues, visualizing fresh blood surging in with new supplies of growth materials. This is what I mean by concentration.

Since you need to concentrate, practice it constantly, not only in your workouts but throughout the day. Spend a few minutes a day concentrating on any one object or concept. Think about it totally and keep your mind on it as long as possible before other thoughts intrude. Then keep forcing your concentration back on target for at least 10–15 minutes. Soon you will develop a tremendous ability to concentrate.

If you can afford the expenditure, take some transcendental meditation classes. TM is the essence of concentration, and I'm sure you will find TM techniques a great help in your workouts. Frank Zane has worked quite a lot with them, and his physique speaks volumes for their effectiveness in bodybuilding training.

BASIC VERSUS ISOLATION MOVEMENTS

For the sake of definition, an isolation movement is one that works a single muscle more or less in isolation from the rest of the body. In certain instances—Incline Flyes for the upper chest and Bent Laterals for the rear deltoids—an exercise can be isolated even to a particular section of a muscle. A basic exercise is one like the Bench Press (for the chest, shoulders, and triceps), which works several muscle groups at one time.

Each of these types of exercises have their values, so don't get the idea that I'm opting for one or the other. Traditionally, basic exercises build muscle mass, and isolation movements develop more shape and muscular detail in a muscle group. Used together, they build almost everything a bodybuilder needs, but there is a specific way to combine these two types of movements for optimum results.

If you really want the full effect of a basic exercise, always do the isolation movements first in your routine. Unfortunately, many people will tell you to do just the opposite—finish up with isolation exercises after doing the basic movements. This is totally invalid, however, because any perceiving and experimenting bodybuilder can give the isolation-basic movement order a try and tell the difference quite easily.

This order of exercises is called the Weider Pre-Exhaustion Principle. To use this method to its best advantage, you can try a number of exercise combinations. Here are a few suggestions.

Thighs—Leg Extensions + Sissy Squats + Squats

Chest—Flyes + Pulley Crossovers + Bench Presses

Deltoids—Side Laterals + Press Behind Neck

Give any one of these combinations a little trial and you will feel the difference in your workouts very quickly.

HEAVY VERSUS LIGHT TRAINING

There are basically two schools of thought on how heavily to train. One advocates working out as heavily as possible, while the other recommends training with moderate poundages. The heavy group claims that a massive and dense-looking physique can be built only by using maximum resistance. Such a physique *can* be built that way, but unless you're as tough as a turtle, training consistently with heavy weights will probably lead to joint problems. Regardless, I do urge you to experiment with this technique. After one joint injury, however, you would be a fool to continue using it.

The moderate-poundage advocates have demonstrated that superb physiques can be built by using moderate, or even relatively light, poundages. And since far less stress is placed on the joints when using lighter weights, this appears to be the most sensible of the two ways to train.

SPECIALIZATION

By now you should have noticed a lagging body part or two, the ones that aren't responding as quickly as the others. When this time comes, it is crucial that you immediately start a campaign to bring the lagging group(s) back into line with the rest of your body. As you will recall, it is a balance between all of the muscle groups that contest judges look for. This balance is the one quality that sets a true superstar apart from the pack.

The way to start a body part moving back into line is to concentrate on it. You have been more or less treating all of your muscle groups with the same intensity so far, but now it's time to treat the sub-par ones differently. And what you need to do is show no mercy to the pitiful wretches.

Bomb them harder. Blitz them more often. Bury them under tons of weights. Hit them with less rest between sets. Put more mental effort into it. In short, hound the lagging areas as hard as you can until they give up and grow.

I must also introduce the Weider Muscle

"No pain, no gain," bodybuilders say. Mike Mentzer vividly illustrates this philosophy in action.

Priority Training Principle. With this training method, you should do a lagging muscle group first in your routine, when both your mental and physical energies are at peak levels. This will allow you to bomb a muscle group to the limit, using every intensity-training technique in your bodybuilding arsenal.

An extension of Muscle Priority Training involves devoting an entire training day to the lagging muscle group. This method works particularly well when your legs are lagging behind the rest of your body. Lou Ferrigno brought up his lagging thighs in this manner during his late teens by Squatting and doing other heavy thigh training on a single day each week and then training the rest of his body the next day. It worked well for him, so this extension of Muscle Priority Training should work just as well for you.

115

SUPERSETS

Back in the early 1950s the Supersets Training Principle was one of the first that I included in the Weider System. It was an effective way of increasing intensity in training. And over the years this has proven to be such a valid technique that it remains very popular even today.

As I originally visualized it (and the technique was so revolutionary that it met with great opposition from the "authorities" of the day), supersets consisted of two exercises for opposing muscle groups, done one after the other with no rest in between. As an example, Curls for the biceps were immediately followed by Lying Barbell Triceps Extensions. Or Leg Extensions could be supersetted with Leg Curls for the thighs or Bench Presses with Lat Pulldowns for the chest and back.

Done in the above manner, supersets still have considerable merit, but bodybuilders in the past few years have been intensifying their training even further by supersetting an exercise for one muscle group with another for the same muscle. As an example, they might superset Flyes with Bench Presses or Side Laterals with Presses Behind Neck. This results in brutal training intensity, and sometimes it takes brutal intensity to get results, especially on the lagging body parts we discussed earlier.

When we arrive at the new training programs at the end of this chapter, you will find some supersets, but only a few. This way you can gradually get used to them. Also, the supersets will fall between antagonistic muscle groups, not within a muscle group, because we will reserve the latter degree of training intensity for use just before competition.

FORCED REPS

Another of my best training techniques is the Weider Forced Reps Training Principle, which allows you to push a muscle far past the point of normal fatigue and normal failure. And when one of the little critters is pushed that far, its only possible response is to *grow!*

You will need a training partner to help you with forced reps. Let's say you are doing a set of Bench Presses with forced reps at the end of the set. At the end of eight full-range reps, you fail on the ninth repetition three-fourths of the way up in the movement. Now the forced reps start. Your partner pulls up on the bar enough to get you to the end of the rep, but instead of putting the bar back on the rack, you do one, two, or maybe even three more reps with your partner helping you more and more on each repetition. This is forced reps in action.

The real trick to doing forced reps is finding a partner who can judge how much to help you on each exercise. He has to take off just enough of the resistance for you to make it to the end of a rep, but not so much that the rep has no oomph to it. But when a partner has this technique down, you're gonna burn, brother, and you're gonna *grow.*

HEAVY-DUTY TRAINING

As part of his Heavy-Duty Training System, my pupil Mike Mentzer takes forced reps even farther and throws in supersets as well. By working with the greatest possible intensity, he has built an incredibly herculean physique on a mere three to five total sets per body part. Here is how he does it.

I did a back superset with him once that was pure murder on the guy, but that's how he grows. Mike started with Pullovers on a Nautilus machine, using a totally ponderous poundage. He did about six or seven full repetitions before he could no longer finish a rep. Then I helped him as little as possible to do two or three more forced reps.

Then Mike immediately jumped to a lat machine and followed the same procedure, doing Lat Pulldowns with a parallel-grip handle to the back of his neck. At the end of the Pulldowns set I did most of the

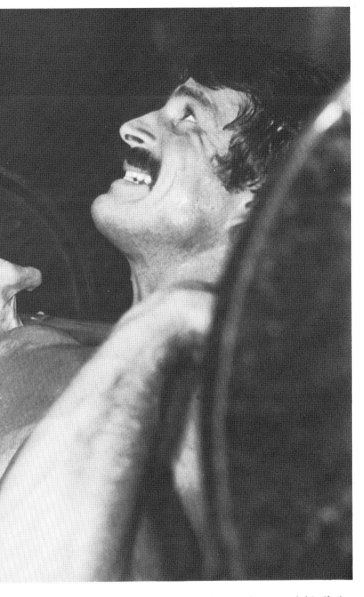

Few bodybuilders train with the super-heavy weights that Mike Mentzer uses in all of his workouts. His "Heavy-Duty System" is an application of the Weider Overload Training Principle.

pulling, and he resisted as well as he could as the bar returned to the start. He did three or four such brutally hard repetitions, using the Weider Retro-Gravity Training Principle (explained earlier in this book).

This is what Mike Mentzer's Heavy-Duty System is all about, and it is rooted soundly in the Weider System. It brings good results, and the more pain you can stand in a set, the better the results you will get from it. As I have often said, "No pain, no gain!"

GAINING WEIGHT

Now might be a good time to begin exploring the old system of bulking up and training down, which was popularized by the great Bill Pearl, a three-time Mr. Universe winner who now heads the IFBB Professional Judges Committee. This method consists of training as heavily as possible and eating a lot of food, which helps you gain plenty of weight, even though much of it might be fat. Then this cycle is followed by one in which you train down by dieting and training very fast, usually prior to a competition (more on this in Chapter 6).

The advantage of this method is that you do gain muscle mass. On the other side of the coin, however, you also gain a lot of fat, which is difficult to take off later. Unfortunately, once you develop new fat cells, you will have them for the rest of your life. When you lose weight they will shrink in size but they will still be there. And when you eat a few too many calories they begin to fill up very quickly.

Still, this bulking up method is very popular, and you should give it a try at least once to see how it works for you. Later, you can also try the opposite method of training up for a contest, instead of down, a method that also has its advocates, notably Frank Zane, a three-time Mr. Olympia winner.

We will cover weight gaining in two phases, diet and exercise. Everyone likes to eat, so let's start with diet. While still adhering to a balanced diet, you will finally be able to eat all the food you want to, even including some ice cream now and then. Your food supplements should include a lot of B-complex vitamins, because they are essential for appetite stimulation, and they also help build muscle mass. Whatever else you take is up to you, but be sure you are getting the multiple vitamins and chelated minerals that we discussed earlier, plus some vitamin C with bioflavonoids.

Since you don't want your stomach to bulge outward excessively, we will try the proven method of eating six small meals each day instead of three very large ones.

This will also put a smaller load on your digestive tract each time you eat.

Buy a blender and some Weider Olympian milk and egg protein powder. Mix up a quart of milk (raw milk if possible) in your blender with 1–1½ cups of the protein powder and a little fruit for flavoring. Carry this around with you in a thermos bottle and take a swig whenever you feel the slightest hunger pangs, even if they come in the middle of your workout.

Eating a good meal just before you go to bed will tend to pack weight on you as well, because you won't be able to burn off its calories while sleeping. Be sure, however, to eat only easily digested foods. Fifteen tacos will probably keep you awake for the rest of your life, and you will need your sleep to grow on. Right?

So you can have an idea of the framework on which you can model your own diet, here is one I have used successfully in the past. (Remember to take supplements with every feeding.)

Breakfast
1. A ham and cheese omelette with five or six eggs
2. Half a pound of steak
3. Two or three glasses of milk (raw if possible)

Morning Snack
1. Roast beef sandwich on whole-grain bread
2. Milk shake with protein powder and ice cream

Lunch
1. Half a roast chicken
2. One or two vegetable dishes
3. Piece or two of fruit
4. Milk

Afternoon Snack
1. Yogurt with fruit
2. Nuts and seeds
3. Milk

Dinner
1. Some type of beef entrée
2. One or two vegetable dishes
3. One or two baked potatoes
4. Milk

Bedtime Snack
1. Hard cheese or cold cuts
2. Milk

Note the heavy emphasis on milk in this diet, as well as the total lack of salads. Milk is a tremendous weight-gaining food, while salad takes up room in your stomach that should be used for food that is going to do you some nutritional good. When you are training down, however, things work in the opposite way. Then you will cut out all milk products and eat a lot of salads.

As to your weight-gaining workout program, it will be heavy, with low reps, a limited number of exercises, and longer-than-usual rests between sets (1½–2 minutes each time), and it will include only two workouts per week for each body part. Here is what I have in mind for you (raise the weight each set in a pyramid and then lower it on the last set for a pump out).

Monday–Thursday
1. Standing Calf Machine: 6 x 20–10
2. Squat: 1 x 20; 1 x 15; 1 x 12; 1 x 10; 1 x 8; 1 x 4–6; 1 x 20
3. Stiff-Leg Deadlift: 1 x 20; 1 x 15; 1 x 10; 1 x 20
4. Shrug: 3 x 10–15
5. Bent Rowing: 1 x 15; 1 x 12; 1 x 8; 1 x 6; 1 x 20
6. Bent-Arm Pullover: 3 x 8–12
7. Barbell Curl: 5 x 8–12
8. Reverse Curl: 3 x 8–12
9. Incline Situps: 1–3 x 25–50

Tuesday–Friday
1. Seated Calf Machine: 6 x 20–10
2. Incline Press: 1 x 15; 1 x 10; 1 x 6; 1 x 3–4
3. Bench Press: 1 x 15; 1 x 10; 1 x 6; 1 x 3–4; 1 x 20
4. Upright Rowing: 5 x 6–8

5. Bent Laterals: 3 x 8–12
6. Lying Triceps Extensions: 5 x 8–12
7. Leg Raises: 1–3 x 25–50
8. Wrist Curls: 3–5 x 10–15

It is essential that you always do a little bit of abdominal work while gaining weight to keep some muscle tone in your midsection. When you train down you will be doing a lot more abdominal training, but for now one to three sets per workout will suffice.

In the Monday–Thursday workout, the Stiff-Leg Deadlifts will take care of your hamstrings, so you won't need to do Leg Curls. On Tuesdays and Fridays, the Bench Presses and Incline Presses are heavy frontal deltoid work, so I have included no Military Presses or Presses Behind Neck in this workout. The Upright Rows will hit your medial deltoid heads, and the three sets of Bent Laterals will stimulate the posterior deltoid heads.

You should bulk up over a six- to eight-week cycle, so this single program should be enough, and you won't need a second one to switch to after a few weeks of training. At least this one will give you an idea of how to train for weight gain. Then, in the next chapter, I will present a discussion of how to make up your own routines. At that point, you should be able to come up with a couple more bulk-up programs on your own.

CHEST EXPANSION

Another way to gain weight—and to improve your overall body structure—is to set about enlarging your rib cage. If you are still in your mid- to late-teens, which I consider the ideal time to begin bodybuilding, it won't be very difficult to do this. If, however, you are past the age of 20 or so, it can be done only with a degree of difficulty.

Rib cage expansion is accomplished by combining an exercise that promotes deep breathing with one that stretches the chest, supersetting back and forth between the

two for one to three sets each. This will gradually stretch the cartilage that attaches your ribs to the sternum (breast bone). Younger men have more pliable cartilage in their rib cages, so it is easier for them to enlarge their rib boxes than it is for men in their twenties and older.

The combination you will use is three supersets of Breathing Squats with Breathing Pullovers. Breathing Squats are fairly simple to do. They are just regular Squats with various numbers of huge breaths between each Squat. Here are the numbers to remember:

Reps	Breaths
1–10	3
11–20	4
21–25	5

It is essential to use a reasonably light weight on Breathing Squats, say somewhat less than your body weight. Emphasis must be placed more on breathing than on the weight you lift while Squatting; hence the lighter suggested poundage.

Breathing Pullovers are a lot different from the Bent-Arm Pullovers presented earlier. For one thing, your arms should be held almost straight (they will be bent slightly to prevent strain on your elbow ligaments). For another, a light weight (about 30–50 pounds) is used, so emphasis can be placed on stretching the rib cage.

Start the movement by lying back on a flat bench while holding a light barbell above your chest in the same position it would be in if you had just finished a Bench Press rep. Your hands should be placed at about shoulder width. Keeping your arms bent slightly, let the bar travel in a semicircle down and to the rear as far behind your head as it will go. As the bar is traveling back, take as deep a breath as possible. Hold your breath as the bar returns to the starting position and then let it out. That is a Breathing Pullover.

Your chest expansion program consists of three supersets of Breathing Squats and

Breathing Pullovers. Do 25 reps of each movement and rest about three minutes between supersets. Here is a good weight-gain routine formed around this superset (the bracket indicates the superset):

Monday—Wednesday—Friday

{ 1. Breathing Squat: 3 x 25
{ 2. Breathing Pullover: 3 x 25
3. Lat Pulldown: 5 x 8—12
4. Bench Press: 5 x 6—10
5. Upright Rowing: 5 x 8—12
6. Barbell Curl: 5 x 8—12
7. Lat Pushdown: 5 x 8—12
8. Calf Machine: 5 x 15—20
9. Incline Situps: 2—3 x 15—25

Give this program a try and I'm sure you will achieve great results, particularly if you are still in your teens. If you are older, however, you will still get results. You will just have to work harder for them.

Breathing Pullovers—near start (above) and finish (below).

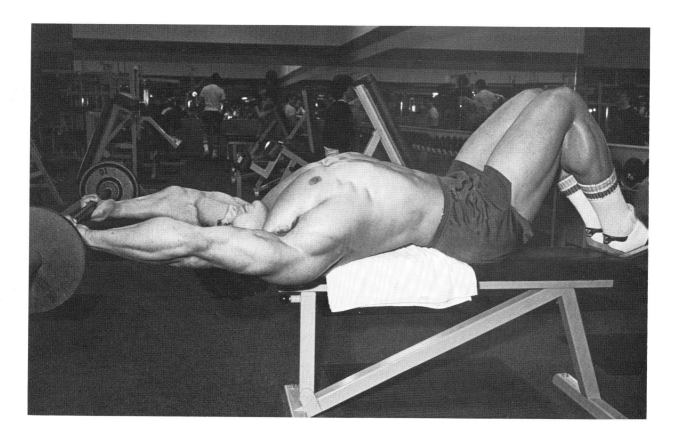

LEVEL THREE EXERCISES

Except for a few more movements for a couple of body parts in Chapter 5, this is about the last of the exercises you will need for your general pool. And over the years you will occasionally learn new movements that you can add to your repertoire.

Thighs

Lunges. This is a favorite exercise of most of the top bodybuilders, who use it to bring out frontal thigh cuts. Start the movement as if you planned to Squat with a light weight, except that both feet should be pointing directly forward. Next, step out with your left foot as far forward as you can and then lunge forward onto your bent left leg as if you were a fencer trying to thrust at an opponent. In the bottom position of the movement, your left knee should be ahead of your left ankle, and your right leg should be held relatively straight. Push back to the starting point and repeat for the required number of repetitions.

Lunges—start (above), midpoint (below), and finish (below right).

Front Squats. The only differences between Front Squats and Back Squats are the grip you use and the fact that Front Squats tend to hit the thigh muscles directly above your knees more than the Back Squat. To assume the correct grip on the bar, step up to a squat rack and extend your arms under the bar. Step forward so the bar rests along the tops of your deltoids and against the base of your neck in front of you. You can then cross your arms over the bar, step back, and do your set. As long as you don't allow your elbows to drop, the bar will remain solidly in this position.

Sissy Squats. Although this exercise doesn't involve any added resistance, it does cut up the frontal thighs to an unprecedented extent. The movement is most easily done at the ends of a set of parallel bars, which you can grip lightly for balance as you do the exercise. Set your feet at shoulder width and point your toes directly forward. Begin the movement by moving your knees and hips forward, leaning back at the same time until your torso is parallel to the floor. Your head should be held back at the bottom of the movement. From this bottom position, simply push yourself back to the starting point with thigh strength.

Front Squat—bottom position.

Sissy Squat—start (below left) and near finish (below right).

Donkey Toe Raise—start. Models: Lou Ferrigno and Casey Viator.

Calves

Donkey Toe Raise. This is a very effective calf movement, particularly if a heavy training partner is available. Place your toes and the balls of your feet on a block of wood and bend over until your torso is parallel to the floor. Place your hands on a low exercise bench to support your body in this position. Your partner should then hop up astride your hips, sitting as far backward as possible, since sitting near your shoulders will apply little resistance to your calves. If your training partner is too light, he can hold barbell plates or a dumbbell against his abdomen or on your back. Keeping your legs locked out, simply rise up and down on your toes in this position.

Back

Good Mornings. This is an odd name for an exercise, but the movement itself is very effective for developing the lower back. Start with a light barbell across your shoulders as in the starting position for a Squat. Your feet should be set at about shoulder width and your toes should be pointed almost directly forward. With your knees slightly unlocked, slowly bend forward until your torso is below an imaginary line drawn parallel to the floor. Return to the starting position and repeat for the required number of repetitions.

Good Mornings—start.

Good Mornings—finish.

Bench Rows. This movement is very similar to Bent Rowing with a barbell, except that you will be lying facedown on a bench instead of merely bending over at the waist. Such a position is excellent if you have had any lower back injuries, since lying down on a bench removes all pressure from your spine. To do the movement, simply adjust a bench so it is high enough to allow you to hang the weight at straight arm's length at the bottom of each movement. Then simply row the weight up and down.

Bench Rows—midpoint.

T-Bar Rows—finish.

T-Bar Rows. Another rowing exercise—
one that has become extremely popular
with the bodybuilding champions in southern California—is done with a T-Bar apparatus. This is the same as all other types of
Rows except that there will be a little more
up-and-down oscillation of the upper body
as you do the movement.

Chins:
   Behind Neck Variation (above left).
   Front of Neck Variation (above right).

Chins. About 10–15 years ago, this was the king of the lat movements, and it is still a fine exercise if you are strong enough to do at least eight to ten reps per set. You have all done Chins before but usually with a reversed grip. Bodybuilders always do them with palms facing forward, and they pull up to a point where the bar touches as low on the chest as possible or until it touches the trapezius at the backs of their necks.

Chest

Dumbbell Incline Press. Dumbbell Bench Presses done at all angles will give you a greater stretch at the bottom of the move- ment than the barbell version in each case. This is because the bar will touch your chest and terminate the downward phase of the movement long before your hands can reach as low a level as they can achieve when you use dumbbells.

Dumbbell Bench Press. The same range- of-motion advantage exists here as on the Dumbbell Incline Presses. Once you get to the point where you are using very heavy weights in this movement, however, you will need to know how to get the dumbbells into position for the movement. Start by sitting at the end of the bench. Grasp the dumbbells and rest them on your thighs just above your knees. Without changing this position, rock backward. The bells will still be braced against your knees when they are at arm's length above your chest. Then simply lower your legs to the normal position for Bench Presses and press away. To return the dumbbells back to the start- ing point, simply bring your knees up to them and rock your body forward.

Dumbbell Incline Press—start.

Dumbbell Bench Press—finish.

Decline Press—start.

Decline Presses. This is another angle from which you can work your chest, and you can do your Bench Presses with either a barbell or two dumbbells in this position. Decline Presses tend to stress the lower and outer edges of the pectorals the most. Any bench used for Declines should be rather narrow at the lower end so you can have an unrestricted range of motion for your arms.

Narrow-Grip Bench Presses. You can experiment with different grip widths at all three of the angles of Bench Presses that I have mentioned. Narrow-Grip Bench Presses done on a flat bench put considerable stress on the inner edges of your pectorals as well as on your triceps.

Shoulders

Dumbbell Presses. With Standing (or Seated) Presses using two dumbbells, you can also achieve a longer range of motion than when using a barbell. Several variations of Dumbbell Presses exist, besides doing them seated or standing. You can press the dumbbells up either together or alternately, and you can press them with your palms facing each other or facing forward.

Dumbbell Press—start.

Pulley Side Lateral—finish.

Pulley Side Laterals. Nothing beats this movement for capping off the medial head of the deltoids so the whole muscle group looks like half a cantaloupe. With a low pulley and a single handle, grasp the handle with your body turned so the arm faces directly away from the pulley. This means that the cable should be running across the front of your body during the entire movement. Round your arm and keep it in this position for the whole exercise. Then simply do Lateral Raises in this position.

Pulley Bent Lateral—finish.

Pulley Bent Laterals. This movement can be done to stimulate the posterior deltoids with either two pulleys (the cables crossed beneath your chest) or with one pulley at a time. Either way, the movement provides a complete range of motion with resistance along the full range.

Arms

Scott Curls. I probably should have described this movement sooner, because it is one of the greatest biceps exercises of all, particularly for the lower part of the muscle. Lean over a preacher bench with your elbows about eight to ten inches apart. Take an under-grip on the bar so your hands are set about six inches wider on each side than shoulder width. Straighten your arms fully and then curl the weight up as high as possible. Lower back to the starting point and repeat for the required number of repetitions. This movement was made famous by Larry Scott, winner of the first two Mr. Olympia competitions.

Scott Curl—midpoint.

Incline Curl:
  Start (above).
  Near finish (below right).

Incline Curls. This movement is for biceps fullness and peak. Lie back on an incline bench with a dumbbell held in each hand. Hang your arms straight down and make sure they are completely straight at the beginning of the movement. Simply curl the weights up and down from this position, bringing them forward and slightly outward as you curl. You will find that lying back like this makes the movement very strict, so you will feel a superior stimulation in your biceps muscles from doing Incline Curls.

134

Reverse Curls. This old standby forearm movement is the same as a Barbell Curl, except that it is done with a reversed grip. You will also notice that you can use only about 60 to 70 percent of the weight you can handle in a regular Barbell Curl. I have personally found Reverse Curls to be more stimulating when done with a narrow grip (about six inches between your index fingers). Regardless of the width of your grip, you will feel this movement in the large *supinator longus* muscles on the outsides of your forearms near your elbows.

Reverse Curls—start (left) and finish (below).

Incline Triceps Extension—near finish.

Incline Triceps Extensions. If you have been searching for a new angle from which to pump your triceps, this is it. Lying back on an incline bench and doing Triceps Extensions will stimulate the long inner head of your triceps quite strongly. If you have an EZ-curl bar handy, you might also try this movement using that type of bar rather than the standard straight bar.

Wrist Roller (above) and Wrist Roller,
machine variation (right).

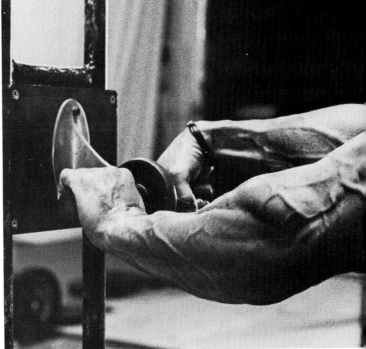

Wrist Roller. Grasp the wrist roller apparatus with your palms down and with one
hand on each side of the cord. Raise your
arms until they are straight out in front of
your body, parallel to the floor, and then
roll the weight up. By the way your wrists
are facing you can stimulate different parts
of your forearms (the palms-down position
builds the inner side, while the palms-up
approach builds the outsides of the muscles). The direction in which you wind up
the cord will also influence which parts of
the forearms you are stimulating most.

Abdominals

Knee-Ups. Sit on the edge of a flat bench and lean back at a 45-degree angle. Brace your body in this position with your arms and angle your legs outward so they assume a straight line with your torso. From there, pull your knees up to your chest and then lower your legs back to the starting position. Because of its low intensity, you will need to do a lot of reps in this exercise, but it is a great lower abdominal movement.

Knee-Ups—start (above) and finish (below).

138

Side Bends. A good companion exercise for Twisting is the Side Bend. Start by standing erect with a broomstick behind your neck, your hands grasping it at the ends. Then bend rhythmically back and forth as far as you can to each side. This will tone and define the external obliques on your sides.

Side Bend—start.

Cable Pulldowns. If you have been looking for a movement with which to bomb your serratus and intercoastals, try this one. Kneel down about two feet back from an overhead pulley, to which is attached a rope handle. Grasp the handle and extend your arms and body fully toward the pulley, being sure to keep tension on your frontal abdominals, serratus, and intercostals as you stretch. Then, keeping everything tensed, simultaneously bend over, blow out all of your air, and do a Mini Bent Arm Pullover with your hands. At the finish position, your forehead should almost be touching the floor and your hands should actually be touching the floor about eight to twelve inches in front of your head. Return to the starting point and repeat for the required number of repetitions.

Cable Pulldown—start (above left) and near finish (above right).

LEVEL THREE ROUTINES

This is the last chapter in which I will actually make up training routines for you, because in Chapter 5 I will teach you how to do this for yourself. By now you know far more about how your own individual body responds than I do, so you will be able to formulate better workout programs for yourself than I can.

The training programs in this chapter will involve a few supersets, which will be indicated by brackets enclosing the exercises involved. You will be spending about six months at Level Three, so I will give you six training programs of graduated intensity.

PROGRAM 1

Monday–Thursday

1. Standing Calf Machine: 4 x 15–20
2. Donkey Toe Raise: 4 x 20–30
{ 3. Leg Press: 4 x 12–15
{ 4. Sissy Squats: 4 x 12–15
5. Leg Curls: 5 x 10–15
6. Good Mornings: 3 x 15–20
7. Rotating Dumbbell Shrugs: 4 x 15–20
8. T-Bar Rows: 4 x 8–12
9. Bent-Arm Pullover: 4 x 8–12
10. Bench Rows: 4 x 8–12
11. Dumbbell Curls: 4 x 8–12
12. Incline Curls: 3 x 8–12
13. Reverse Curls: 3 x 8–12
14. Wrist Curls: 4 x 15–20
15. Reverse Wrist Curls: 4 x 15–20
{ 16. Roman Chair Situps: 2–3 x 50
{ 17. Side Bends: 2–3 x 50–100
{ 18. Cable Pulldowns: 2–3 x 20–30

Tuesday–Friday

1. Seated Calf Machine: 4 x 15–20
2. Calf Press: 4 x 15–20
3. Bench Press: 4 x 12–6
4. Incline Dumbbell Press: 3 x 6–10
5. Parallel Bar Dips: 3 x 10–15
{ 6. Press Behind Neck: 3 x 6–10
{ 7. Bent Laterals: 3 x 8–12
8. Cable Side Laterals: 3 x 12–15
9. Incline Triceps Extension: 4 x 8–12
10. Lat Pushdown: 3 x 8–12
11. One-Arm Triceps Extension: 3 x 8–12
{ 12. Bench Leg Raise: 2–3 x 20–30
{ 13. Cable Pulldowns: 2–3 x 20–30
{ 14. Twisting: 2–3 x 50–100

Some individuals might criticize these training schedules as being too long, but even now we should be paying attention to attaining full muscular detail. These programs are heavily weighted with calf and abdominal training, because these, not the arms or pecs, are the muscle groups that will win contests for you in later years.

PROGRAM 2

Monday–Thursday

1. One-Leg Toe Raise: 5 x 15–20
2. Seated Calf Machine: 5 x 15–20
3. Incline Press: 4 x 10–6
4. Decline Press: 4 x 10–6
5. Flyes: 4 x 8–12
6. Upright Rowing: 4 x 8–12
{ 7. Front Laterals: 4 x 8–12
{ 8. Bent Laterals: 4 x 8–12
9. Pulley Rowing: 4 x 8–12
10. Lat Pulldown: 4 x 8–12
11. Bent-Arm Pullover: 4 x 8–12
12. Stiff-Leg Deadlift: 4 x 10–15
13. Barbell Shrug: 5 x 15–20
14. Incline Situps: 3 x 20–30
15. Cable Pulldowns: 3 x 20–30
16. Twisting: 3 x 50–100

Tuesday–Friday

{ 1. Standing Calf Machine: 5 x 15–20
{ 2. Hack Machine Toe Raise: 5 x 10–15
3. Leg Press: 5 x 20–10
{ 4. Leg Extension: 5 x 15–20
{ 5. Leg Curl: 5 x 15–20
{ 6. Barbell Curl: 4 x 8–12
{ 7. Incline Triceps Extension: 4 x 8–12
{ 8. Scott Curls: 3 x 8–12
{ 9. Lat Pushdown: 3 x 8–12
{ 10. Reverse Curl: 3 x 8–12
{ 11. Dumbbell Triceps Extension: 3 x 8–12
{ 12. Wrist Curl: 5 x 15–20
{ 13. Reverse Wrist Curl: 5 x 15–20
{ 14. Incline Leg Raise: 3 x 15–25
{ 15. Twisting: 3 x 50–100
{ 16. Side Bend: 3 x 50–100

PROGRAM 3
Monday–Thursday
{1. Seated Calf Machine: 5 x 10–15
{2. Hack Machine Toe Raise: 5 x 15–20
{3. Bench Press: 5 x 10–6
{4. Pulley Crossovers: 5 x 10–15
5. Incline Dumbbell Press: 5 x 10–6
{6. Bent-Arm Pullover: 5 x 8–12
{7. Lat Pulldown: 5 x 10–15
8. Bench Row: 5 x 6–10
{ 9. Upright Row: 5 x 8–12
{10. Press Behind Neck: 5 x 10–6
11. Cable Bent Laterals: 5 x 8–12
{12. Roman Chair Situps: 3 x 50
{13. Bench Leg Raise: 3 x 20–30
{14. Twisting: 2–3 x 50–100
{15. Side Bends: 2–3 x 50–100

Tuesday–Friday
{1. Standing Calf Machine: 5 x 20–25
{2. Toe Press: 5 x 10–15
{3. Scott Curl: 5 x 8–10
{4. Incline Triceps Extension: 5 x 8–10
{5. Incline Curl: 4 x 10–12
{6. Lying Triceps Extension: 4 x 10–12
{7. Alternate Dumbbell Curl: 3 x 12–15
{8. Lat Pushdown: 3 x 12–15
{ 9. Reverse Curl: 5 x 10–12
{10. Wrist Curl: 5 x 15–20
{11. Front Squat: 5 x 10–15
{12. Leg Extension: 5 x 10–15
{13. Stiff-Leg Deadlift: 5 x 10–15
{14. Leg Curl: 5 x 10–12
{15. Knee-Up: 3 x 100
{16. Cable Pulldown: 3 x 20–30
{17. Side Bends: 3 x 100

PROGRAM 4
Monday–Thursday
1. Standing Calf Machine: 6 x 15–20
2. One-Leg Toe Raise: 6 x 15–20
{3. Leg Extension: 3 x 10–15
{4. Squat: 3 x 10–15
{5. Leg Press: 3 x 10–15
{6. Sissy Squat: 3 x 10–15
7. Leg Curl: 5–7 x 10–15
{8. Incline Triceps Extension: 3 x 10–12
{9. Lat Pushdown: 3 x 10–12
{10. Dumbbell Triceps Extension: 4 x 8–12
{11. Barbell Curl: 4 x 8–12

{12. Scott Curl: 3 x 8–12
{13. Reverse Curl: 3 x 8–12
{14. Wrist Curl: 5 x 15–20
{15. Reverse Wrist Curl: 5 x 15–20
{16. Incline Leg Raise: 5 x 20–30
{17. Incline Situps: 5 x 20–30

Tuesday–Friday
{1. Seated Calf Machine: 7 x 15
{2. Calf Press: 7 x 20
3. Incline Press: 5 x 10–6
{4. Parallel Bar Dips: 5 x 10–15
{5. Pulley Crossovers: 5 x 10–15
6. Military Press: 5 x 10–6
{7. Bent Laterals: 5 x 10–15
{8. Side Laterals: 5 x 10–15
{ 9. Bench Row: 5 x 10–6
{10. Bent-Arm Pullovers: 5 x 10–15
11. Lat Pulldown: 5 x 8–12
{12. Side Bend: 3 x 100
{13. Twisting: 3 x 100

PROGRAM 5
Monday–Thursday
1. Seated Calf Machine: 5 x 6–10
{2. Calf Press: 4 x 10–15
{3. Hack Machine Toe Raise: 4 x 10–15
{4. Leg Press: 4 x 10–15
{5. Sissy Squats: 4 x 10–15
{6. Leg Extension: 4 x 10–15
{7. Front Squats: 4 x 10–15
{8. Stiff-Leg Deadlift: 4 x 10–15
{9. Leg Curl: 4 x 10–15
{10. Upright Row: 3 x 10–15
{11. Shrug: 3 x 10–15
12. Bench Row: 5 x 10–6
13. Seated Pulley Rowing: 5 x 8–12
14. Bent-Arm Pullover: 5 x 8–12
{15. Scott Curl: 5 x 8–12
{16. Barbell Curl: 5 x 8–12
17. Concentration Curl: 3–4 x 10–12
{18. Reverse Curl: 4 x 8–12
{19. Wrist Curl: 4 x 15–20
{20. Incline Situps: 3 x 20–30
{21. Roman Chair Situps: 3 x 50–100

Tuesday–Friday
1. Standing Calf Machine: 15 x 15–20
{2. Flyes: 4 x 10–15
{3. Bench Press: 4 x 10–6

4. Incline Press: 4 x 10–6
5. Dips: 4 x 10–15
6. Seated Pulley Rowing: 10 x 8–12
7. Lat Pulldown: 5 x 8–12
{8. Side Laterals: 5 x 8–12
{9. Press Behind Neck: 5 x 10–6
{10. Front Laterals: 4 x 8–12
{11. Bent Laterals: 4 x 8–12
{12. Incline Leg Raise: 3 x 20–30
{13. Knee-Ups: 3 x 50
{14. Twisting: 3 x 100
{15. Side Bends: 3 x 100

PROGRAM 6
Monday–Thursday
{1. Seated Calf Machine: 8 x 15–20
{2. Calf Press: 8 x 15–20
{3. Parallel Bar Dips: 5 x 10–15
{4. Incline Dumbbell Press: 5 x 10–6
{5. Pulley Crossovers: 4 x 10–15
{6. Decline Press: 4 x 6–10
{7. Upright Rowing: 4 x 8–12
{8. Dumbbell Shrugs: 4 x 10–15
9. Press Behind Neck: 10 x 10–6
{10. Side Laterals: 4 x 10–15
{11. Bent Laterals: 4 x 10–15
12. Chins: 10 x 8–12
{13. Bent-Arm Pullovers: 4 x 8–12
{14. Seated Pulley Rowing: 4 x 8–12
{15. Wrist Curl: 5–7 x 15–20
{16. Reverse Wrist Curl: 5–7 x 15–20
{17. Incline Situps: 5 x 20–30
{18. Twisting: 5 x 100

Tuesday–Friday
{1. Standing Calf Machine: 6 x 8–10
{2. Hack Machine Toe Raise: 6 x 10–12
{3. Leg Extensions: 5 x 10–15
{4. Sissy Squats: 5 x 10–15
{5. Leg Curls: 8 x 10–15
{6. Squats: 8 x 10–15
7. Hyperextension: 5–7 x 10–15
{8. Scott Curl: 5 x 8–12
{9. Alternate Dumbbell Curl: 5 x 8–12
{10. Incline Curl: 3 x 8–12
{11. Reverse Curl: 3 x 8–12
{12. Incline Triceps Extension: 5 x 8–12
{13. Lat Pushdown: 5 x 8–12
{14. Dumbbell Triceps Extension: 3 x 8–12
{15. Lying Triceps Extension: 3 x 8–12
{16. Incline Leg Raise: 5 x 20–30
{17. Side Bends: 5 x 100

PUMPING OUT

In the next chapter we will cover a variety of Level Four (Precompetitive Bodybuilding) training techniques and round out your pool of weight-training exercises. Chapter 5 will then be followed by a chapter outlining the exact training and nutritional philosophies of one of the sport's greatest champions, Chris Dickerson.

Ron Teufel (above left), Carlos Rodrigues (above right), and Tom Platz (right) have all won high-level bodybuilding championships. Not everyone has the potential to equal these champs, but anyone can develop an outstanding physique through bodybuilding training and nutrition.

5

Level Four— Precompetition

This phase of your training will last for a considerable length of time, perhaps for as long as two or three years. It will consist of a long buildup toward your first competition, and it will be followed by a six- to eight-week precontest sharpening phase to strip all the fat from your body before you step on stage. There are five key goals that you should try to reach at Level Four.

1. Gain muscle mass all over your body, trying to reach a body weight equal to 2.5– 2.7 pounds per inch of your height when in contest condition. Therefore, if you are 5'10" in height, you should weigh at least 175–189 pounds. Any less than this and you will have considerable difficulty winning your first show.

2. You should especially gain muscle mass in your deltoids and calves.

3. Endeavor to balance each body part with the rest of your body.

4. Gradually build up the overall intensity of your bodybuilding workouts.

5. Continue to experiment with various bodybuilding techniques in an effort to evolve your own personal training philo-sophy. No bodybuilder ever develops a "perfect" training philosophy, so all the champions are still experimenting with new training and nutritional concepts, even after they have won Mr. Universe and Mr. Olympia titles.

If you achieve each of these five goals while you are training at Level Four, you will be in a very advantageous position to win your first bodybuilding competition. And you *will* win it, unless you become impatient and rush into a show before you have paid sufficient dues in the gym via hard, consistent, and dedicated training. In other words, be *sure* you have developed a contest-winning physique before you enter competition.

HARD GAINERS

The average advanced bodybuilder will increase his muscular body weight by six to eight pounds each year for the first two or three years of training and four to six pounds per year after that. But there are some "hard gainers" who are able to gain only two or three pounds of muscle mass per year.

By now many readers will probably think they are hard gainers, but most are not. Unfortunately, many young bodybuilders are so impatient to reach championship caliber that they expect to gain five to ten pounds of muscle *each month*, when any realistic veteran bodybuilder is overjoyed to gain that much muscle mass in a year. A gain of six pounds per year amounts to only a half-pound increase each month. That doesn't seem like much, but if you go to a butcher shop tomorrow and look at a lean six-pound beef roast, you will immediately understand that six pounds of muscle mass is a lot! So, be patient; your gains will come, but they will come slowly and steadily.

Still, some readers will truly be hard gainers. If you are, don't despair, keep pumping iron, and be very careful to avoid overtraining. By paying close attention to your diet and by training consistently to 100 percent of your abilities, you will ultimately achieve excellent results from bodybuilding. Many Mr. America and Mr. Universe winners have been hard gainers and have still succeeded by totally dedicating themselves to bodybuilding. You can do the same.

There is actually an advantage in being a hard gainer if you intend to compete one day. While most bodybuilders have to fight like demons to reach peak muscularity, hard gainers invariably are extremely muscular at all times, regardless of what they eat. So, while everyone else is exhausted and bitchy in the gym, you can be eating virtually everything you want to eat before a contest, have extremely energetic workouts, and feel great the whole time!

If you genuinely are a hard gainer, you will make your fastest gains by doing short, high-intensity, heavy workouts like Mike Mentzer recommends in his Heavy-Duty Training System. Long training programs, like the ones presented in this book, will drain your energies excessively, and you will become chronically overtrained. You will recuperate much more quickly and efficiently if you do shorter and more in-tense workouts, and you can't expect muscle growth to occur unless full recuperation takes place first.

SMALL BONES

One excuse many bodybuilders make for not being able to gain muscle mass is having a light, small-boned skeletal structure. Small bones have nothing to do with a lack of muscle mass gains, which is usually caused by overtraining, inconsistent workouts, or insufficient training intensity.

Having a light skeletal structure can actually be an advantage, because it allows a bodybuilder to have small knees and narrow hips, two requisites for developing an esthetically pleasing physique. Frank Zane, three-time Mr. Olympia winner, is an excellent example of this, because he has a light skeletal structure and has still developed an incredible physique. Indeed, many bodybuilding fans feel he is the greatest bodybuilder of all time!

MAKING UP YOUR OWN ROUTINES

I can't make up training routines for you forever, so you will soon be set adrift on the bodybuilding sea, where you will sink or swim according to how well you plan your own training program. If you are an inherently lazy person, you could probably even avoid this problem by merely substituting new exercises for those recommended in the programs already outlined.

Unless you make up your own routines from scratch, however, you will miss half the benefit you should be receiving from your bodybuilding training. By now you will know explicitly which exercises, sets, reps, and exercise combinations do and don't put muscle on your body. And if you don't take advantage of this knowledge by making up programs tailored exactly to your unique body, you won't gain as quickly as you should.

You have already mastered many of my Weider Training Principles in previous chapters, and I will teach you several more in this chapter. These training techniques should *always* form the foundation of any bodybuilding training schedule you make up for yourself. Building on this sound foundation will ensure that you get great results from each new workout, but you should adhere to several other general rules when you make up a new routine.

You will probably recall that I have already suggested changing your training programs every four to six weeks. This helps prevent boredom, and it allows you to experiment with all the exercises and training techniques that you have already discovered to work well for you, plus any new concepts you might read or hear about in the future.

From my constant harangues about the vital importance of good body proportions to a competing bodybuilder, you have undoubtedly already concluded that you should include in your routines movements for every muscle group (except for the neck, which grows simply from peripheral shoulder, chest, and back exercises). And if some body part is lagging, you should hit it harder than your other muscle groups during each workout. You should also use the Weider Muscle Priority Training Principle for weak body parts, training them first in your workout, when your physical and mental energies are at maximum levels.

Next, you should *never* train your arms in a workout before you have trained your torso muscles (chest, shoulders, and back). This is necessary because your arm muscles are much smaller and weaker than those of your torso. When you do a torso exercise that also involves your arms (e.g., Chins for your back or Bench Presses for your chest), the intensity of exercise you can give to your torso muscles is limited by the strength of your arms. Because your arms are so small and weak, they always fatigue and give out long before the pectorals, deltoids, and lats have been fully fatigued.

Let's take the Bench Press as an example of this phenomenon. The exercise stresses the pectorals, deltoids, and triceps. When you do a set of Bench Presses and fail to complete a rep at the end of the set, it is invariably because the triceps gave out, not the pectorals or deltoids. If you train your triceps before your chest or shoulders, or your biceps before your back, your arms will be even weaker than normal, and your torso muscles will receive proportionately less stimulation.

As you might already have guessed, there is a method by which bodybuilders can make their arms temporarily stronger than their pectorals, deltoids, and lats, allowing them to blitz their torso muscles far more intensely than normally. This technique is called the Weider Pre-Exhaustion Training Principle, and I will discuss it in greater detail later in this chapter.

Generally speaking, when you sequence exercises for your body, it is best to train the large muscle groups before the smaller ones. This is because you have limited energy reserves, and when you are fatigued toward the end of a workout it is much easier to continue training a small body part like your biceps than a larger one like your thighs. Here is a list of the size of each muscle group, proceeding from largest to smallest:

1. Thighs
2. Latissimus dorsi
3. Pectorals-Calves
4. Trapezius-Erector spinae
5. Deltoids
6. Triceps-Biceps-Forearms
7. Abdominals

Despite the above list and my advice that you should do the largest body parts first in your workout, virtually every champion bodybuilder I have trained does his calf and/or abdominal training first in his workout as an effective warmup for bombing the rest of his body. It is also a good idea to do forearm training last in your workout, because your forearm muscles will become so pumped up that it will be difficult to grasp a barbell or two dumbbells for any other exercises once you have finished training your forearms.

Some bodybuilders prefer training their deltoids before their pectorals. Thirty years ago Steve Reeves, who played in the famous film *Hercules,* revealed to me that this sequencing resulted in better deltoid development for him. Other bodybuilders would disagree with him, so give Steve's method a try and see if it works for you. If not, then train your pectorals before your deltoids.

PHA TRAINING

As in other walks of life, bodybuilding training has occasionally spawned fads. One of these was the PHA (Peripheral Heart Action) System used widely during the mid-1960s. It is unfortunate that PHA Training went the way of all fads, because it was a very effective system, particularly for the health improvement it afforded through increased cardiorespiratory conditioning and the fact that the body could be worked as a unit prior to contests, rather than in parts on each training day.

PHA was developed by Bob Gajda, who won the 1966 Mr. America and 1967 Mr. World titles using the system. Gajda was a college student of exercise physiology while reaching his peak as a bodybuilder, and one of his professors sparked Bob's interest in this type of workout by lecturing on peripheral heart action. This is a method by which blood circulates through the arms and legs via muscle contractions, pushing it past one-way valves in the arterial system.

Gajda theorized that numerous muscle contractions all over the body would stimulate blood circulation even further, which in turn would induce muscle growth with less-than-normal overall body fatigue. Since Bob felt that the muscle contractions should take place everywhere, he began to train with series of four to six exercises, each for a different body part. And he did these series with minimal rest between sets.

Steve Reeves, the 1947 AAU Mr. America winner, was the first modern bodybuilder with a good V shape to his torso. He starred in ten Italian "muscle movies" which greatly popularized bobybuilding worldwide.

This system was essentially a variation of Circuit Training, a form of weight training that used a series of 10–20 exercises to build endurance. Circuit Training had been in existence for nearly 30 years before Gajda evolved PHA Training. The short-series programs worked quite well, because they developed both quality muscle tissue and terrific cardiorespiratory fitness.

I suggest that you give PHA Training a try, because it might also work quite well for you, especially close to a contest when you are trying to cut up. Don't be discouraged at first if your exercise poundages go down and your fatigue levels go up, because you will merely need a short breaking-in period to normalize both factors.

Here is a sample three-day-per-week PHA program that you can try. (Six-day PHA training can also be done. Simply emphasize one half of the body one day and the other half the next day, but always while including at least one exercise per muscle group each day.)

Monday—Wednesday—Friday
Series I
1. Leg Press: 5 x 10–15
2. Incline Situps: 5 x 20–30
3. Bench Press: 5 x 6–10
4. Calf Press: 5 x 15–20
5. Barbell Bent Row: 5 x 8–12

Series II
1. Barbell Incline Press: 5 x 6–10
2. Side Bend: 5 x 50
3. Press Behind Neck: 5 x 6–10
4. Barbell Curl: 5 x 8–12
5. Barbell Shrug: 5 x 15–20

Series III
1. Squat: 5 x 10–15
2. Lying Triceps Extension: 5 x 8–12
3. Incline Leg Raise: 5 x 20–30
4. Leg Curl: 5 x 10–15
5. Dumbbell Curl: 5 x 8–12

Series IV
1. Narrow-Grip Bench Press: 5 x 6–10
2. Seated Calf Machine: 5 x 15–20
3. Lat Pulldown: 5 x 8–12
4. Pulley Pushdown: 5 x 8–12
5. Leg Extension: 5 x 10–15

Series V
1. Seated Pulley Rowing: 5 x 8–12
2. Seated Twisting: 5 x 50
3. Side Laterals: 5 x 8–12
4. Hyperextension: 5 x 10–15
5. Flyes: 5 x 8–12

Series VI
1. Parallel Bar Dips: 5 x 10–15
2. Standing Calf Machine: 5 x 15–20
3. Wrist Curl: 5 x 15–20
4. Bent Laterals: 5 x 8–12
5. Bent-Arm Pullovers: 5 x 8–12

One thing you will notice once you get used to PHA Training is that you will be able to do many more total sets with it than you normally can do with the pump system. The preceding programs require only five sets per exercise, but in only a few weeks you could comfortably do as many as 10 sets per movement!

QUALITY TRAINING

The Weider Quality Training Principle is universally used by champion bodybuilders to develop maximum muscle density for competitions. It consists of progressively reducing the rest intervals between sets—to as little as 10–15 seconds—during a peaking phase.

The use of this principle will result in a drastic reduction of your training poundages, but in combination with a definition diet it definitely produces maximum muscularity.

Since you shouldn't want to go into a contest totally ignorant of how to train correctly for it, you should probably give the Weider Quality Training Principle a trial sometime during your buildup phase, just to determine how your body reacts to it. And don't forget to record your experiences with Quality Training in your workout diary, because such notes will be invaluable once you decide to peak for your first competition.

TRI-SETS AND GIANT SETS

The Weider Tri-Set and Giant Set training principles are an intensity progression from my Supersets Principle. Tri-Sets are groupings of three exercises—usually for a single body part but occasionally for two or three muscle groups—done consecutively and with no rest between exercises.

Tri-Sets are ideal for muscle groups with three distinct sections, such as the deltoid with its three heads. Here is an example of a deltoid Tri-Set, using a bracket to indicate that the exercises are done as a group:

1. Side Laterals (medial deltoid head)
2. Press Behind Neck (anterior deltoid head)
3. Bent Laterals (posterior deltoid head)

When you are training a muscle group that has more than three aspects, you can use a Giant Set consisting of four to six exercises. And you will find such a super-intense Giant Set to be very effective. As an example, here is a Giant Set you can do for your chest:

1. Incline Dumbbell Press (upper pectoral)
2. Pullover (rib cage)
3. Flyes (outer pectoral)
4. Parallel Bar Dips (lower pectoral)
5. Cable Crossovers (inner pectoral)

Tri-Sets and Giant Sets are very fatiguing, but they drastically increase training intensity, which in turn accelerates muscle growth. Most bodybuilders use Tri-Sets and Giant Sets just prior to a contest or in the off season only on a lagging muscle group.

Giant Sets can also be done for two or three body parts. To conclude this discussion of Giant Sets, here is one that you can try for your chest and back:

1. Bench Press
2. Chins
3. Incline Dumbbell Press
4. Seated Pulley Rowing
5. Decline Flyes
6. Bent-Arm Pullovers

As a word of caution, even some of the Olympian-level champions have found Tri-Sets and Giants Sets too intense to be used for more than two or three weeks prior to competition. Approach using them yourself with caution.

PRE-EXHAUSTION

Using the Weider Pre-Exhaustion Training Principle is the best way to overcome the problem of your arms being weak links when doing torso exercises, as well as that of your back being a weak link when doing Squats for your thighs. By eliminating these weak links through Pre-Exhaustion you will be able to bomb your chest, back, deltoids, and thighs much harder than ever before.

The weakness of your arms or lower back becomes a problem only when doing basic exercises for the torso muscles or Squats for your thighs, because your arms or lower back tire and force you to terminate a set before your pectorals, deltoids, latissimus dorsi, or thighs have been max-

Multi-title winner Boyer Coe is one of the hardest training bodybuilders of the present day. He has seldom placed out of the top three or four places in international professional bodybuilding competition.

imally stimulated. But what if there was a training method by which you could temporarily make your arms or lower back stronger than your torso or thigh muscles? Then you could use basic exercises to bomb your torso and thighs to the limit.

This method does exist and is the Weider Pre-Exhaustion Principle. Using this technique, you first do an isolation movement for a torso muscle group or the thighs. This prefatigues that muscle group, making it weaker than your arms or lower back for five to ten seconds. So, if you immediately superset this isolation movement with a basic exercise for the same muscle group, you can do that exercise until your torso muscles or thighs fail to complete a rep. And you won't need to worry about your arms or lower back failing during the basic exercises, because they have been made much stronger in relation to your torso muscles or thighs through Pre-Exhaustion.

Here are several time-tested Pre-Exhaustion supersets that you can use in your own bodybuilding workouts:

Chest: Flyes + Bench Presses
Upper Chest: Incline Flyes + Incline Presses
Lower Chest: Decline Flyes + Decline Presses
Deltoids: Side Laterals + Presses Behind Neck
Lats: Bent-Arm Pullovers + Lat Pulldowns
Thighs: Leg Extensions + Squats

With a little thought you will be able to come up with numerous other Pre-Exhaustion supersets.

MUSCLE CONFUSION

The human body is a very adaptable organism, but it constantly seeks the comfort of being in a state of equilibrium wherein it doesn't have to adapt to new stresses. In bodybuilding the human body reaches this equilibrium, and the muscles cease to grow, when the same exercises and routines are used for long periods of time. And this happens even though you may be

progressively increasing training intensity in each exercise.

If you change your routines for each workout—perhaps never again using the same program for a body part—your muscles are confused by the changes, can't adapt to them by reaching equilibrium, and are forced to grow much faster. This concept is the Weider Muscle Confusion Principle, which also applies to what you eat, how much you sleep, and what time of the day you do your bodybuilding workouts.

Lou Ferrigno is one of the greatest proponents of the Weider Muscle Confusion Principle. He constantly changes the exercises he does for each body part, the angles at which he does his exercises, the total number of sets per muscle group, the reps he does for each set, and even the amounts of weight he uses for each exercise.

"I need this type of variety," Lou told me, "because it keeps my muscles off balance and they are forced to continue growing at a fast rate. Variety like this also keeps my interest level quite high for my training."

REST-PAUSE TRAINING

Rest-Pause Training is one of the most intense forms of bodybuilding. It has become quite popular recently, but few bodybuilders understand that I evolved the Weider Rest-Pause Training Principle in the early 1950s!

As you will recall, the heavier the weights you use in an exercise, the larger the muscles stressed by that movement will become. Unfortunately, fatigue products accumulate so quickly in the muscles when you are using very heavy weights that you often can do only one or two reps per set. And you really need about six to eight repetitions in a set to promote maximum muscle growth.

I wondered how it would be possible to force the fatigue toxins from a muscle while it is working, so a bodybuilder could do far more repetitions with a heavy weight. Unfortunately, while the muscle is being trained these toxins stay in the muscle. Then I read in a physiology book that 50 percent of the fatigue toxins have been flushed from the muscle after only 10 seconds of rest, and 75 percent have been eliminated after 15 seconds.

I immediately concluded that a bodybuilder could do *many* reps with a heavy weight if he took a 10- to 15-second rest-pause between each rep or two. Since this would flush out most of the toxins, a set could be continued for up to eight to ten total reps. And in actual practice this technique works exceedingly well!

Mike Mentzer told me that he gets his best muscle growth rate from Rest-Pause Training. Using Machine Incline Presses as an example of how he utilizes this training technique, Mike will pick a weight with which he can do only one or two repetitions and then he will force them out, rest 10–15 seconds, and immediately do one or two more. After another 10–15 seconds rest he will do one or two more reps, but usually with a weight that is 10–20 percent lighter. Finally, he will rest 10–15 more seconds and do a last one or two reps of Machine Incline Presses. The whole "set" blows up his pecs and frontal delts to an almost unbelievable degree.

Rest-Pause Training is so severe that you will probably be able to use it only once per week for each muscle group. And you should use Rest-Pause Training on only one exercise per body part. But when you do use it in your workouts you will experience super results from the Weider Rest-Pause Training Principle!

STRETCH MARKS

Should your muscles or fat deposits expand in size too quickly, the skin over certain areas of your body (most frequently where your pectorals tie in with your deltoids) will be stretched to the point of tearing. This causes stretch marks, the bane of all bodybuilders. These stretch marks are red or purple streaks that are somewhat tender to the touch at first. Later they become light-colored scars on the skin. While a few bodybuilders are completely free of stretch marks, many of the greatest champions of the sport have them all over their bodies, even on their forearms.

In most cases stretch marks can be prevented (or at least minimized) in two ways: (1) Maintain a balanced diet, liberally supplemented with vitamins and minerals; (2) Avoid adding too much fat to your body too quickly, which happens when bodybuilders bulk up excessively. If you do notice a stretch mark developing, you can minimize its spread by rubbing vitamin E lotion on and around the stretch mark. Rubbing this lotion on every morning and evening will help heal your skin and keep the skin tears from spreading.

OUTDOOR TRAINING

In some instances outdoor training can be a joy, while in others it can be disastrous to both you and the sport. If you have some equipment you can drag into your backyard on a sunny day, do so. Training outdoors can be far more enjoyable than working out in a dark, dingy basement. The sun kissing your face and a soft breeze ruffling your hair—what more could a man want from life?

Sometimes, however, such outdoor workouts become exhibitionistic—as occasionally happens at the famous "Muscle Beach" outdoor weight pen on Venice Beach in southern California—which can do far more harm than good for the sport. In such a case, the average person will immediately think that you and all other bodybuilders are a bunch of freaks.

When training outside you must also pay heed to temperature extremes, especially if it is 100 degrees F. (about 40 degrees C.) or hotter. Then you can fall victim either to heat stroke or to body dehydration. So, when it's hot, try to train in the morning and be sure to drink water or other fluids during your workouts.

Another problem with outdoor training which you probably won't have to contend with if you live outside southern California, is smog. When it is extremely smoggy it can actually be a health hazard to train outdoors. Then it is better to train in an air-conditioned gym.

BODY WRAPS AND LIFTING BELTS

The longer you bodybuild, the greater will be the poundages you use in each exercise. And the heavier the weights you use, the greater the strain on your joints and the greater the potential of injuring one of them. Therefore, most advanced bodybuilders use weight-lifting belts and/or body wraps, particularly over a joint that has previously been injured.

Weight-lifting belts are made of thick leather and are either four or six inches in width across the back of the belt. In weight-lifting and powerlifting competition the belt can be no more than four inches in width. But the six-inch belt gives more support, so I suggest you buy it for bodybuilding workouts. These belts cost $30–$40.

Cinched tightly about your waist, a lifting belt will give you mid-body stability when doing heavy overhead lifts, Squats, and heavy back exercises. It protects your back from injury and also holds in your stomach during heavy lifts. I have seen few champions go without a lifting belt when doing Squats, Military Presses, Deadlifts, and Barbell Bent Rows.

Body wraps come in two types— neoprene rubber body bands and elastic fabric bandages. The neoprene bands do not give as much support as elastic bandages, but the rubber holds in perspiration and heat against the skin. Since moist heat has a beneficial effect on healing and preventing injuries, many top bodybuilders wear these bands around their knees, elbows, and waists (to protect their lower backs), particularly if these joints have previously been injured.

Elastic bandages can be wrapped tightly around the knees, elbows, ankles, or wrists to protect old injuries to these joints. Still, while they give great support to a joint,

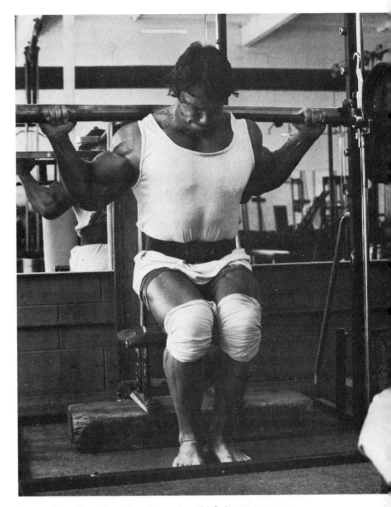

Seven-time Mr. Olympia winner Arnold Schwarzenegger uses both a weightlifting belt and knee wraps while doing heavy Squats in a Smith machine.

they don't hold in moist heat like the rubber body bands. So, for maximum protection to previously injured joints— particularly the knees—a few champion bodybuilders will first don the rubber bands, then will put on a sweat suit, and finally will wrap elastic bandages around the joint over the rubber and cloth. Dennis Tinerino—a former Mr. America, Mr. World, and Mr. Universe—is one of these men and he swears by this procedure!

ADVANCED FOOD SUPPLEMENTATION AND DIET TIPS

My final advice to you on food supplementation and general diet involves a series of things you should and shouldn't do.

Here are nine things you *should* do with food supplements and other foods from now on.

1. If you ever have trouble sleeping, take three to five tryptophane tablets 30 minutes before retiring. Tryptophane—one of the eight essential amino acids—is a natural tranquilizer.

2. When you are too rushed to prepare and/or eat a full meal, at least drink a high-protein milk shake. You can whip one up in only a minute or two and drink it just as quickly. Or you can keep one in a thermos bottle in the fridge for emergencies.

3. Supplement your diet with 800–1200 IU of vitamin E and two or three chelated iron tablets each day. Each of these food supplements will help provide additional training energy, but they should never be taken at the same time. Taken together, vitamin E and iron tend to cancel out each other's effects.

4. Begin to consume your flesh products more from white meats like fish and poultry and less from red meats like beef and pork.

5. Eat a couple of pieces of fruit for training energy.

6. Experiment with various caloric intake levels to determine how low you have to go for your body to begin losing fat. You will definitely need to know this if you intend to compete soon.

7. If you can afford them, start taking both vitamin B-12 and vitamin B-15 tablets. Both are good for increasing training energy.

8. Begin to (or continue to) experiment with individual vitamins and minerals—but continue to take multiple vitamins and minerals—to see which ones work best for you.

9. Be sure to take your supplements with your meals, because they tend to work better in your body when taken with other foods.

On the other side of the coin there are five things you *shouldn't* do with your diet and food supplements.

1. Don't overemphasize dessicated liver tablets in your diet just because you read somewhere that it increased some swimming lab rat's energy and endurance. Dessicated liver *does* increase training energy, but largely because it is a superior source of protein that is also high in carbohydrates (about 30 percent of liver calories are derived from its carbohydrate content). This combination is far more important for promoting workout energy than some mystical "energy" ingredient that liver is supposed to have.

2. Don't depend on kelp tablets to improve your metabolism and burn off body fat, because the iodine in them can actually have the opposite effect. Kelp is, however, an excellent source of trace elements, and it should be taken for those nutrients.

3. Don't drink liquid amino acids without taking tryptophane tablets with them. Liquid amino acids are made from animal by-products in such a way that they are always low in tryptophane, one of the eight essential amino acids that the human body can't manufacture on its own.

4. Don't overdo anything nutritionally. I have known hundreds of bodybuilders—many of them champions—who have actually make themselves ill by consuming excessive amounts of food supplements.

5. Again, don't neglect a balanced diet just because you like to take a lot of pills and powders. Food supplements aren't magic muscle-building potions by any stretch of the imagination. Vitamins, minerals, and protein powders should be treated only as *supplements* to a balanced diet.

HOW TO WATCH A BODYBUILDING CONTEST

Since you will be entering competition soon, it is vitally important that you first attend several shows to familiarize yourself with how they are conducted and what the judges look for in each bodybuilder. You will be able to learn when a competition will be held in your area by reading either the "Coming Events" column in *Muscle & Fitness* or the posters that contest

Athletes are compared in both pairs and groups. This was a back pose comparison between Carlos Rodriguez (left) and Bill Grant at the 1979 Diamond Cup professional competition.

promoters put up in major gyms and YMCAs before their events.

Most amateur contests feature a guest poser as part of the program. This will be a bodybuilder who has won national and/or international titles, and he will give an exhibition toward the end of the evening's program. Seeing this champion pose will be an excellent opportunity for you to see what you will eventually look like, as well as how esthetically and athletically you will pose.

Keep in mind when watching this cham-

pion that, unless he is posing on a weekend just before a major competition, he isn't likely to be in his best condition. During his off season he will be fatter than normal (what we call "smooth"), but you will still be able to appreciate his huge muscle size, great body proportions, and the way the muscles flow from one into another (what we call "tie-ins"). He will retain these qualities—but be startlingly more muscular—for a competition. You should also take careful note of how smoothly and impressively the guest poser actually poses.

At the Diamond Cup, Mohamed Makkawy (Egypt) and Henry Caulker (Barbados-Canada) compare front double-biceps poses. Caulker has won Mr. Canada and Makkawy is a former Mr. Universe.

At a professional competition, of course, you will see all the superstar contestants at or near their best condition, and all will pose impressively.

Most contests—both amateur and professional—will be prejudged in the morning or early afternoon of the day of the show, and the prejudging is where most of the action takes place. In most cases the evening show becomes merely a public presentation, since most of the decisions have been made at the prejudging. At night the only decision usually made is among the weight-class winners to determine an overall champion.

Watch carefully how contestants are judged, because soon you will be undergoing the same procedure yourself. The IFBB has developed a super-fair judging system, which is used worldwide as well as by the American Physique Committee (the amateur bodybuilding federation in America that is affiliated internationally with the IFBB). So, I will describe how this judging system works.

To begin with, there are seven judges, each of whom can award a score of one to 20 to every contestant in each of three judging rounds (although normally judges never give a contestant less than 10 points). In every round the high and low scores given to each contestant are elimi-

156

nated, and the remaining scores are totaled. The highs and lows are thrown out to prevent a judge from unfairly ranking a contestant. This seldom happens, but such a safeguard is necessary to protect contestants from the rare possibility of an incompetent judge being included on the panel (which happens only at the local or state levels, incidentally).

Amateur contestants are judged according to weight classes, so a man who is 5' tall isn't handicapped by being forced to compete against one who is 6'5" tall. These weight classes are 70 kg. (154 lbs.), 80 kg. (176 lbs.), 90 kg. (198 lbs.), and over 90 kg. Professionals are usually judged without such class distinctions. Occasionally, however, over-200- and under-200-pound categories are used.

Round I of the IFBB system of judging consists of four semirelaxed facing poses, done with the arms held down at the sides. Each contestant is viewed singly facing forward, from the right side, facing away from the judges, and from the left side. Then all the contestants are brought onstage and comparisons are made among various bodybuilders using the same four poses. Finally, the judges score each contestant.

Round I allows the judges to appraise each contestant's overall symmetry (body outline, such as how good a V-shape a contestant has), general body proportions, muscle tone, and general appearance (tan, skin tone, etc.).

In Round II the contestants pose individually and then are compared in groups in seven compulsory poses. These poses are front double biceps, front lat spread, side chest (either side), back double biceps, back lat spread, side triceps (either side), and front abdominal pose (with both hands held behind the head and one leg extended to show thigh and calf development). Round II allows the judges to assess how each contestant compares with the rest while his muscles are under tension.

Round III consists of free posing, for 60 seconds in amateur shows and for an unlimited amount of time in pro contests (us-

In Round III of the IFBB Judging System, the athletes are allowed to free-pose individually. This is one of Sergio Oliva's most awesome free poses.

ually a maximum of two or three minutes, since posing is very strenuous work). During this judging round contestants become extremely artistic and innovative in their posing. Watch carefully how they make transitions between poses and how they adapt standard poses to fit their unique physiques. It is generally felt that Ed Corney, Boyer Coe, and Chris Dickerson are the leaders in free posing today.

As mentioned earlier, each contestant is scored in each of the three judging rounds. He could receive up to 100 points per round (five 20-point scores after the high and low scores have been eliminated), so after three rounds of judging he could have a maximum of 300 points. And in Round IV, the pose-down, he can be given an extra point for each first-place vote he is awarded,

At IFBB pro competitions the stars shine! Danny Padilla (left) goes *mano a mano* with Mike Mentzer in the above photo. Below is the lineup for the 1980 Florida Grand Prix, won by Chris Dickerson (far left).

Above, at the 1980 Louisiana Grand Prix, Casey Viator (far left) won convincingly. Below left, Chris Dickerson edged out Robby Robinson (left) and Roy Callender (right) at the 1980 New York Grand Prix. At the same show, Steve Michalik (left to right), Bill Grant, Tom Platz, and Boyer Coe fought it out for fourth place.

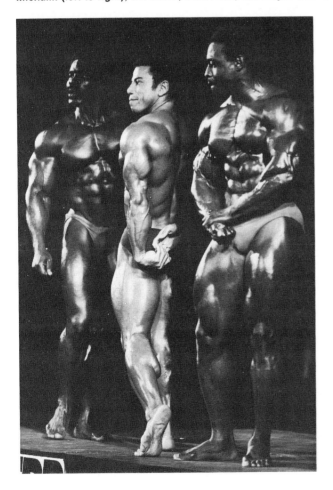

making 307 points the maximum a contestant can receive. In the 1981 World Cup, Boyer Coe was the first professional bodybuilder to receive the maximum score of 307 points.

The top five men after the first three rounds are included in the pose-down, which consists of two to three minutes of man-against-man warfare. The contestants give all they can to receive a judge's vote, since in a close contest the pose-down round points can be decisive. And the winner is invariably the happiest man in the auditorium!

Aside from the way the contestants are judged and how they pose, soak up everything else you can at the show. It will all come in handy some day, because the contest scene is the culmination of many years of sacrifice and hard training. It is the climax of bodybuilding and will sustain you for many more years of hard training.

PEAK CONTRACTION AND CONTINUOUS TENSION

The Weider Peak Contraction Principle and Weider Slow Continuous Tension Principle are used widely by champion bodybuilders to bring out the utmost in contest muscularity and muscle density. You should give each principle a try in your training and determine how well they work for you.

The Weider Peak Contraction Principle relies on the fact that a muscle has the maximum number of fibers contracted only when it is fully flexed. You can easily prove this to yourself merely by flexing your arm and seeing how much more the biceps bunch up in height when your arm is flexed than when it is straight.

Peak Contraction involves having maximum resistance on each muscle group when it is fully contracted. The Machine Curls mentioned in Chapter 3 are an example of this training principle in action. Numerous other movements allow you to take advantage of the Peak Contraction Principle, because they exercise each muscle group with maximum intensity and efficiency.

The Weider Slow Continuous Tension Principle advocates moving a weight in any exercise slowly and over that muscle's full range of motion with maximum tension built into the muscle it works. This technique builds tremendous intensity into an exercise, because when a movement is done with a quick cadence, momentum usually does a lot of the work a muscle should be doing over part of its range of motion. And building maximum tension into a working muscle is one of the best ways to bring out the greatest possible number of muscle striations.

CONTEST PEAKING

Once you decide to enter a contest, you must commit yourself to an all-out training, dietary, and psychological assault to win the title for which you will be competing. A majority of fledgling bodybuilders are either unable or unwilling to make this type of commitment, so they fall by the wayside. Only the champions survive—sort of a "bodybuilding Darwinism" in action. To commit yourself to winning is to set yourself apart from the masses.

Training effectively for a contest involves peaking both the intensity of your training and the strictness of your diet. From hard training and a balanced diet, you will gradually increase the intensity of your training and tighten your diet. And through six to eight weeks of following this peaking procedure your muscle quality and muscularity will improve dramatically. This should put you into the condition that I know will make you a champion bodybuilder!

"Pushing" and Quality Training

As Lou Ferrigno so aptly describes it, "Contest training makes you push like a dog." You will find that the incentive of wanting to appear at your best onstage will give you enormous training drive. You will push harder, faster, and with more concentration than ever before. Your training will become more and more intense until every muscle in your body cries out for you to stop. If you keep going, *that's* pushing.

Earlier you had a chance to think about Quality Training, but now you can live it. With every workout in your peaking phase, you simply *must* endeavor to shorten the rests between sets. When you get your rest intervals down into the 10- to 15-second range you will be training almost nonstop, and you will be where you want to be in terms of Quality Training.

With shortened rest intervals comes an inevitable reduction in the poundages you can handle in each exercise. The trick here is to keep them up for as long as you can, because the heavier the weights you use when Quality Training, the greater the muscle density you will end up with. Still, the weights will go down, and that is nothing to be ashamed of. It has happened to every great champion who has cut his rest intervals as much as you have.

Precontest Diet

When you diet for a contest you will have two options—either restrict carbohydrates in your diet or restrict your total caloric consumption. Both methods are popular among top bodybuilders, and it appears that both methods work well. You should simply read all the pros and cons enumerated here for each diet before you decide which one to try. Then, after you have tried one type of diet, give the other one a trial for your next contest to see if it might not do the job even better for you.

The most popular precontest diet has involved restricting carbohydrate intake. Several weeks (usually eight to ten) before a contest a bodybuilder takes out his booklet of carbohydrate contents for each food (available for a dollar or less in most drugstores) and uses it to cut his carbohydrate intake to about 120 grams per day. Each week he reduces this level by 10 or more grams, until it is at 20–30 grams per day for the last two or three weeks. This draws on the body's fat for fuel and reduces body water retention (one gram of carbohydrate retains four grams of water in the body). Thus, the bodybuilder ends up looking quite muscular.

There are three keys to effective utiliza-tion of the carbohydrate restriction method of precontest dieting.

1. *Progressively* restrict carbohydrate intake. Cutting too much all at once will be very difficult to do, and it is also unhealthy to cut carbs too drastically in one fell swoop.

2. Don't blow the diet (this caution also holds for the caloric restriction diet).

3. Never go to zero carbohydrates, because this will kill your energy levels and result in a considerable loss of muscle mass.

The second type of precontest diet is a little more difficult to keep track of even with a calorie counter, but it is a far more sensible method of dieting. It involves progressively cutting back on the calories you eat from your normal level down to a level of 1,500–2,000 calories per day. Some bodybuilders may even need to go lower than 1,500 calories per day (Danny Padilla is one of these men), while some might be able to eat as many as 2,500 calories per day and still cut up (as Greg DeFerro can easily do, since he was eating more than 4,000 calories per day when he won the Mr. International title).

It's a simple fact that when you take in fewer calories than you burn off each day, you begin to lose body fat. For each 3,500 calories you do burn off, you will lose one pound of fat. This has been scientifically proven.

One gram of fat yields nine calories when metabolized in the body for energy, while one gram of protein or one gram of carbohydrate will yield only four calories. Therefore, bodybuilders who restrict calories in their diets will cut back drastically on their fat intake. Generally they eat chicken breasts (without the skin, which is high in fat), fish, green vegetables, and a limited amount of fruit when peaking for competitions. It is certainly a restricted diet but still one that is better balanced nutritionally than the low-carbohydrate precontest diet.

The trick with both types of diet is to learn and to take note of how your body reacts to a diet. Be sure to see *how much* calorie or carbohydrate reduction it takes you to go from "X" amount of weight to being ripped to shreds for a competition. If you do this correctly, you will never blow your timing for a competition, because you can always regulate your diet according to how you appear in the mirror at certain checkpoints close to the contest. A smidgen too fat, and out goes the apple or the succotash each day. It's that simple to peak on time nutritionally for a competition!

Precontest Supplements

It is a popular and effective method among top bodybuilders to increase food supplementation levels drastically prior to a contest. Go ahead and take all you can, but keep in mind that you will receive a greater effect from this supplement increase if you have kept your intake threshold for vitamins and minerals low until your peaking cycle starts.

There are a couple of B-complex vitamins—choline and inositol—that many bodybuilders take to increase fat metabolism, but I'm not fully convinced of their value. Go ahead and experiment with them, however.

Too many bodybuilders take kelp tablets to speed up their metabolisms, but I have already mentioned that this can have the opposite effect. And finally, if you do take dessicated liver tablets and you are on a carbohydrate reduction diet, you should remember, as I've already pointed out, that liver contains about 30 percent carbohydrate.

MENTAL TRICKS

The importance of a strong link between the mind and body has been explored and verified thoroughly by such champion bodybuilders as Arnold Schwarzenegger (Mr. Olympia seven times), Frank Zane (Mr. Olympia three times), Andreas Cahling (Mr. International once), and Tom Platz (Mr. Universe once). In fact, most champion bodybuilders agree that it is vital to have the mind fully oriented toward gaining muscle mass and muscle density.

To assure the correct degree of concentration, it is necessary to focus your mind strongly on the muscle(s) being worked during every set of every exercise you do. Try to visualize and feel the working muscle(s) contracting and extending under a heavy load. "Don't feel the *weight*," Jusup Wilkosz (Mr. Universe) emphasizes. "Feel the *muscle!*"

Arnold Schwarzenegger has taken this mind–muscle link even further. "When I was working my biceps," he stated, "I imagined them as huge mountains while I concentrated on them. This had the effect of preparing my mind to accept my biceps as already being huge, so the actual muscle growth became a mere formality."

Visualization, which draws its effectiveness from a psychological construct called *self-actualization,* is another mental technique bodybuilders use. It is very similar, in fact, to what Arnold Schwarzenegger just described.

The visualization technique consists of spending a few minutes each day vividly imagining your body the way you wish it soon to be. If this image is real enough to you, it programs your subconscious mind to make choices that will assure the achievement of such a goal. And it thus becomes easier to go to the gym regularly or to avoid progress-stalling junk foods in your diet.

Of all bodybuilders, Frank Zane is recognized as the best exponent of visualization. Each time he has won the Mr. Olympia title, Frank has been able to visualize the win in every detail—the setting, how he would look, the feeling of excitement at competing, etc. And he was able to make his images so real that he had actually "won" his competition before he even walked onstage.

If you would like to try using visualization, set aside 15 minutes each night before you fall asleep. Lie in bed totally relaxed and close your eyes. Then try mentally to project images of your future physique on the backs of your eyelids. Do this every day and soon you will be able to conjure up very vivid images of your body. At this

Frank Zane, Mr. Olympia winner of 1977-1978-1979, shows that a man with a small-boned frame can be a winner, even at the highest levels of competition. Each time he has won this title, Frank has been able to visualize the win in every detail.

point you will be positively programming your mind for bodybuilding success.

BODYBUILDING DRUGS

No issue in our sport these days evokes such emotion as that of bodybuilding drugs. I am personally against the use of such drugs in bodybuilding, but still the policy of *Muscle & Fitness* magazine has long been to publicize the positive and negative qualities of such drugs, to educate objectively the bodybuilding public about them. If the drugs exist, bodybuilders will take them, and I feel that it is best to give them objective information about the drugs. For more detailed information than I will present here about bodybuilding drugs, I suggest that you read *Muscle & Fitness* each month.

There are basically five types of bodybuilding drugs—anabolic steroids, androgenics, thyroid stimulants, amphetamines, and analgesics. Steroids are artificial male hormones with the androgenic (pertaining to the development of secondary sex characteristics of males) properties removed. Most bodybuilders take steroids, and a few take pure androgenics (such as testosterone), for six weeks before competing. Both types of drugs result in temporary increases in muscle mass.

Thyroid stimulants are used to speed up the metabolism and help the body to get cut up. But they also result in a loss of muscle mass, so it seems silly to take such drugs when a week or two more of strict dieting will give a bodybuilder the same degree of muscularity while maintaining muscle mass. Some bodybuilders also take amphetamines in an effort to kill their appetites and have more workout energy. Again, these drugs are counterproductive in bodybuilding, since they also eat away at muscle tissue.

Analgesic drugs are pain killers such as Darvon and aspirin. These drugs have been used widely in the past to mask the pain of inflamed ligaments and tendons, but recently they have been replaced by the widespread use of DMSO (di-methyl sulfoxide). Use of DMSO apparently reduces inflammations (even arthritis, supposedly) all over the body, but sufficient research has not been done on this drug for the FDA to have approved it for sale legally. DMSO is a solvent widely used in various industries and hobbies, however, so it is easily available.

BASIC POSING

The first thing you should do when learning to pose is to look at the photos in *Muscle & Fitness* of champion bodybuilders posing. Pick out a pose that you particularly admire and try to imitate it in the mirror. Obviously you won't look like the superstar in the magazine, but you might look pretty good in that pose nonetheless. By trying out numerous poses you will soon come up with a collection of stances in which you look fairly good.

As you are doing each pose, keep in mind that it can be done in thousands of ways. Simply by shifting your hips a little, narrowing the stance of your feet, changing the tilt of your shoulders, or whatever, you subtly change a pose. Play with every pos-

On this and the following page, Boyer Coe shows how a basic double biceps pose—one of his best shots—can be changed to a new pose by slightly altering his leg and arm positioning.

sible variable when adapting a pose to your body, and sooner or later you will master it. No two champions do the same pose identically, as can easily be ascertained by cutting out from *Muscle & Fitness* photos of 20 champions doing double biceps poses from the front and laying them side by side.

The first poses you should try to master are the seven compulsory stances discussed earlier in this chapter. Not only are they essential poses for one of the three judging rounds, but they will also form the backbone of your free-posing routine.

As you are working on your compulsory poses and various optional stances, you should also be practicing how to stand in the Round I positions. These stances are actually poses and can be improved on with practice. Again, just a slight change in

foot or hand position or a minor twist of the torso can improve one of these stances 100 percent.

Finally, you will need to develop transitions between poses and learn how to arrange your poses in logical sequence. The two best ways to do this are to attend contests and observe how contestants move between poses and sequence poses, and to view 8mm films of the champions posing. These films are often advertised in *Muscle & Fitness* magazine.

Eventually, you can develop a posing routine that is a work of art. Never neglect posing practice, because you will never win a contest unless you can show yourself to your best advantage. Ed Corney spends as much time practicing his posing as he spends training in the gym. Need I say more?

Casey Viator in a basic front pose . . .

166

. . . and in a basic back pose that any beginner can duplicate.

Mike Mentzer demonstrates one of the many types of twisting back poses that can be done.

And here is Mike's unique version of the basic double-biceps pose from the back.

Dennis Tinerino demonstrates two variations of the same basic pose. By kneeling or lunging it is changed dramatically. Or, a simple two-inch move of each hand reveals an entirely new pose.

LEVEL FOUR EXERCISES

This is the last group of exercises that I will give you in this book, but don't make the mistake of assuming that these are all the exercises in existence. We have hardly scratched the surface, because there are *hundreds* of other bodybuilding movements and scores of variations on the ones I have given you so far. You can pick up the rest of the bodybuilding exercises you will be using in the future by staying alert in the gym and watching what people are doing in *Muscle & Fitness* for various body parts. Or, ideally, you can read Bill Pearl's superb book, *Keys to the Inner Universe*, which lists, explains, and fully illustrates literally hundreds of exercises for each muscle group.

Thighs

Partial Squats. At some point in your bodybuilding career you will be training for power, and that is the time that you can experiment with Partial Squats. Except for the depth to which you squat, these are the same as the Full Squats. The gradations upward from a Full Squat are Parallel Squat (the thighs go down just to a point parallel to the floor), Bench Squat (you squat down to a bench), Three-Quarters Squat, Half Squat, and Quarter Squat. Be very sure to wrap your knees with elastic bandages for all Partial Squats, because you will be using very heavy weights, particularly on the Quarter Squats.

Partial Squats:
   Start, in power rack (above right).
   Finish, to three-quarters (right).

Decline Flyes—finish.

Chest

Decline Flyes. We have already done Flyes at virtually every other angle, so why not on a 30-degree decline bench, too? Simply lie with your head at the lower end of the bench and do your Flyes. You will find that Decline Flyes are excellent for carving a clean line around the lower edge of your pectorals.

Prone Incline Laterals—finish.

Shoulders

Prone Incline Laterals. This is an excellent movement for both the side and rear sections of your deltoids. It is also an excellent movement for stressing your trapezius and other upper back muscles. Lie facedown on a 45-degree incline bench with two dumbbells in your hands and your arms hanging straight down. Face your palms inward and hold them at this angle throughout the exercise. Bend your elbows slightly. From this basic starting position, raise the dumbbells straight out to the sides in semicircles until they reach shoulder level. At the top of the movement, rotate your thumbs downward, pause for a second, and lower back to the start.

174

Side Incline Laterals. For the medial head of your deltoid you can exercise one shoulder at a time by lying on your side on an incline bench and doing Lateral Raises. Start by lying on your right side and holding a light dumbbell in your left hand. The plates of the dumbbell should be resting on your left thigh at the start of the movement. Raise the dumbbell straight out to the side until it is directly overhead. Lower it back to the starting point and repeat the movement.

Side Incline Laterals—midpoint.

Arms

Dumbbell Kickbacks. This is one of the best exercises for working the triceps muscles with peak contraction. Take a dumbbell in one hand and bend over so your torso is parallel to the floor. Press your upper arm into the side of your torso so that your forearm hangs down at a 90-degree angle from your upper arm. From this position, move only your forearm and the dumbbell until your entire arm is straight. Return to the start and repeat. Be sure to do an equal number of repetitions and sets for both arms.

Dumbbell Kickbacks—finish.

Zottman Curl. For both the biceps and forearm muscles, nothing can equal the Zottman Curl. This is an Alternate Dumbbell Curl with a wrist twist. Curl each dumbbell upward with your palm facing upward. Then, at the top of the movement, rotate your wrist so your palm is facing down as you lower the dumbbell back down to the starting position. This movement takes some practice to achieve good coordination, but you will have little difficulty if you remember, "Up, palm up; down, palm down."

Zottman Curl—midpoint.

Standing Triceps Extension—finish.

Standing Triceps Extension. This is simply another variation of the barbell or dumbbell Triceps Extension we have done lying, seated, and on an incline. This movement stresses the large inner head of the triceps.

Decline Triceps Extension—midpoint.

Decline Triceps Extension. Again, with this movement you are dealing with a Barbell Triceps Extension at a different angle. You will simply be lying on a decline bench as you do the movement. Each new angle will have a slightly different effect on your triceps development. It is always a good idea to experiment with all possible angles of each movement to evolve an ideal workout for your individual body.

PUMP OUT

This chapter brings to an end my instructions on how to train. In the final chapter, I will present a discussion of how Chris Dickerson prepares himself for competitions. Chris is one of the greatest professional champions our sport has produced, and his training philosophy will give you an idea of how everything I have described fits together.

Chris Dickerson, Pro Bodybuilding superstar.   Bill Pearl, Chris Dickerson's mentor.

6

Level Five—
How a Champion Does It

If you have followed the instructions given in this book sequentially, you will almost be ready to compete in your first body-building contest. Or you will have already competed, probably lost, and are now trying to improve 100 percent for your next competition.

In this final chapter, I will give a detailed account of how a top pro bodybuilding champion, Chris Dickerson, diets, mentally programs himself, rests and recuperates, and trains. These factors will be discussed for use both in the off season and while peaking for a major competition, such as the Mr. Olympia, an annual super show-down of famous Mr. Universe winners.

CHRIS DICKERSON'S BODYBUILDING CAREER

Chris Dickerson was a late starter as a bodybuilder, since he was already 23 years of age when he first walked into Bill Pearl's Gym in Pasadena, California, during the summer of 1962. "I was 5'6" tall and weighed 145 pounds when I started," Chris recalls. "I had a fairly athletic build, with naturally large calves, from years of playing soccer, my favorite sport.

"I had been taking voice lessons toward my goal of becoming an opera singer, and my voice teacher had suggested that I take up weight training to build up my lungs. That's how I discovered Bill Pearl's Gym, which was bodybuilding's gain and opera's loss!"

As was Bill Pearl's custom when he was still actively involved in the gym business, he personally wrote out Dickerson's first training routine, one of over 100,000 he wrote for his gym members during nearly 30 years in the gym business. "But I remember Chris that first day quite distinctly," Pearl said recently. "He had such terrific calves that everyone in the gym kept asking Chris to flex them. I think that all of the attention embarrassed him some-what, because he wore sweat pants instead of shorts to the gym every day after that first workout, and he still wears a full sweat suit to train even to this day!"

The first basic routine Pearl wrote for Dickerson was just what Chris's body had apparently been lying dormant and waiting for, because his muscles all began to grow rapidly from his first week of three-day-per-week workouts.

"Bill Pearl's bodybuilding philosophy is one that stresses overall body proportions that are perfectly balanced," Chris said, "so he didn't let me do a single set of calf work at first, except when I sneaked in a couple when he wasn't looking. Instead of wasting time and energy further improving an ex-ceptionally strong body part—and throw-ing the body's proportions even farther off—he wanted me to concentrate on all my weaker areas, until they eventually became as good as my calves.

"Bill has always been my primary trainer (although, of course, I also rely heavily on Joe Weider for advice), even when I lived for a few years in New York City. So, he should be given a lot of credit for the suc-cess I've achieved over the years. Of course, I had to do the workouts myself, but he often trained right along with me to provide me with that little extra push I always need just before a competition, when my strict diet has drained away much of my usual energy supplies. Overall, Bill Pearl has influenced me beneficially on so many levels—as a brother, a confidant, a father-figure, a hero-image, a trainer, and a totally objective critic of my physique.

"This final role that Bill Pearl plays is extremely valuable to a pro bodybuilder of my stature, because it's the minor flaws that blow a contest like the Olympia or one of the Grand Prix shows. If someone, as Bill does for me, can spot such minor flaws and point them out to me, I can usually correct one or two within six to eight weeks. Of course, if my calves were three or four inches smaller in girth, it would take several years to correct such a major

fault. But with Bill Pearl as my constant critic over the years, I never developed such major flaws, even though some pro bodybuilders did.

"To be sure that I'm as close to perfection as possible for a major competition—and so I'm certain I will have a training partner who will kill me in my workouts—I'll go up and spend four to six weeks at Bill's ranch in Oregon before a show. His ranch sits high on a ridge overlooking the Rogue River Valley in southern Oregon, which is such beautiful and peaceful country that I can be totally relaxed there, forget about the frenetic pace of LA and all my problems there, and concentrate totally on body-building.

"Bill has a 'home gym' in a barn that he cleaned up, paneled, installed with mirrors, and then loaded with more equipment than 95 percent of all professional gyms I've ever seen have in their own inventories. It's almost the equal of his old gym in Pasa-dena, as well as Gold's and the World gyms in southern California! With Bill as my training partner in that gym, I'm guaran-teed to reach the *absolute best condition I'm capable of achieving* for a big show like the Olympia!"

Returning our story to 1964, Chris Dick-erson entered his first competition—after nearly two years of steady training at Pearl's Gym—and placed third in the Mr. Long Beach Show. "I was delighted," he recalls nostalgically. "To this day, I love that small trophy more than any other I've ever won. I display it on the same shelf as my Overall Grand Prix trophy, which I won in 1980 in a grueling five-contest duel with Casey Viator. Even though I've won 150 bodybuilding trophies since that first one, to me it's still the most important award I've ever received."

In the fall of '64, Chris moved back to New York City, where he continued to train as hard as he could, keeping in touch with Bill Pearl by phone. So whenever I devel-oped a new Weider Training Principle, Chris would be trying it in his own work-out that same night, because I would in-

Chris Dickerson: "Bill Pearl's bodybuilding philosophy is one that stresses overall body proportions that are perfectly balanced."

variably be so excited that I would have to call Bill Pearl myself the minute I finally had a new principle totally conceptualized.

Bill would try the new principle, and he would relay the new technique to Chris, almost as soon as I had hung up after telling him about it. So, while Bill was using it in his workouts in California, Chris was using it in his own training sessions in New York. They would compare notes a couple of weeks later, and Bill would then give me their collective conclusion about how the new principle worked for them.

Usually, they would give total approval of the new Weider Training Principle, or sometimes they would suggest a slight change to adapt it to an actual gym setting. Only then did I have the full confidence that a new Weider Training Principle was ready for publication in *Muscle Builder* (later changed to *Muscle & Fitness*) magazine. If it worked for Bill and Chris, it would certainly work for the masses of bodybuilders reading the magazine.

While living in New York, Dickerson won 11 titles in 12 months, losing only once to Jim Haislop in the Mr. North America competition. Haislop won the Mr. America show a year later, however, so that lone defeat was nothing for Chris to be ashamed of. Besides, his East Coast wins were against established and better publicized bodybuilders, and his titles included Mr. New York City, Mr. New York State, Mr. Eastern USA, Mr. Eastern America, Mr. East Coast, and other similar high-level regional titles.

Longing for the sun, warmth, and beaches of California instead of the cold and blizzards of New York City, Chris returned to California in early 1966, making a beeline directly to Bill Pearl's Gym on arrival. He trained hard enough to win the '67 Mr. California contest, as a dark horse when compared to the best Californian amateurs of the day—Chuck Collras, who competes these days in Past-40 shows; Don Peters, who now owns and operates a fine gym, Don Peters Gym and Fitness Center, in Reseda, California; and John Balik, who

is a nutrition consultant and writes articles on nutrition and profiles of top bodybuilders for *Muscle & Fitness*, where he is also one of our top photographers.

In 1968 Chris hit the big time nationally, winning the AAU Mr. USA title over Boyer Coe, against whom Chris regularly competes today on the professional bodybuilding circuit. Then in 1969 he lost the Mr. America title to Coe by a mere half point. But Chris Dickerson bounced back in 1970 to win the America convincingly over Ken Waller and Casey Viator, both of whom are also prominent professional bodybuilders today. In fact, during the 1980 Grand Prix of Bodybuilding, Chris won three of the contests and Viator took the other two.

It was the custom until 1978 for the AAU Mr. America to go to London to enter the NABBA Mr. Universe, which Chris did in 1970. He defeated Franco Columbu in the short class but lost out in the race for the overall title. In 1973, however, he did win the amateur Mr. Universe title, followed by the professional Mr. Universe award in 1974.

Then, late in 1976, Chris severely injured the pec-delt tie-in on one side of his body while doing heavy Bench Presses. "It was a rookie mistake," he admits. "I just wasn't warmed up enough to use as heavy a poundage as I had on the bar, and I tore the pectoral muscle near its insertion point badly enough to be unable to train my chest for two years. For a while I trained around the injury and then totally stopped working out for an extended period of time. Eventually, my body weight was up to 215 pounds, which at 5'6" in height is very heavy. I should say that I was then downright fat!"

So, late in 1978, he began semiserious training again and was overjoyed to find that there were even a few chest movements he could do without pain. Then, fortuitously, he received a letter in February of 1979 from Warren Langman, who was then promoting the Diamond Cup that August in Vancover, British Columbia. Langman was offering a total of $30,000 in

prizes, which made Chris think hard about competing again.

"People had been coming up to me for a couple of years asking, 'Chris, why don't you compete these days?'" Dickerson says. "It's nice to be asked, you know, even if you're as far out of shape as I'd been six months before receiving Warren Langman's letter. Langman thought enough of me to invite me to compete, even though he knew I'd been out of shape for nearly three years.

"Ironically, the 1979 Diamond Cup competition was scheduled to be held on the same day as my fortieth birthday. 'Wouldn't it be nice,' I fantasized, 'to be standing up onstage in my best lifetime condition for that show on my fortieth birthday?' So, I started training full-bore for it. I *did* achieve my lifetime best physical condition, but was narrowly edged out for the $20,000 diamond offered as first prize by an incredible Roy Callender. But I took home a check for $5,000 as the second-place finisher, and I was on my way as a pro bodybuilder!"

Chris Dickerson competed in his first Mr. Olympia show that fall, placing a respectable sixth behind Frank Zane, Mike Mentzer, Boyer Coe, Robby Robinson, and Dennis Tinerino, all of whom he defeated within the next year. Still, Chris was disappointed with his finish at that initial Olympia.

"I went in with too little publicity," he noted, "so the crowd didn't react to me with the wild enthusiasm that they reserved for the five men who finished in front of me. And I didn't feel I was quite as cut up for the Olympia as I had been at the Diamond Cup a couple of months before. I decided to go all-out for cuts for my next show, the Canada Cup in November of '79."

Chris was so defined at the Canada Cup that he looked like a living anatomy chart, even when standing totally relaxed. He won easily for his first pro victory, avenging his Olympia losses to Mentzer, Robinson, Coe, and Tinerino in the process. Zane habitually competes only in the Mr. Olympia show each year, so Chris would have to wait 10 more months to defeat the '79 Olympia winner.

Dickerson had a greater year—both financially from prize money and in terms of the number of victories he amassed—during 1980 than any professional bodybuilder in history. In one year he placed first in three of the five Grand Prix shows (at Miami, Santa Monica, and New York City), took the overall Grand Prix title, won the World Couples Championships with Stacey Bentley as his partner, won the Canada Cup for a second consecutive year, and placed no lower than second in his other three outings. (The Grand Prix stops at Lafayette, Louisiana, and Pittsburgh were both won by Casey Viator, and the Mr. Olympia was won by Arnold Schwarzenegger.)

The 1980 Mr. Olympia competition, held in early October at the incredibly sumptuous Sydney (Australia) Opera House, proved to be the most controversial Mr. Olympia contest held since I invented the show in 1965 to give all the languishing former Mr. Universe winners something more to compete in each year. It is history that Arnold Schwarzenegger—who had won six consecutive Mr. Olympia titles between 1970 and 1975, then retired to devote more time to his business affairs and pursue a career as an actor—suddenly whipped himself back into contest shape and entered the contest at the last possible moment.

To the chagrin of all the other contestants and a large portion of the audience, Arnold won his seventh Mr. Olympia title, with Chris Dickerson placing second, scantily rewarded by finally avenging his '79 Olympia loss to Frank Zane, who placed third in the '80 show. Mike Mentzer slipped to fourth, and Boyer Coe fell from third in '79 to fifth at the '80 Mr. Olympia.

As this book is being written in early 1981, the smoke of controversy following the 1980 Mr. Olympia still has not cleared, despite the passage of four months. Most of the contestants feel that Arnold Schwarzenegger was allowed to clown and cavort excessively onstage, drawing attention to himself at a disproportionate rate.

No contestant, when polled, would have had Arnold placed higher than third. So if

Dickerson struts his stuff on the posing platform against the superstars of bodybuilding.

Schwarzenegger had been placed below the first-place spot he ended up taking, then Chris Dickerson probably would have been the 1980 Mr. Olympia. Indeed, many bodybuilding aficionados are now calling him the "Uncrowned Mr. Olympia."

Unfortunately, we won't be able to see if Chris Dickerson is a true Mr. Olympia until the 1982 Mr. Olympia competition, which is scheduled to be held in Birmingham, England. This is because virtually all the 1980 Mr. Olympia contestants, including Chris, were so incensed by Arnold Schwarzenegger's tactics at that show that they have organized a boycott of the 1981 Mr. Olympia show to be promoted by Arnold.

Still, Mr. Olympia or not, Chris Dickerson was the most consistent and successful bodybuilder actively competing at the time I wrote this book. So, it is fitting that he should be the subject of this chapter, since his nutritional and training philosophies are obviously among the best in the sport. Read them carefully and see how your own methods compare to his. Then make a few adjustments—based on what Chris Dickerson does in his own training and diet—and you should soon come up a winner yourself!

CHRIS DICKERSON'S NUTRITIONAL PHILOSOPHY

Chris's overall nutritional philosophy has changed drastically over the years that he has competed at a high level. "The only concession I've had to make to advancing age as a bodybuilder has been in the area of nutrition," Chris wrote in a recent issue of *Muscle & Fitness* magazine. "Everyone's metabolism begins to slow down at 30, and I just can't get ripped up anymore on the type of diet I used to follow in the late '60s and early '70s. I can't use milk products during my precontest phase anymore, and I can't eat junk foods more often than once or twice a week in the off season. I used to drink milk right up to the day of a show as late as when I won the 1974 Pro Mr. Universe title, and I could eat a little junk food

almost every day until about the age of 35, without getting more than 10–12 pounds heavier than contest condition.

"During my off season cycles nowadays, I try to follow a nutritionally well-balanced diet that includes some milk products, white meats (poultry and fish), red meats (beef and pork), eggs, whole grains, fresh fruits and vegetables, green salads, seeds and nuts, and other health-producing foods. Since cooking destroys many of the vitamins, minerals, and enzymes naturally contained in a food, I try to eat my foods either raw or as lightly cooked as possible.

"I supplement my diet with extra vitamins and minerals in a tablet or capsule form all year-round, but I use less supplements during the off-season than just before a contest. When my precontest diet becomes very tight for the last four to six weeks before peaking, I simply must use food supplements to provide those necessary nutrients that aren't contained in such a strict precontest diet. Without supplements, I could potentially develop nutritional deficiencies that would keep me from reaching my highest possible peak.

"My precontest diet starts 2–2½ months before a show. (The exact time I start dieting depends on how much extra fat I'm carrying at the time I initiate my diet.) If I'm 12 pounds over my contest weight, for example, I'll start gradually eliminating from my diet those foods (like grains, seeds, and nuts) that keep me from being able to cut up, beginning about 2½ months before the contest. If I'm only eight to ten pounds overweight, on the other hand, I can wait an extra two or three weeks before starting gradually to eliminate these types of foods from my daily diet.

"I gradually cut back on what I've been eating in the off season, over a two- to four-week period, until I get down to my strictest diet four to six weeks before competing. At its tightest, my diet consists of only broiled fish, broiled and skinless chicken breasts, salads, one piece of fruit three to five times a week (which depends on my energy levels for each workout; usually I'll

eat an apple, seeds, stem, and all), water, and black coffee. (The skin of a chicken is very high in fat and should be removed before broiling a chicken breast, which keeps the fats in the skin from sinking into the breast meat and drastically increasing its caloric content.) It's quite a struggle to stay on this type of diet, because it's so low in calories (about 1,200–1,500 per day, versus the 3,500–4,000 that I consume during the off season), but it rips me to shreds in four to five weeks.

"I used to follow a low-carbohydrate diet, which worked well enough for me to win Mr. USA, Mr. America, and two Mr. Universe titles. But since I moved back to

California in early 1979 to train for the pro shows, I've followed a low-fat diet, which is naturally low in calories, since one gram of fat yields nine calories when metabolized in your body for energy as compared to the four calories yielded by one gram of protein or carbohydrate. And since the body prefers to use carbohydrates or stored body fat for its energy needs, I feel a little more energetic in my workouts when I'm on a low-fat diet than when I was on the low-carbohydrate regimen.

"The only time I'll eat more than a single piece of fruit each day during my precontest cycle is the night before competing and the morning of a show, when I'll eat raisins and other high-calorie fruit. This fills my muscles with glycogen, making them appear larger than before I eat the carbohydrates, since each gram of carbohydrate that ends up in my muscle tissue holds four grams of water. So, if you don't overdo it, eating carbohydrates for 24 hours before competing will make your muscles look bigger, and you will also get a much better pump when you have consumed a high-carbohydrate meal or two than if you have starved yourself.

"Be careful to eat natural carbs, and *do not* pig out too much before competing, because if you overdo your sugar intake, it will fill the muscles, then your liver, and finally—if there is too much sugar in your bloodstream—it spills over into your skin, particularly around your waist. When that happens, the water that the carbs attract to your skin will make you look smooth and puffy. Therefore, try to hold your carbohydrate down to about three-quarters of a gram per pound of body weight that last 24 hours (e.g., 150 grams if you weigh 200 pounds).

"The final point in my dietary philosophy that I'd like to emphasize is that I avoid *all* sodium-containing foods for at least the last seven to ten days before competing. This means that I can't use any diet sodas or any artificial sweeteners (both of which have sodium-saccharide in them), and it even means that I must avoid celery, which has loads of sodium in it. I avoid sodium—as all other champion bodybuilders do—because one gram of sodium in my body will hold **50 grams** of water! Could you imagine what a sprinkling of sodium chloride (common table salt) on my chicken breast the night before competing would do to my hard-earned muscular definition? There wouldn't be a cut left on my whole body, even though I was virtually devoid of fat, because my skin would be bloated with water!

"Such attention to tiny details of both diet and training can make the difference between winning $25,000 for first place and $10,000 for second. So, I am *very* careful about what goes into my body for the last four to six weeks before I compete."

CHRIS DICKERSON'S PHILOSOPHY OF REST AND RECUPERATION

"Rest and recuperation are vitally important to any bodybuilder, from novice to Olympian competitor," Chris Dickerson told me recently. "Indeed, without rest—which allows for proper recuperation of the body between training sessions—your body will simply fail to respond efficiently to the training, nutrition, and mental stimuli you give it.

"I've seen young, inexperienced, overly enthusiastic bodybuilders do marathon workouts and then miss out on their sleep by running around with their friends most of the night. This combination of overly long workouts and too little sleep causes them to recuperate so little between workouts that they can actually begin to *lose* muscle instead of making gains in muscle mass. What a horrible return for all those long hours of hard training effort that they put in every day!

"It's little wonder that this type of fellow soon gives up his training completely, unless some experienced bodybuilder has noticed the kid's mistake and has convinced the unfortunate guy that doing *half* the training he has been putting in would give him *twice* the rate of muscle growth he has ever experienced. But, alas, few of these 'supertrainers' will listen even to a Mr. Universe winner like myself. My God, even a bodybuilder of my experience, and with recuperative abilities that took me more than 15 years of steady training to acquire, would overtrain in a week doing the 50-sets-per-body-part routines that some of these guys spend all day in the gym doing!

"Except for the last three to four weeks prior to a contest—when it's actually desirable to overtrain *slightly*—less training is usually better than more. Resist the desire to do those extra two or three sets of Presses Behind Neck once you have a full pump in your delts, because they will add nothing to stimulate muscle growth further, and they might be the straw that breaks your recuperation-camel's back. Train less, sleep more, and you will recuperate so fully and efficiently that your muscle growth rates will astound you. My own growth rates—even at 41—are astonishingly fast when I am careful to oversleep and undertrain.

"I've discovered that I personally need a minimum of 7½–8 hours of sleep each night if I am to recuperate fully both physically and mentally. I also have to keep my mind tranquil, even though this can be extremely difficult with the distractions that automatically come into my life before a major event like the Mr. Olympia show. You can expend tremendous amounts of mental and emotional energy when you have some heavy problem on your mind, e.g., an im-

pending divorce or a recent death in your immediate family. For full recuperation—and consequently for the fastest rate of muscle growth—you have to plug every energy leak, including mental and emotional leaks."

CHRIS DICKERSON'S PHILOSOPHY OF MENTAL APPROACH TO BODYBUILDING

"A proper mental attitude is essential, because your mind literally controls your body," Chris said. "The mental outlook of any champion bodybuilder going into a competition is consistently superpositive. Each champion has already rehearsed his victory in his mind a thousand times. He is so sure he is going to win that the actual act of winning is often somewhat of an anticlimax. It's merely a matter of playing out the scenario before an audience.

"I'm no different from any other champion in this respect. I spend hours visualizing my victories, seeing myself in vivid detail the way I expect to look onstage. And this visualization allows my subconscious mind to help me look and act like I imagine myself to be. As long as my image is totally positive, I end up being completely positive myself. And I win again and again in reality, just as I've already won again and again in my imagination."

CHRIS DICKERSON'S TRAINING PHILOSOPHY

"In championship bodybuilding today it is impossible to train with any principles that aren't included in the Weider System," Chris Dickerson complimentarily wrote in an article for *Muscle & Fitness* at the end of his supersuccessful 1980 competitive season. "In all my workouts, I follow the Weider System.

"Like almost every champion bodybuilder, I cycle my training over the course of a year. My goals in the off season are, first, to improve my weak areas so they compare more favorably with the rest of my body and, second, to continue adding muscle mass over my entire physique. In my precontest cycles I strive to achieve maximum definition and to refine my body even more than I had for my latest previous competition. Every show I try to get better and better, and if I didn't consistently improve, I don't think I'd stay in the sport.

"In general terms, my off season training philosophy calls for a total of eight to fifteen sets per body part (sometimes slightly more on a lagging muscle group). I train six days a week on a split routine, doing each body part two or three times per week, except my abdominals, for which I do four or five total sets each day as a warmup for the major part of my workout.

"My reps are generally in the range of six to ten in the off season, and the weights are as heavy as I can handle on the final one or two sets of each exercise. I always do two or three progressively heavier sets to warm up my muscles for each exercise before using my heavy workout poundages, a practice I have scrupulously adhered to since I started to go back to training after my disastrous pectoral injury.

"I always use strict form on all sets, both in the off season and before a competition—even when I'm using my heaviest weights—except for a cheating rep or two at the end

of a set, just to push my muscles past their normal point of muscular failure. When you go two or three reps (*never more!*) past failure, you can stimulate your working muscle(s) 20–30 percent harder than if you terminated the set at the point of normal failure.

"The secret to cheating correctly is to cheat to make the rep *more difficult* to complete, not *easier* to finish. Instead of just swinging up all the reps of a set of Barbell Curls—getting little, if any, growth stimulus from the cheating set—you could stimulate your muscles very hard by doing a set of Barbell Curls until you finally fail to get the last rep past the halfway point. Already, this set has been *more difficult* to do than the type of swinging Curls just described, but you can cheat to make the set even more difficult by swinging the

barbell *just enough* to get it barely past the sticking point, then curling it up on your own the rest of the way. Finally, lower it slowly in a negative-style rep, resisting the downward movement of the bar as hard as you can.

"Before a contest, I'll begin six to eight weeks early to increase gradually the total number of sets I do to 18–25 per muscle group, and I favor doing as many isolation movements as possible. So, while I will still do a Seated Press Behind Neck and/or Seated Dumbbell Press in my precontest shoulder workout, I'll do almost entirely Dumbbell and Cable Laterals for the rest of my shoulder training, leaving out the Upright Rows and Machine Presses I usually do in the off season for deltoid thickness.

"Since my deltoids are already quite thick-looking from the high volume of

Overhead Presses that I do during my off season cycle, I do only one or two Overhead Pressing movements in my precontest deltoid workout, just to maintain the mass. And I do all the variations of Dumbbell and Cable Laterals—to the front, to the sides, bent-over, etc.—to shape the deltoid masses, giving them the coconut-shaped roundness, and to carve all the little cat-clawed striations within each of the three distinctly separated delt heads.

"I also train much faster prior to a contest (20–30 seconds of rest between sets, versus 45–60 seconds in the off season). As a result of this training speed, my muscles harden up, because I'm then using the Weider Quality Training Principle.

"'As a natural consequence of the greatly increased workout volume and pace—and due to generally low energy levels resulting from my low-calorie precontest diet—my exercise poundages must be reduced to the point where I'm using only 50–60 percent as much weight before a show as I'd used when I could eat as many calories per day as I wanted to for training energy and was able to rest twice as long between sets. But while the training poundages I use in every exercise are lighter in an absolute sense than they were in the off season, they are in actuality *relatively* just as heavy as they were in the off season, if not heavier. Believe me, the lighter weights actually *feel* heavier to me when I'm cooking through a workout and dieting on only 1,200 calories per day!

"I caution novice bodybuilders to remember that my methods are appropriate only for high-level competitive bodybuilders. You'll have to pay your dues with less severe workouts for several years before embarking on one of my routines. The biggest mistake that younger, inexperienced bodybuilders make is that they overtrain. Don't make this mistake, because it will only slow your progress."

To be absolutely certain that you have a complete picture of Chris Dickerson's training philosophy, here is a typical back routine that he uses prior to a contest. (Note: he does no trapezius or lower back training, because those areas were overdevel-

oped during a time when he specialized in Olympic-style weight lifting, and they maintain their size and shape merely from the shoulder, lat, and leg work Chris does.)

1. Chins (to the front of his neck): 4–5 x 10–15 (with extra weight strapped to his waist for the final two or three sets)
2. Dumbbell Bent Rows: 4–6 x 8–10
3. Pulldowns Behind Neck: 4 x 8–10
4. One-Arm Pulley Rows: 4 x 8–10
5. Seated Pulley Rows: 4 x 8–10

As Chris notes, "I work hardest on the Dumbbell Bent Rows, because I consider that to be one of the best—if not *the* best—lat exercises. I also put a lot of energy into the Seated Pulley Rows, because they are the last exercise in my routine, and I want to be sure to exhaust thoroughly my lats by the time I finish my back workout."

CHRIS DICKERSON'S SUMMARY OF HIS SUCCESS FORMULA

In concluding why he has been successful and other bodybuilders—including many with better natural potential to succeed in the sport—have failed, Chris Dickerson said, "If you're lucky enough to have good heredity and you are persistent enough to stick with hard and consistent training for a long period of time, my four bodybuilding philosophy factors—nutrition, recuperation, mental approach, and training—will help you become a champion yourself one day.

"Success won't come to you overnight, because, as they say, 'Rome wasn't built in a day.' Neither was I, since I've trained steadily and consistently hard since 1962, except for that year and a half off with my injury. In that time, approximately 17 years as I write this, *I have not missed a single workout* that I had planned to take, except when I was either too ill to train or too badly injured to work out efficiently. And in those 17 years of workouts, I've had both good and bad training sessions, but I always—even on the bad days—gave the exercises 100 percent of what I had to give them. And those are probably the main reasons why I am where I am today—I've paid my dues for 17 years, and I've always given every workout 100 percent effort."

Right on, Chris! You're a true champion, both as a bodybuilder and as a gentleman. I'm proud to have had a positive effect on your progress and your ultimate success in bodybuilding!

OUR FINAL SET TOGETHER

Sadly, we have come to the final set of our long workout together in this book. I have given you as much knowledge as you will ever need to succeed in competitive bodybuilding—or just to look trim and muscular, if that is your goal—and I am now throwing the bodybuilding ball to you. As I said at the beginning of this book, the beauty of bodybuilding is that you succeed spectacularly or fail miserably totally on your own merits.

Through strong self-discipline and consistently hard training you **can** develop an outstanding physique. You are the only one who can make decisions on how to train and eat, but you are ultimately the product solely of your own endeavors. **You will literally create yourself!**

I have now given you all the help I can through this book, and I will continue to give you the latest training, dietary, psychological, and other scientific training advances in my articles—as well as those of my staff of writers—in each monthly issue of *Muscle & Fitness* magazine. And you can always feel free to write to me and tell me about your progress.

If you have made particularly phenomenal progress using the instructions, nutrition information, exercises, and training routines of this book, send me before and after photos of yourself in a swimsuit, plus details of how much bodybuilding has affected and changed your life. If your story and pictures are outstanding and interesting enough, I'll publish them in *Muscle & Fitness!*

So, we have done the last rep of our final set together as training partners. It's time for you to go out on your own and succeed or fail on your own merits. I'm sure you **will** succeed, however, so give everything in your life and your workouts 100 percent effort. Go for it, and go for it hard!

Gary Leonard—1980 Mr. America.

Glossary

BAR—The steel shaft forming the handle of a barbell or dumbbell. Barbell bars vary in length from four to seven feet. The weight of this bar must be taken into consideration when adding plates to form a required exercise poundage.

BARBELL—Consisting of a bar, sleeve, collars, and plates, this is the basic piece of equipment for weight training. Barbells can be either adjustable (allowing the weights to be changed) or fixed (with the plates welded or otherwise fastened permanently into position).

BODYBUILDING—A type of weight training in which the primary objective is to change the form or appearance of one's body. Often bodybuilding can be a competitive sport for both women and men.

COLLAR—The cylindrical metal fastener that holds barbell or dumbbell plates into position on the bar. There are inside collars and outside collars, both of which are held in position on the bar by a set screw or special clamp.

DUMBBELL—This is merely a short-handled barbell that is intended primarily for use in one hand. The bar of most dumbbells is 12–14 inches long. A dumbbell has all the other characteristics of a barbell.

EXERCISE—Each individual movement done in a weight training program (e.g., a Bench Press or a Squat). This is also sometimes called a *movement*.

INTENSITY—The amount of actual work done by a muscle or muscles during an exercise or entire workout. Intensity is normally increased either by adding weight to the bar or machine being used or by increasing the number of repetitions done for an exercise.

OLYMPIC LIFTING—The main international form of weight lifting, in which the Snatch and Clean and Jerk are contested to see which athlete can lift the most combined weight in the two exercises.

PLATES—The flat cast-iron or vinyl-covered concrete discs that are fitted on the ends of a barbell or dumbbell bar to make up the training poundage for a particular exercise.

POWER LIFTING—A form of competitive weight lifting in which the Squat, Bench Press, and Deadlift are performed to see which athlete can lift the most combined weight in the three exercises.

REPETITION—Each individual complete cycle of an exercise (e.g., the full bending and straightening of the arms in a Bench Press). This term is often abbreviated to *rep*. Normally several repetitions (usually six to twelve) are done of each exercise in a training program.

ROUTINE—The complete program of exercises done on an individual training day. This is also called a *program* or a *schedule*.

SET—A distinct grouping of repetitions in a particular exercise (usually six to twelve), after which a trainee takes a rest interval of 30–90 seconds, followed by additional sets of the same movement.

SLEEVE—The hollow metal tube fitted over the bar of an adjustable barbell or dumbbell. This sleeve helps the bar rotate more easily in the hands during an exercise. To aid a trainee in gripping the bar when his hands are sweaty, this sleeve is

usually scored with shallow crosshatched grooves called *knurlings*.

WEIGHT LIFTING—A form of weight training in which athletes compete in weight classes to see who can lift the most combined weight in either the two Olympic lifts (Snatch and Clean and Jerk) or the three powerlifts (Squat, Bench Press, and Deadlift). The weight classes now used in international competition are 52 kg. (114½ lbs.), 56 kg. (123½ lbs.), 60 kg. (132¼ lbs.), 67½ kg. (148¾ lbs.), 75 kg. (165¼ lbs.), 82½ kg. (181¾ lbs.), 90 kg. (198¼ lbs.), 100 kg. (220½ lbs.), 110 kg. (242½ lbs.), and unlimited (over 110 kg.).

WEIGHT TRAINING—A form of physical exercise using weight resistance provided by barbells, dumbbells, or exercise machines. Weight training can be pursued toward numerous goals—bodybuilding, improving sports performance, increasing strength, competing as a weight lifter, gaining weight, losing weight, rehabilitating an injury, increasing aerobic conditioning, improving health, providing a greater sense of personal well-being, etc.

WORKOUT—The program or routine of exercises done to its completion on each training day. This is also called a *training session*.

Annotated Bibliography

BODYBUILDING BOOKS

1. Bass, Clarence. *Ripped*. Albuquerque, NM: Ripped Enterprises, 1980.

COMMENT: This is a uniquely personal account of how 42-year-old Clarence Bass, a busy and successful attorney with a wife and son, found the time and motivation to develop a unique system of training and dieting that reduced his body fat level to an unprecedented 2.3 percent of his total body weight. And with his approach to training and dieting to get ripped, Clarence has won his weight class at both the Past-40 Mr. USA and Past-40 Mr. America competitions, plus the Most Muscular Man trophy at the Past-40 Mr. USA show and numerous Best Abdominals and Best Legs subdivision trophies in national competition.

While his training methods are an adaptation of what Mike Mentzer and others have been using—and are thus of only moderate interest to any aspiring muscle builder reading *Ripped*—Clarence Bass has developed a unique, controversial, and highly effective nutritional philosophy that has helped him reach his 2.3 percent body fat level not once but several times. His discussion of how, what, and why he eats meal-by-meal is supremely interesting and entertaining to read, and any bodybuilder who is serious about competing would be a fool not to buy *Ripped* for his reference library. As Boyer Coe said after reading *Ripped*, "It's a great bodybuilding book. Everyone should have one." Mike Mentzer echoed Coe's recommendation, saying, "I enjoyed reading *Ripped*

and profited from the book." And finally, Andreas Cahling enthusiastically endorsed *Ripped*: "An outstanding account of a journey through the confusing terrain of bodybuilding. The book gave me plenty of ideas to try in my own dietary and training philosophies, and it would be a great educational tool for any bodybuilder." *Ripped* is available only by mail order from Ripped Enterprises, 305 Sandia Savings Building, 400 Gold St. S.W., Albuquerque, NM 87102. The cost of a copy of *Ripped* is $9.95 (plus 10 percent extra for fourth-class postage, and 20 percent extra if you would like the book mailed to you via first-class mail). Foreign orders (except Canada) should include an additional 30 percent for postage and handling, and all foreign orders must be remitted in U.S. currency or its equivalent. New Mexico residents must add four percent sales tax.

2. Coe, Boyer, and Summer, Bob. *Getting Strong, Looking Strong*. New York: Atheneum, 1979.

COMMENT: Boyer Coe is one of the most enduring and successful bodybuilders of all time. He has competed several times per year since 1964, winning the Mr. USA, Mr. America, Mr. Universe (four times), Mr. World (five times) titles, and the Professional World Cup Championships in early 1981, his seventeenth year of competition. Working with Bob Summer, a noted bodybuilding journalist, Boyer has produced a book that is exceptionally easy to understand, outlining his methods for training from the first workout a young bodybuilder takes up to the Mr. Olympia level, a contest in which Boyer has twice placed third and will no doubt one day win, due to his tenacity in the gym and the dramatic year-to-year progress he makes in improving his physique.

Unfortunately, this excellent bodybuilding manual received poor distribution around America and is only available in a handful of bookstores. I recommend this book highly, so if you can't lcoate one in a bookstore, send Boyer Coe a money order of $13 (which includes postage and handling charges), and he will send you this profusely illustrated 145-page hardcover book within 24 hours of receiving your order. Send your order for *Getting Strong, Looking Strong* directly to Boyer Coe at P.O. Box 5877, Huntington Beach, CA 92646.

3. Coe, Boyer, and Morey, Dr. Stan. *Optimal Nutrition.* Huntington Beach, CA: Boyer Coe Enterprises, 1979.
COMMENT: Usually I approach self-published books like this with a high degree of suspicion, just waiting to pounce on the glaring faults that most self-published books contain in their slavish effort to please the publisher/subject's vanity and ego. But after reading only a few pages of Coe's and Morey's short book (it's less than 100 pages in length, but what a wealth of information it contains!), I was hooked on reading the incredible collection of facts and theories—heretofore either unpublished or unavailable to the bodybuilding community—that *Optimal Nutrition* contained. Stan Morey is a former bodybuilding champion who has earned two doctorates, one in biochemistry (the study of nutrition) and one as an M.D. He has shunned developing a medical practice and instead runs a gym and health food store in Tampa, Florida, from where he advises scores of champion bodybuilders—as well as hundreds of fast-rising future stars—on their nutrition and medical problems.

So, essentially, no pair of writers in the sport can equal the combined knowledge of Coe and Morey, and *Optimal Nutrition* completely proves this. The book covers such topics as quality of protein, vitamins, and enzymes for optimal digestion, how to buy supplements wisely and economically, essential macrominerals, a total cycled nutritional plan for competitive bodybuilders (the exact one Boyer uses to get himself into such hard and massive condition) and numerous other topics vital to the success of any bodybuilder who hasn't been able to reach top condition for a show. And each concept in the book is explained in normal bodybuilding language, which is then backed up by a clearly written scientific explanation of how and why each nutrient works in the human body. Again, this valuable addition to all bodybuilders' libraries is unavailable in bookstores. You can order it directly from Boyer Coe for $13 (which includes postage and handling) at P.O. Box 5877, Huntington Beach, CA 92646.

4. Columbu, Franco, and Fels, George. *Coming On Strong.* Chicago: Contemporary Books, Inc., 1978.
COMMENT: This profusely illustrated book is Franco Columbu's autobiography, which traces his life from a poor shepherd boy on the island of Sardinia to his Mr. Olympia victory in 1976 and to the fame and wealth he has achieved as a bodybuilder, author, and Doctor of Chiropractic. I found this book so extremely interesting that I stayed awake half the night to finish it. Franco's superb success story and his inside look at high-level competitive bodybuilding often led me to think for 10–15 minutes about something he had said, which I take as a sign of profundity in any book. I'm sure that you'll be inspired when you read this book. The soft-cover book sells for $5.95 in most book stores.

5. Columbu, Franco, and Fels, George. *Winning Bodybuilding.* Chicago: Contemporary Books, Inc., 1977.
COMMENT: This informative manual on basic and advanced bodybuilding techniques was the first book of its kind written by an established bodybuilding superstar and published by a national company. And once it was released, *Winning Bodybuilding* sold so well (it's the bestselling bodybuilding book of all time) that it unleashed a flood of similar books. Profusely illustrated with photos by master bodybuilding photographers like Art Zeller and Jimmy Caruso, *Winning Bodybuilding* is a clearly written and easily understandable book telling readers how to progress from total novice in bodybuilding to the quality of physique that can win bodybuilding competitions. I recommend this book highly. The soft-cover edition of *Winning Bodybuilding* is available at most book stores for $4.95.

6. Gaines, Charles, and Butler, George. *Pumping Iron.* New York: Simon and Schuster, 1974.
COMMENT: *Pumping Iron* has become a classic book of photos and essays on bodybuilding, popular not only within our sport but with the general public as well. The book was incredibly successful, selling more than 200,000 copies by the end of 1980. The book also inspired a reasonably successful film of the same title.

Pumping Iron is still available at many bookstores, in a large-format softcover edition costing less than $10.

7. Kennedy, Robert. *Natural Body Building for Everyone.* New York: Sterling Publishing Co., Inc., 1980.
COMMENT: Robert Kennedy has been writing articles for virtually every bodybuilding magazine in the world for nearly 20 years, and he publishes his own bodybuilding magazine, *Muscle Mag International,* in Canada. In this book, Bob distills all the voluminous knowledge he has gained over more than 20

years in the sport into an eminently authoritative and easily readable 190-page book, selling for $5.95 in bookstores across America.

8. Lurie, Dan, and Lima, John J. *Dan Lurie's "Instant Action" Body-Building System.* New York: Arco Publishing, Inc., 1980.

COMMENT: Since this book was written by two former business associates of mine, I would prefer not to give it a comparative rating. Suffice it to say that this 110-page book sells for $4.95 in major bookstores across America. It is a large-format softcover book organized as one-page "lessons," much like the old bodybuilding courses that Charles Atlas and George Jowett sold through the mails 30–50 years ago.

9. Mentzer, Mike, and Friedberg, Ardy. *The Mentzer Method to Fitness.* New York: William Morrow and Company, Inc., 1980.

COMMENT: Mike Mentzer, the sport's true intellectual, is one of the greatest bodybuilders of all time. He has won Mr. America, Mr. North America, Mr. Universe, and several professional bodybuilding titles. And the articles he writes each month for *Muscle & Fitness* magazine draw more mail than do all the rest of the articles combined that are published in each issue.

If you ignore the cute cover—no doubt intended by the book's publishers to appeal to the average man or woman who lifts weights recreationally—and get into the meat of the book, you will be entranced by the valuable bodybuilding knowledge that Mike has revealed in this 190-page, softcover book, selling nationwide for $6.95.

10. Murray, Jim. *Inside Bodybuilding.* Chicago: Contemporary Books, Inc., 1978.

COMMENT: Jim Murray, a former editor of *Strength & Health* magazine, presents an authoritative and progressive body of information on how to go from beginning bodybuilder to having a championship physique. The first five chapters lead a young bodybuilder through these stages, using clear photos and descriptions of numerous bodybuilding exercises. The book also explains basic training techniques and presents a number of progressively more intense training routines.

The strongest feature of *Inside Bodybuilding*, however, is a chapter included to illustrate how a champion bodybuilder—in this case, the magnificent Boyer Coe—trains and diets for bodybuilding competition. This book is excellent, particularly for beginning and intermediate bodybuilders. It is available in a large-format, softcover edition, and costs $4.95 in bookstores across America.

11. Pearl, Bill. *Keys to the Inner Universe.* Pasadena, CA: Physical Fitness Architects, 1979.

COMMENT: This fabulous and superbly authoritative book is so complete that it is as thick as the Los Angeles telephone directory. In nearly 650 pages, Bill Pearl presents the accumulated knowledge he gained from more than 30 years of experience as a high-level competitor (Bill has won the Mr. America, Mr. USA, and Mr. Universe titles, the Universe four times) and a gym owner who has personally written training programs for more than 100,000 students. This encyclopedia of bodybuilding includes a biography of Bill Pearl, hundreds of training tips, and the most complete listing of exercises ever assembled. Each movement is illustrated with exceptionally clear drawings, its performance is explained in great detail, and its level of difficulty is rated. For the shoulders alone, Bill has included more than 110 different exercises. Indeed, at least 100 exercises are included for virtually every muscle group in your body. And finally, *Keys to the Inner Universe* is illustrated with scores of photographs tracing Bill Pearl's magnificent 20-year competitive career. Several of the photos are in color, and many of the black-and-white pictures have never been published before.

Bill Pearl's *Keys to the Inner Universe* receives my highest recommendation, and I suggest that every serious bodybuilder buy the book and refer to it often. *Keys to the Inner Universe* is available only by mail order from Physical Fitness Architects, P.O. Box 4625, Pasadena, CA 91106. It is available in a softcover edition for $32.95 and in a beautifully bound collector's edition for $52.95 (add 10 percent for postage on each book ordered).

12. Schwarzenegger, Arnold, and Hall, Douglas Kent. *Arnold: The Education of a Bodybuilder.* New York: Simon and Schuster, 1977.

COMMENT: Most bodybuilding aficionados—and even virtually every competing bodybuilder with whom I've talked—agree that Arnold Schwarzenegger is the greatest bodybuilder of all time. Certainly, no one has even remotely approached his competitive record, which boasts 14 world championships, including seven Mr. Olympia titles.

Arnold's book is really two volumes in one. The first half consists of a riveting autobiography of how Arnold discovered bodybuilding and became the sport's superstar; the second half of Arnold's book consists of six chapters detailing Schwarzenegger's training philosophies for all bodybuilders, from rank beginner to Mr. Olympia.

In addition to an exciting and informative text, *Arnold: The Education of a Bodybuilder* is crammed with well over 100 brilliant photographs, from John Balik's sparkling cover photo to black-and-white masterpieces by Jimmy Caruso, Albert Busek, George

Butler, and numerous other accomplished bodybuilding photographers.

Overall, *Arnold: The Education of a Bodybuilder* is one of the best bodybuilding books currently on the market. It is available in nearly all bookstores for $9.95 in a hardback edition and $5.95 for the softcover version.

13. Snyder, George, and Wayne, Rick. *3 More Reps* (Book 1 and Book 2). Warrington, PA: Olympus Health and Recreation, Inc., 1979.

COMMENT: George Snyder has been a tremendous asset to the sport of bodybuilding as a gym owner, as a promoter of the highest-quality professional competitions, and as the co-author and publisher of these two fine volumes of inside information about the training and nutritional philosophies of most of the sport's superstars. Rick Wayne—who did most of the actual writing from tape recordings of training seminars held at George Snyder's Olympus Gym–Spa in Warrington—is a former editor-in-chief of my magazine, *Muscle & Fitness,* and one of the most prolific and popular writers the sport has ever had. He has found time between training to win a host of international titles, including the IFBB Mr. World competition, and to write well over 1,000 published articles and three books on bodybuilding.

Book 1 of *3 More Reps* includes detailed chapters describing the training secrets and dietary techniques of six of the sport's all-time greats—Arnold Schwarzenegger, Franco Columbu, Frank Zane, Robby Robinson, Mike Mentzer, and Ed Corney. Book 2 treats nine more superstar bodybuilders—Kal Szkalak, Boyer Coe, Rick Wayne, Ken Waller, Dave Draper, Danny Padilla, Leroy Colbert, Mike Katz, and Bill Grant.

Both books are profusely illustrated and can be purchased only via mail order for $14.95 in a softcover edition and $19.95 in the hardcover version (add 75¢ for each book to cover postage and handling. Send your order to Olympus Gym–Spa, Route 611, Warrington, PA 18976.

14. Weider, Joe. *The IFBB Album of Bodybuilding All-Stars.* New York: Hawthorne Books, Inc., 1979.

COMMENT: I wrote this book and chose the best photographs from more than 100,000 in our magazine's photo files to honor the greatest athletes our sport has produced, beginning with Eugen Sandow, who toured America with Flo Ziegfeld and caused such a sensation that he singlehandedly started the American bodybuilding movement. For Sandow and nearly 30 other champions, I have written a short profile of the man and included several of his best photos (there are also 14 sparkling color plates included in the book). Some of the champions I have honored are John C. Grimek, Steve Reeves, Bill Pearl, Larry Scott, Sergio Oliva, Arnold Schwarzenegger, Lou Ferrigno, Frank Zane, Franco Columbu, Boyer

Coe, and Mike Mentzer (who also wrote the foreword to the book). This is a beautifully designed, large-format, hardcover book that would look good on anyone's coffee table or would read well in any library. This book is available for $19.95 in most bookstores across the country.

15. Zane, Frank and Christine. *The Zane Way to a Beautiful Body.* New York: Simon and Schuster, 1979.

COMMENT: While Frank Zane and his wife Christine wrote this book primarily to appeal to average out-of-shape persons, Frank did include an extensive section toward the end of the book detailing his exact training programs and his workout and dietary philosophies. Also included is a discussion of the mental techniques he is so famous for using to peak out perfectly enough to have won three consecutive Mr. Olympia titles. Overall, *The Zane Way to a Beautiful Body* is an excellent reference work for bodybuilders at all levels of experience. A profusely illustrated, 250-page hardbound book, *The Zane Way* is available in most bookstores for $12.95.

ANATOMY

1. Gray, Henry. *Anatomy, Descriptive and Surgical.* London: Crown Publishers, 1968.

COMMENT: This is the classic anatomy book, which is used in medical schools throughout the nation and world.

BODYBUILDING DRUGS

1. Coe, Boyer, and Morey, Dr. Stan. *Steroids.* Huntington Beach, CA: Boyer Coe Enterprises, 1979.

COMMENT: Boyer Coe and Dr. Stan Morey also teamed up for this shorter (75-page) book about the dangers, the safe use of, and the effects of steroids and other bodybuilding drugs on the human body. This is a very honest treatment of a most controversial topic. The information is presented in clear layman's language but is still backed up by references to numerous published scientific studies on the use of steroids, HCG, testosterone preparations, and other drugs commonly used by today's champion (and even novice) bodybuilders. Like the other two Coe books discussed previously, *Steroids* can be purchased by mail order directly from Boyer Coe at P.O. Box 5877, Huntington Beach, CA 92646. The price of this book is $13 (postpaid).

2. Wright, James E., Ph.D. *Anabolic Steroids and Sports.* Nantick, MA: Sports Science Consultants, 1978.

COMMENT: This book is very relevant to bodybuilding. Reading it originally prompted me to retain Dr. Wright as a research consultant for the Weider Research Clinic and as a much-respected and widely read author of articles for *Muscle & Fitness* each month. This book is typical of Dr. Wright's reliance on scientific studies dealing with anabolic drugs, pure androgenics, and other such muscle-building drugs. It is a totally objective treatment of the benefits and dangers of anabolic steroid use, which should be on any bodybuilder's library shelf. It can be ordered by sending a check for $10.95 (which includes postage and handling) to Sports Science Consultants, P.O. Box 633, Nantick, MA 01760.

FLEXIBILITY

1. Anderson, Bob. *Stretching.* Fullerton, CA: Anderson, 1975.
COMMENT: This is a quite complete and informative book, which includes scores of stretching movements, along with drawings on how to do each one and what areas each stretch works. Regular stretching workouts promote muscle flexibility, which dramatically reduces the chances of incurring a training injury and losing your workout momentum while laying off training for two to four weeks until the injury heals. I suggest you invest in this book and use the exercises in it on a regular basis to avoid crippling muscle and joint injuries.

GENERAL WEIGHT TRAINING

1. Carnes, Ralph and Valerie. *Playboy's Book of Fitness for Men.* Chicago: The Playboy Press, 1980.
COMMENT: For general fitness training—which includes calisthenics, stretching, and aerobic training, along with bodybuilding workouts—this book is quite good. But it gives little valuable advice for competitive or precompetitive bodybuilders. You will, however, find several almost comical errors in spelling the names of body builders like Zabo Koszewski. Also included are several misconceptions about exercise physiology and commonly used weight training techniques, as well as some erroneous exercise descriptions that are passed off as fact. Still, the softcover, 232-page book is a good value at $7.95, particularly if you read other weight-training books along with it.

2. Dobbins, Bill, and Sprague, Ken. *The Gold's Gym Weight Training Book.* Los Angeles: J. P. Tarcher, Inc., 1977.
COMMENT: Gold's Gym is the most famous place where Olympian bodybuilders work out; this book has little to do with competitive bodybuilding, despite the title. As a manual of weight training for the average person, however, it is excellent.

3. Murray, Jim. *Contemporary Weight Training.* Chicago: Contemporary Books, Inc., 1978.
COMMENT: Jim Murray—who wrote *Inside Bodybuilding,* which I reviewed earlier in this bibliography—has aimed this short book (90 pages, including an index) primarily at young teenagers, who are just beginning to train with weights. As such, *Contemporary Weight Training* serves its purpose quite well, but this book would be of little value to any bodybuilder with more than six to eight months of training under his belt. This is a softcover book, costing $4.95 and available in most major bookstores.

4. Ravelle, Lou. *Bodybuilding for Everyone.* New York: Pocket Books, 1977.
COMMENT: As with the previous two books in this bibliography, *Bodybuilding for Everyone*—despite its title—is a book dealing with weight training in general. Actually, the approach this book takes is rather dated, but since it is a pocketbook-type paperback priced at less than $2, you might want to invest in one nonetheless.

5. Reynolds, Bill. *Complete Weight Training Book.* Mountain View, CA: Anderson-World, Inc., 1976.
COMMENT: Now in its ninth printing, this $4.95 softcover bestseller was written by the present editor-in-chief of my *Muscle & Fitness* magazine. With 75 different routines and 200 photos included, this book can't be topped for men and women interested in using weight training to achieve any imaginable goal, including preparing for bodybuilding competition. The *Complete Weight Training Book* receives my highest recommendation as a book on general weight training and bodybuilding.

6. Sing, Vanessa. *Lift for Life!* New York: Bolder Books, 1977.
COMMENT: It's unfortunate that this well-written and informative book hasn't received wider distribution, because it is an excellent weight-training manual for anyone interested in shaping up, losing weight, or improving sports performance. A 150-page softcover book, *Lift For Life!* sells for $5.95 and is well worth the price.

INJURY TREATMENT AND REHABILITATION

1. Mirkin, Gabe, and Hoffman, Marshal. *Sports Medicine Book.* Boston: Little, Brown & Co., 1978.
COMMENT: This large-format, softcover book will tell you virtually everything any bodybuilder would ever need to know about why injuries occur, how to prevent them, and how to help them heal more completely and quickly.

KINESIOLOGY

1. Wells, Katharine E., and Luttgens, Kathryn. *Kinesiology: Scientific Basis of Human Motion.* Philadelphia: W. B. Saunders Co., 1976.
COMMENT: This has long been the standard reference work on the complicated subject of which muscles are activated when any particular movement is made by the body.

NUTRITION

1. Neve, Vickie. *Pat Neve's Bodybuilding Diet Book.* Phoenix, AZ: Phoenix Books, 1980.
COMMENT: This is an interesting and valuable book that traces Pat Neve's bodybuilding career (he has won Mr. USA, two Mr. America class victories, and several world records in powerlifting). The book contains scores of recipes for bodybuilders, as well as Neve's exact precontest diet day-by-day and food-by-food. Not widely distributed, the book can be ordered by sending $6.95 to Phoenix Books, 6505 N. 43rd Pl., Paradise Valley, AZ 85253.

2. *Nutrition Almanac.* New York: McGraw-Hill Book Co., 1973.
COMMENT: As mentioned in the text of this book, the *Nutrition Almanac* is virtually indispensable to any serious bodybuilder, particularly because of its large number of very complete tables of nutritional values for various foods.

PHYSIOLOGY

1. Astrand, Per-Olof, and Rohdahl, Kaare. *Text Book of Work Physiology.* New York: McGraw-Hill Book Co., 1977.
COMMENT: This is the standard text for most university exercise physiology classes. It is extremely detailed and informative but can still be fairly easily read by any bodybuilder, even one without much of a scientific background.

FOREIGN LANGUAGE BODYBUILDING BOOKS

1. Szekely, Dr. Laszlo. *Culturism.* Romania: Editura Sport-Turism, 1977.
COMMENT: Dr. Szekely is the leader of Romania's bodybuilding movement, and his book is excellent *if* you can read Romanian.

2. Wilkosz, Jusup. *Was Wurde bloss die Emma dazu sagen?* Stuttgart: Ha We-Verlag, 1980.
COMMENT: Well illustrated, this is Jusup's German-language diary of how he won his 1980 Mr. Universe title. I recommend it to anyone who can read German.

MAGAZINES

I can say without prejudice—even though I publish it—that *Muscle & Fitness* is absolutely the best bodybuilding magazine ever published, and each issue becomes better than the last one. It is 200 pages long, double the size of its nearest competitor, and most of the pages are now printed in full color. Bill Reynolds, editor-in-chief, is the best in the business at his job, which demands that he be a jack-of-all-trades: an editor, an excellent photographer (both posed pics and contest photos), a public relations

man, and one of the best writers in the game. He has written or ghost-written eight books that have been published to date, and he is even a Ph.D. candidate in physical education at the University of California at Berkeley.

Our editorial staff is headed by Managing Editor Dave Prokop. Dave worked for eight years at *Runner's World* magazine and is a national record holder in the 50-mile run on a track.

In addition to having great writers and editors in the sport, *Muscle & Fitness* offers the best possible photography and art work. Bob Gardner, one of America's most highly acclaimed studio photographers, shoots most of the magazine's covers and color studio photos. The photographic efforts don't stop with posed studio photos, however. Exercise photos are taken of the stars of the sport actually working out in the gyms. In addition, *Muscle & Fitness* covers all the major contests photographically, as well as editorially.

Muscle & Fitness is a first-class operation from start to finish, which is why virtually all the superstars of the sport—Schwarzenegger, Ferrigno, Columbu, Zane, the Mentzer brothers, Cahling, Dickerson, Callender, Viator, et al—are closely associated with the magazine and appear exclusively in *Muscle & Fitness*. Circulation has quadrupled in the past three years, from about 95,000 copies sold per issue in 1978 to slightly more than 400,000 sold each issue as of early 1981.

Muscle & Fitness is also published in German, French, Flemish, Italian, Japanese, Swedish, Spanish, Tagalog, and numerous other languages. It has been selected every year since 1947 to be the official journal of the IFBB, which has 117 nations affiliated with it. The IFBB distributes copies of *Muscle & Fitness* to the national federations' officials, as well as to the members of the International Olympic Committee and to heads of national athletic federations for almost every sport in every nation imaginable.

Muscle & Fitness is published monthly and is available on all large and most smaller newsstands for $3 per issue. Or you can save $8 over the newsstand price for 12 issues by subscribing for a year to *Muscle & Fitness* for $28. Subscribers almost invariably receive their latest copy of the magazine at least a week before it appears on local newsstands. To order a year's subscription, send a check for $28 along with your clearly printed name and address to Joe Weider, 21100 Erwin St., Woodland Hills, CA 91367. You should have your first issue within three or four weeks, but please allow six weeks.

In all fairness, there are numerous other bodybuilding magazines clogging the newsstands, some of them fairly good and others so badly produced and so lacking in useful information that Ricky Wayne has dubbed them "muscle rags." You can look for these magazines on the newsstands or write for subscription rates (which seem to change with the direction the wind is blowing) to the addresses listed below for each magazine in the following alphabetical list.

1. *American Athlete* (a monthly newsletter that is notable for its honest and unbiased reporting of contests and issues in the sport); published and edited by Ron Griffen. Address: P.O. Box 3567, Washington, DC 20007.

2. *Bodybuilder* (a bimonthly magazine of fairly low quality that debuted in mid-1979; it has a double-page color centerfold in each issue but appears to struggle for good articles, especially outside of northern California, where their biggest contributor, Allan Bolte, lives); edited by Alan Paul. Address: Charlton Publications, Charlton Building, Derby, CT 06418.

3. *Bodypower* (a magazine that debuted in early 1981 and is issued bimonthly; covers bodybuilding, powerlifting, and weight training for athletes); edited by Bill Kumagai. Address: Family Publications, P.O. Box 1084, Reseda, CA 91335.

4. *Iron Man* (one of the oldest and most highly respected magazines dealing with bodybuilding, weight lifting, and powerlifting; *Iron Man* is issued bimonthly but with no color pictures inside the mag; has coverage of all major competitions and personality profiles of the top American and international bodybuilders, as well as training and nutrition articles); published and edited by Peary Rader. Address: Box 10, Alliance, NE 69301.

5. *Muscle Digest* (a 100-page—10–12 pages of editorial color—bimonthly magazine that has demonstrated erratic quality over the past two or three years, since its publisher has had five or six different editors during that time; runs the same type of information as *Iron Man* magazine); edited by John Meade. Address: 10317 E. Whittier Blvd., Whittier, CA 90606.

6. *Muscle Mag International* (a bimonthly, Canadian-published magazine that has always been of excellent quality, though financial problems caused by a long Canadian postal strike in late 1977 and early 1978 reduced the magazine temporarily from 110 pages, 16 in color, to 64 pages, 8 in color; but recent issues are almost back up to the size and quality of the magazine before the postal strike; barring another strike, this is always an interesting publication, heavy on profiles of big-time bodybuilders and exercise technique articles; the *Muscle Mag International Annual* comes out each spring, with the 1980–81 issue being 240

pages in length); edited by Robert Kennedy. Address: Unit Two, 270 Rutherford Rd. S., Brampton, Ontario L6W 3K7, Canada.

7. *Muscle Training Illustrated* (issued nine times per year; has improved in both editorial and artistic quality following an editorial staff change in early 1980; recent issues have had 85–90 pages; covers all aspects of the sport of bodybuilding); edited by Denie, who uses no last name but who is one of the most capable photographers and writers in the game. Address: 1665 Utica Ave., Brooklyn, NY 11234.

8. *Muscle Up* (a sister publication of *Bodybuilder* magazine, which was reviewed in item #2 above; all information for *Bodybuilder* also applies to *Muscle Up*; this is merely issued bimonthly on alternate months with *Bodybuilder*).

9. *Muscular Development* (a bimonthly magazine that used to be the best muscle magazine in the bodybuilding industry, but has slipped badly in recent years, particularly when Bill Reynolds, their West Coast editor and primary contributor of profiles and photos of the California stars, left them to become my editor-in-chief in early 1978); edited by John C. Grimek, the first AAU Mr. America winner in 1940. Address: P.O. Box 1707, York, PA 17405.

10. *Muscle World* (another bimonthly publication put out by Charlton Publications, along with *Bodybuilder* and *Muscle Up*; but *Muscle World* is of considerably better quality, because it is put together both editorially and artistically by Robert Kennedy, editor of *Muscle Mag International*). Address: See address for *Bodybuilder*.

11. *Power and Fitness* (a sister publication of *Bodypower*, which was reviewed above; all the information for *Bodypower* also applies to *Power and Fitness*, which is issued bimonthly on alternate months with *Bodypower*).

COURSES FROM THE CHAMPIONS

All the champion bodybuilders who have issued mail order courses have them advertised in *Muscle & Fitness* magazine. But just in case you don't have a copy of the magazine handy, here is an alphabetical list of the champions, the courses they have to sell, the prices for each course, and an address to which you can write to order the courses.

1. Balik, John: Four courses—*You Can't Flex Fat* ($5), *Total Muscularity* ($5), *The Complete Cycle* ($5), *Anabolic Steroids* ($5). U.S. and Canadian orders add $1 for postage and foreign orders add $3 for

postage; California residents add 6 percent sales tax. Address: John Balik, P.O. Box 337, Santa Monica, CA 90406.

2. Cahling, Andreas: Four courses—*Viking Power Arms and Shoulders* ($5), *Viking Power Chest and Back* ($5), *Viking Power Legs and Abs* ($5), *Viking Power Training Secrets* ($6). U.S. and Canadian orders are postpaid, while foreign orders should add $1 per book for airmail postage; California residents must add 6 percent sales tax. Address: Andreas Cahling, P.O. Box 988, Santa Monica, CA 90406.

3. Coe, Boyer: Seven courses and three books—*Massive, Ripped Thighs & Calves* ($5), *Arm Perfection* ($5), *Dynamic Deltoids* ($5), *Complete Chest Development* ($5), *Advanced Back Training* ($5), *Intensified Waist Training* ($5), *Power Posing* ($5), *Steroids*, with Dr. Stan Morey ($13), *Optimal Nutrition*, with Dr. Stan Morey ($13), *Getting Strong, Looking Strong*, with Bob Summer ($8). All courses and books are postpaid, but California residents must add 6 percent sales tax. Address: Boyer Coe, P.O. Box 5877, Huntington Beach, CA 92646.

4. Columbu, Franco: Ten courses and six books—*Power* ($5), *Chest and Abdominals* ($5), *Shoulders* ($5), *Arms and Forearms* ($5), *Back* ($5), *Thighs, Calves, and Abdominals* ($5), *Photo Album* ($5), *Nutrition* ($5), *Definition* ($5), *Spinal Problems and Injuries* ($5), *Weight Training and Bodybuilding: A Complete Guide for Young Athletes* ($6), *Coming on Strong*, with George Fels ($10 hardcover, $7 softcover), *Starbodies: The Women's Weight Training Book*, with Dr. Anita Columbu ($8), *Weight Training for Young Athletes*, with Dr. Dick Tyler ($7), *Winning Weightlifting and Powerlifting* ($10 hardcover, $7 softcover), *Winning Bodybuilding*, with George Fels ($10 hardcover, $7 softcover). All U.S. and Canadian orders are postpaid; foreign orders add $3 per order; California residents must add 6 percent sales tax. Address: Franco Columbu, P.O. Box 415, Santa Monica, CA 90406.

5. Davis, Steve: Four courses—*Achieving Total Muscularity* ($5), *Foundation of Training* ($10), *Gaining Muscle Size and Density* ($5), *Best of the New Breed—Volume 1* ($10). U.S. and Canadian orders postpaid; foreign orders add $1 per course for postage; California residents must add 6 percent sales tax. Address: Steve Davis Fitness Center, 23115 Lyons Ave., Newhall, CA 91321.

6. Dickerson, Chris: Seven courses—*Calves* ($5), *Thighs* ($5), *Back* ($5), *Deltoids* ($5), *Arms* ($5), *Chest* ($5), *Abdominals* ($5). U.S. and Canadian orders are postpaid; foreign orders add $1 postage for each item ordered; California residents must add 6 percent sales tax. Address: Chris Dickerson, P.O. Box 1123, Santa Monica, CA 90406.

7. Ferrigno, Lou: Twelve courses—*The Mind* ($5), *Basic Principles* ($5), *Intermediate and Advanced Principles* ($5), *Legs* ($5), *Abdominals and Serratus* ($5), *Super-Wide Shoulders* ($5), *The Back* ($5), *Arms* ($5), *Chest* ($5), *Muscular Size & Power* ($5), *Contest Training* ($5), *Photo Album* ($5). Special offer: all 12 courses for $50, a savings of $10; add $1 postage for all U.S. and Canadian orders; overseas customers must add $3 per order; all foreign orders (including Canadian) must remit funds in U.S. currency only; California residents must add 6 percent sales tax. Address: Lou Ferrigno, Box 1671, Santa Monica, CA 90406.

8. Mentzer, Mike: Eight courses—*Heavy Duty Training System* ($7), *Building Heavy Duty Arms* ($4), *Heavy Duty Leg Training* ($4), *Heavy Duty Torso Training* ($4), *Heavy Duty Shoulders* ($4), *The Heavy Duty Journal* ($9.95), *Heavy Duty Nutrition* ($5), *Heavy Duty Training for Women* ($5). Add $1 for postage and handling; Canadian and foreign orders send U.S. currency only; California residents add 6 percent sales tax. Address: Mike Mentzer, P.O. Box 67276, Los Angeles, CA 90067.

9. Padilla, Danny: Four courses—*Chest and Back* ($4), *Shoulders and Arms* ($4), *Legs and Abs* ($4), *Master Bodybuilding and Nutrition Course* ($5). Special offer: all four courses can be purchased for only $14, a savings of $3; add 75¢ with each order for postage; foreign orders add $3 for postage and remit all payments in U.S. currency or equivalent; California residents must add 6 percent sales tax. Address: Dan Padilla, P.O. Box 1840, Santa Monica, CA 90406.

10. Pearl, Bill: Five courses and one book—*Your Key to Broad Shoulders* ($3), *Building Bulk and Power* ($5), *Complete Chest Development* ($3), *Build Big Arms* ($4), *Fabulous Forearms* ($3), *Keys to the Inner Universe* ($32.95 in softcover, $52.95 in the collectors' edition). Add 10 percent of the total order for postage and handling; California residents must add 6 percent sales tax. Address: Physical Fitness Architects, 100 S. Michigan Ave., Pasadena, CA 91106.

11. Platz, Tom: Two courses—*Leg Training Manual* ($5), *Upper Body Mass and Power* ($5). California residents add 6 percent sales tax. Address: Tom Platz, P.O. Box 1262, Santa Monica, CA 90406.

12. Schwarzenegger, Arnold: Ten courses and one book—*Arnold's Own Conditioning Course* ($6), *Build Massive Arms* ($5), *Building a Giant 60-*

inch Chest! ($4), *Building a Wide, Powerful Back!* ($4), *Doorway-Wide Shoulders!* ($4), *Building Legs of an Oak!* ($4), *Developing a "Mr. Universe" Body!* ($4), *The Art of Posing!* (4), *Massive Size, Muscular Weight!* ($4), *Muscular Mass, Sharp Definition!* ($4), *Arnold's Bodyshaping for Women*, with Douglas Kent Hall ($7). All foreign orders must be remitted in U.S. dollars only; California residents must add 6 percent sales tax. Address: Arnold Schwarzenegger, P.O. Box 1234, Santa Monica, CA 90406.

13. Scott, Larry: Thirteen courses—*How to Build 20″ Arms* ($5), *Building a Mr. America Chest* ($3), *Massive Thick Lats* ($3), *Herculean Thighs* ($3), *Cannon Ball Deltoids* ($3), *Mr. America Body* ($4), *Photo Album* ($3), *Slice Your Physique for Definition* ($4), *Secrets of Bulking Up Quick* ($3), *Instinctive Training* ($3), *Posing* ($3), *Mighty Forearms* ($5), *Abdominal Training* ($5). Special offers: any six books for $15, all 13 books for $30. Address: Larry Scott, Box 934, Salt Lake City, UT 84110.

14. Tinerino, Dennis: Seven courses—*Natural Champion Training Philosophy* ($5), *Guide to Sensible Training* ($3), *Secrets of Building Muscular Bulk and Power* ($5), *Shoulders & Back* ($4), *Championship Legs* ($4), *Chest & Arms* ($4), *Waist Trimming & Muscularizing* ($4). Orders from outside the U.S. and Canada should add 20 percent of the total order for airmail postage; all prices are in American currency or equivalent; California residents must add 6 percent sales tax. Address: Dennis Tinerino, "The Natural Champion," P.O. Box 299, Northridge, CA 91328.

15. Zane, Frank: Eight courses and one book—*How to Build Championship Legs and a Small Waistline* ($3), *Develop a Classic Upper Body* ($4), *Total Training for the Total Body* ($3), *Secrets of Advanced Bodybuilding* ($5), *The Mind in Bodybuilding* ($7), *On Posing* ($5), *The Zane Supernutrition Cookbook* ($5), *At a Zane Seminar* ($9.95), *The Zane Way to a Beautiful Body* (hardback only, $14.95). Postage is $1 for up to a $10 order, $2 for up to $19.95, $3 for up to $49.95, and $5 for over $50 each order. To determine foreign postage rates, double the rates listed for American and Canadian delivery. Make all checks payable to Zane; all foreign checks must be payable in U.S. dollars; California residents must add 6 percent sales tax. Address: Frank Zane, P.O. Box 366, Santa Monica, CA 90406.

SEMINAR CASETTE TAPES

1. Bass, Clarence, "Ripped Seminar Cassette," a one-hour, superhonest interview of Clarence Bass by Bill Reynolds, editor-in-chief of *Muscle & Fitness* magazine; $12.95 plus 10 percent for postage, 20 percent for foreign surface-mail postage, and 30 percent for foreign airmail postage. All foreign orders must be sent in U.S. dollars or equivalent; New Mexico residents must add 4 percent sales tax. Address: Ripped Enterprises, 305 Sandia Savings Building, 400 Gold St. S.W., Albuquerque, NM 87102.

2. Cahling, Andreas, "Vegetarian Bodybuilding Seminar," a one-hour interview of Andreas Cahling by Bill Reynolds, editor-in-chief of *Muscle & Fitness* magazine; $15 per tape; add $1 per item for postage; California residents must add 6 percent sales tax; all funds must be remitted in U.S. dollars or equivalent. Address: Andreas Cahling, P.O. Box 929, Venice, CA 90291.

3. Coe, Boyer, "Boyer Coe Seminar Tape," a one-hour talk by one of the sport's most knowledgeable and candid bodybuilders, in which he pulls no punches and uses his own unique style of discussing his bodybuilding secrets; $19.95 postpaid; California residents must add 6 percent sales tax. Address: Boyer Coe, P.O. Box 5877, Huntington Beach, CA 92646.

4. Ferrigno, Lou, "The Incredible Muscle-Up Seminar," an unbelievably open, candid, and informative one-hour interview of Lou conducted by Bill Reynolds, editor-in-chief of *Muscle & Fitness* magazine; $19.95, plus $1 for postage and handling; overseas orders add $3 for postage and send a bank draft in U.S. currency only; California residents must add 6 percent sales tax. Address: Lou Ferrigno, P.O. Box 1671, Santa Monica, CA 90406.

5. Mentzer, Mike, "Heavy Duty Seminar," a one-hour tape cassette covering such topics as Exploring Your Bodybuilding Potential; New Heavy Duty Methods; Rest-Pause, Infitonic and Omnicontractional Training; and The Perfect Routine; $19.95, plus $1 for postage and handling; Canadian and foreign orders please sent U.S. currency only; California residents must add 6 percent sales tax. Address: Mike Mentzer, P.O. Box 67276, Los Angeles, CA 90067.

6. Padilla, Danny, "Giant Killer Seminar Tape"; standing only 5′2½″ in height, Danny had to learn early in the game how to pack on symmetrical muscle fast, "so I could compete against the bigger guys. Everything I've discovered about training and nutrition is on this one-hour cassette tape!" Price is $9.95 plus $1 for postage and handling; foreign orders should add $3 for postage; all foreign customers must remit payment in U.S. currency or equivalent; California residents must add 6 percent sales tax. Address: Danny Padilla, P.O. Box 1840, Santa Monica, CA 90406.

7. Viator, Casey, "The Unreal Seminar Tape," a one-hour, ultra-informative interview of Casey Viator by Bill Reynolds, editor-in-chief of *Muscle & Fitness* magazine, in which Casey tells it all: his steroid usage, his training methods, secrets of attaining his unique mental drive, how he has become so strong, and how any bodybuilder can apply Casey's own Unreal Training System to his own training, doubling or tripling his results; $9.95, plus $1 for postage; California residents must add 6 percent sales tax; add $3 for overseas airmail postage; all foreign customers must remit payment in U.S. dollars or equivalent. Address: Casey Viator, P.O. Box 826, Santa Monica, CA 90406.

TRAINING FILMS

1. Columbu, Franco: Four 50-foot Super 8 films—*Posing* ($10), *Training the Chest, Lats, and Abs* ($15), *Training the Shoulders, Arms, and Forearms* ($15), and *Training the Thighs and Calves* ($15). Learn how to change from one pose to another professionally, as well as how to train properly for the fastest results, by viewing these films of a Mr. Olympia winner actually posing and working out. Foreign orders add $3 for postage and handling; all foreign orders must be remitted in U.S. dollars or the equivalent; California residents must add 6 percent sales tax; U.S. and Canadian orders are postpaid. Address: Franco Columbu, P.O. Box 415, Santa Monica, CA 90406.

Index